Cladistics and Archaeology

Cladistics and Archaeology

Michael J. O'Brien and R. Lee Lyman

With contributions by

Daniel S. Glover and John Darwent

Foreword by

Robert D. Leonard

THE UNIVERSITY OF UTAH PRESS

Salt Lake City

The Defiance House Man colophon is a registered trademark of the
University of Utah Press. It is based upon a four-foot-tall,
Ancient Puebloan pictograph (late PIII) near Glen Canyon, Utah.

08 07 06 05 04 03
5 4 3 2 1

Index prepared by Andrew L. Christenson

LIBRARY OF CONGRESS CATALOGING-IN-PUBLICATION DATA

O'Brien, Michael J. (Michael John), 1950–
  Cladistics and archaeology / Michael J. O'Brien and R. Lee Lyman ;
with contributions by Daniel S. Glover and John Darwent ; foreword by
Robert D. Leonard.
    p. cm.
Includes bibliographical references and index.
  ISBN 0-87480-775-1 (alk. paper)
  1. Archaeology—Methodology. 2. Cladistic analysis.
  I. Lyman, R. Lee. II. Glover, Daniel S. III. Darwent, John, 1969– IV. Title.

CC75.7 .O275 2003
930.1'01'2—dc21
                              2003008908

To the late

E. J. O'Brien

Contents

Illustrations

Tables

Robert D. Leonard

The Carpenter's Apprentice

My FATHER is a carpenter. Family legend has it that he put a hammer in my hand the day I was born. As a child, my first "job" involved using my hammer to break up dirt clods in the backdirt of neighborhood house-basement excavations. I soon moved on to driving nails, and by the time I was fourteen, I was one of the best nailers on my father's carpentry crew. I'm still not half bad.

At sixteen I learned how to read a carpenter's square. Specifically, I was taught via cultural transmission how to use it to cut rafters and stair risers. This knowledge was esoteric and privileged and came with great responsibility. Not just anyone could learn how to use a carpenter's square. For one thing, not everyone had a head for the numbers, but more importantly most people had no opportunity to learn this pivotal skill. The knowledge embedded within the carpenter's square—trigonometry—brought security to one's family. If you knew how to interpret the mysterious tables of numbers etched into steel (nowadays aluminum), you could frame and finish a house from top to bottom. But if you couldn't read the square, stairs and rafters could not be crafted, and any house you began to construct could not be completed. Furthermore, knowledge of how to use the carpenter's square was held closely. In our small town, if you taught someone outside the family how to read the square, they could start a house-building business of their own. By sharing knowledge one created potential competition for the family business and, in uncertain times, put one's family at economic risk.

No one knows the origin of the carpenter's square. Silas Hawes, a blacksmith from South Shaftsbury, Vermont, holds the 1819 patent for the United States, but it was used in Europe for centuries. Even less is known of its counterparts in the rest of the world. My father learned how to use the square from his father and he from his father. When my son is

old enough, I will teach him how to use the square, and I know that he
will do the same. It is our tradition.

In what do *you* apprentice? Do you draw or sculpt? Make quilts using
your grandmother's patterns? Participate in local theatrical productions?
We all apprentice in a great variety of traditions. Apprenticeships can be
formal or informal and are simply more active and intensive venues for
cultural transmission than is, say, listening to the radio. One way to con-
ceptualize these more intensive episodes of cultural transmission is by seeing them as forming parts of intellectual traditions.

Some of our intellectual traditions, such as language or ritual behavior, do not necessarily involve technology. But many traditions in which
we participate are sets of instructions for technology: how to drive a car,
play a guitar, use the carpenter's square, or read a book. Other traditions
tell us how to create or maintain technology: how to throw a pot, knit a
scarf, or change the spark plugs in a car. Other traditions tell us how to
place symbols on technology: the designs on a hand-woven rug, graffiti on
a wall, or our signatures on a legal document. Still other traditions tell us
how to use technology to perform tasks related to subsistence activities:
how to bake bread, till a garden, or milk a cow.

Notice that many if not all of these intellectual traditions involve an
oral and interactive component. For example, if you ever went fishing as a
child, you will remember the gentle touch of an adult—perhaps your
grandfather—reaching over your shoulders to grasp your hands to illustrate the right way to cast a line. You also learned of bait, the behavior of
fish, the importance of shade, small talk, and when to be quiet. The sub-
tleties of fishing couldn't be learned from books then or the Internet
today. If those means were sufficient for learning, we wouldn't need class-
rooms, or grandfathers.

Intellectual traditions permeate our lives and are woven inextricably
into the past. Even the most complex intellectual traditions have threads
that reach back into the Paleolithic. A "bunker-buster" bomb is part of
the same deep intellectual tradition as the atlatl; the ceramic technology
that protects space shuttles continues a knowledge line that began with
Neolithic farmers ten thousand years ago. Harappan clay tablets, Inka
knots, and Mousterian scrapers were complex intellectual traditions of
their times, akin to our books, computers, and stainless-steel knives.

While I learned how to use the carpenter's square through a patrimo-
nial transmission process, most cultural transmission doesn't happen that
way. As the blacksmith Silas Hawes cannot be found in my family's his-

tory, a long-forgotten person who was not a family member passed on the knowledge of the carpenter's square to one of my great-grandfathers. Indeed much if not most of what we learn belongs to intellectual traditions that transcend the family structure.

We learn from books, television, radio, computers, from each other, and through many other venues. Virtually every bit of information our minds process can be used to teach us something. Within this onslaught of information, however, any given intellectual tradition has an integrity that distinguishes itself from other such bits of processed information. For example, why doesn't Plácido Domingo have a pop hit, and why doesn't Ricky Martin sing at the Metropolitan Opera? The answer is simple: they were trained in different musical traditions—intellectual traditions if you will—that are distinct, irrespective of the natural singing talent of the artists. Both singers had and possibly still have mentors; each provides a model for countless opera and pop-star hopefuls. Some of this training may be formal and institutionalized; some admirers may learn simply by listening to the radio or CDs. Either sort of training constitutes cultural transmission and results in the perpetuation, with varying modifications, of the intellectual traditions of pop music and opera. But will these famous singers have crossover hits? Perhaps, but likely not.

Like the songs Domingo and Martin sing, not all intellectual traditions have an easily discerned physical reality. Sometimes we abstract aspects of cultural traditions into simple information packets called memes. While we don't know exactly what a meme looks like, we know that it has a biochemical signature in the brain. We also know that when memes or combinations of memes (memeplexes) relate to the construction, use, or maintenance of technology such biochemical signatures can be expressed in the physical world in technologies that archaeologists ultimately refer to as artifacts with attributes and associations. Replication of what is learned or transmitted occurs across individuals with varying degrees of fidelity but is often remarkably consistent. This is how we can tell a Ford from a Ferrari and French fries from fondue. Varying degrees of fidelity are important, however, as they are a source of both innovation and failure—important learning opportunities. They are also a source of change and potential fodder for evolution.

Archaeologists have long recognized that cultural traditions are reflected by technology and that they also change with time. We look at similarities and differences in the artifacts we study. Using common sense, occasionally statistics, we create types or classes within which we categorize our artifacts. Most often, we hope that our types reflect historical and heritable continuity—another way to say that they are part of the same intellectual tradition.

Yet, despite the fact that we have been looking at what we hope are historical types for a long time, we currently have no reliable methodology that allows us to unequivocally identify intellectual traditions. Furthermore, no methodology takes into account that not only do types change but also the intellectual traditions that create them. For example, in the area where I work in northern Mexico, prehistoric people living from about A.D. 1250 to 1450 made some of the most remarkable ceramics in the western hemisphere. Beautiful red, black, and cream polychromes with geometric, anthropomorphic, and zoomorphic designs constitute a tradition called Ramos Polychrome within the Casas Grandes ceramic tradition. For over one hundred years archaeologists have sought to determine how the Casas Grandes ceramics were related to other traditions in the area. The researchers Bandelier, Brand, and others felt the ceramics were related to Puebloan traditions in the American Southwest; Di Peso posited a strong Mesoamerican influence; Sayles thought they derived from the Mimbres tradition of the American Southwest; LeBlanc and Lister saw them growing out of a general Mogollon tradition of southern New Mexico; Kidder noted their relation to the Lower Gila Style of southern New Mexico and Arizona; Amsden and Sauer saw them as related to the Little Colorado redwares of the four corners area; and Carey and Hewett found them completely unique. Others see both Southwestern and Mesoamerican influences.

In other words, over a hundred years of discussion has not resolved the issue, largely because no methodology exists that will allow us to trace these intellectual traditions through time and across space in a manner that is definitive and replicable, until now.

Cladistics is a component of phylogenetic analysis. Michael J. O'Brien and R. Lee Lyman present it to us here. This is a well-reasoned and thoughtful account written in an engaging manner. The subject matter is complex, both conceptually and in its practical application. Yet, despite this complexity, the authors are able to convincingly demonstrate the power cladistics can play in understanding the past. In many ways this account is a primer, an introduction that will allow readers to pursue cladistics as an avenue to address archaeological problems. As a primer, it provides a beginning for profitable dialogue among those who seek to serve an apprenticeship in this field. I hope that dialogue will include other archaeologists who have read the book, as well as colleagues in anthropology, mathematics, statistics, biology, and paleontology who share such interests.

While the focus of this book is the methodology of cladistics, it is much more than a methodological treatise. It also offers a fascinating philosophical discussion of the matters at hand, embedding that discussion in the history of anthropology as well as evolutionary biology and paleontology. Importantly, it contextualizes cladistics within evolutionary theory and places archaeology at the core of reaching an evolutionary understanding of the human past—in Darwinian terms. Here it builds upon the important work of evolutionary archaeology and human evolutionary ecology. It is more than a simple addition to this literature, however, as it may well revolutionize it.

Tracing intellectual traditions in the past is in itself inherently interesting, but incorporating them within the Darwinian framework adds an additional explanatory dimension of contemporary relevance to our society at large. If one looks at the problems confronting the world today, many if not most are evolutionary problems: global warming, genetic engineering, the loss of biodiversity, extinctions, increasing bacterial resistance to antibiotics, and human competition for the earth's limited resources come to mind. These evolutionary problems will require evolutionary solutions that can only be crafted in terms of past and present conditions. As such, we see research in evolutionary biology and paleontology at the core of these solutions. Archaeology informed by evolutionary theory can provide an equally important perspective on many of the issues confronting the world today, if we choose to make it happen.

Should we take up their challenge, these are the opportunities that O'Brien and Lyman offer us: new understandings of the past and increased contemporary relevance. May we learn to use this tool well, like the carpenter's apprentice.

Preface

ALL OF US at one point or another have been introduced to the Linnaean taxonomic system—an approach to biological classification that dates back to the eighteenth century and the work of Swedish botanist Carolus Linnaeus. Based on their similarities to one another, organisms are placed in a hierarchical set of taxa that become more generalized, and therefore more encompassing, as one ascends through the hierarchy. Thus genera are more general (and higher in rank) than the species they encompass, families are more general (and higher in rank) than the genera they encompass, and so on. In and of itself the Linnaean taxonomic system tells us nothing about the phylogenetic history of various taxa—the manner in which they are related historically—and in fact Linnaeus never intended it to. It was the work of Charles Darwin, especially his notion of descent with modification, that provided taxonomists with the theoretical basis for using Linnaeus's system for phylogenetic purposes. That is, once like is placed with like—say, three species in a genus—descent with modification can be used as an explanation for why taxa placed in the same rank are similar. The unification of Linnaean taxonomy and Darwin's insight produced what eventually became known as evolutionary taxonomy.

By the early 1950s evolutionary taxonomy was the only approach to phylogeny, but a challenge to its supremacy soon arose. A small but vocal subset of taxonomists became increasingly dissatisfied with the fact that evolutionary taxonomy simultaneously monitors organismic similarity and phylogeny. This duality, they argued, opens the classification process to a host of problems, not the least of which is that subjective appraisals of phylogeny often create groups of organisms that should not be placed together in higher taxa. Conversely, nonrigorous assessments of similarity create erroneous groupings from a phylogenetic standpoint. What was needed, they argued, was a rigorous method that classified organisms solely on the basis of similarity. After taxa were grouped into a hierarchical arrangement strictly on similarity, perhaps phylogeny could be examined, but this was a secondary consideration. This school became known first as numerical taxonomy and later as phenetics. The opposition to phenetics was immediate. Evolutionary taxonomists saw it as a vacuous exercise—one that produced theory-free groupings because it completely ignored the evolutionary history of taxa. Pheneticists used any morphological characters to create their groups, whereas evolutionary taxonomists tried to separate analogous characters (those that taxa acquire independent of any historical connectedness) from homologous characters (those that taxa share as a result of a common history). The latter were viewed as useful for inferring phylogeny, whereas the former were not.

But some taxonomists argued that when phylogeny is the issue, not all homologous characters are created equally. Further, they, like the pheneticists, viewed evolutionary taxonomy as a murky enterprise that conflates evolutionary pattern with evolutionary process. Like phenetics, evolutionary taxonomy creates units based on similarity, but are the units true historical entities—the results of evolutionary processes—or are they figments of the method of classification used? Are they sometimes one and sometimes the other? Phylogenetic systematics, or cladistics, arose as a direct challenge to both evolutionary taxonomy and phenetics and attempts to create units that strictly reflect patterns of descent. Cladistics bypasses the analogy-homology problem associated with phenetics and uncouples the association of pattern with process that plagues evolutionary taxonomy.

Phylogeny depends on transmission, irrespective of mode. This means that cultural transmission is as legitimate a mechanism for creating phylogenetic relationships as genetic transmission is. Therefore, cladistics is not limited to organisms but rather is applicable to anything that evolves, such as language, manuscripts, and tools. This book was written to demonstrate the applicability of cladistics to issues that are deeply rooted in archaeology. The fundamental premise of cladistics—that only particular kinds of characters (traits) are useful for creating historically meaningful relationships among taxa—is not difficult to understand, but the analytical techniques themselves require considerable attention and patience to master. Several introductory manuals on cladistics have appeared in recent years, but they tend to cover so much ground that the reader can quickly become lost in detail. In contrast, our approach is to stick more or less to the basics of cladistics and to provide key references that can be read for more detail. Our goal is to show that although cladistics to this point has been used strictly to show phylogenetic relationships among biological taxa, it can easily be extended conceptually and methodologically to include cultural phenomena. Thus, where appropriate, we substitute archaeological examples for biological examples. As a guide to terminology, we include a glossary of some of the more important terms and concepts used. Also, we conclude all but the last chapter with a brief section titled "Starting Points," which contains references to begin with if you are interested in reading further about select topics.

Our hope is that archaeologists and anthropologists interested in using cladistic methods can rely on this book as an introduction to the subject rather than having to try to acquire the basic skills from an extensive and often contentious biological literature. Above all, we hope to make it clear that cladistics not only differs both methodologically and ontologically from evolutionary taxonomy—the approach to phylogenetic reconstruction that is so familiar to most archaeologists and anthropologists—but is superior to it in terms of what it can tell us about historical relationships.

Many individuals have helped us over the past several years as we grappled with developing what has come to be known as evolutionary archaeology. For reading, discussing, and commenting on our earlier musing on some of the topics covered here, we thank C. M. Barton, C. Beck, R. L. Bettinger, A. V. Z. Brower, G. A. Clark, R. C. Dunnell, M. Ereshefsky, R. Ethington, R. Foley, M. Harmon, C. Holden, G. T. Jones, P. V. Kirch, J. L. Lanata, R. D. Leonard, C. P. Lipo, R. Mace, M. Madsen, S. Matthews, H. Neff, F. Neiman, N. I. Platnick, C. A. Pool, E. Saab, Y. Saab, M. B. Schiffer, S. Shennan, M. Siddall, E. Sober, P. A. Teltser, C. S. VanPool, T. L. VanPool, and S. Wolverton. By no means do these individuals necessarily share all our views on archaeological phylogeny, but all have in some important way made us rethink our assumptions, reshape our methods, and/or refocus our arguments. In addition, Marcel Harmon, Robert Leonard, and José Luis Lanata read the manuscript in its entirety and made countless suggestions for improvement. We also thank Jeff Grathwohl, director of the University of Utah Press, for his personal interest in the book, and Kathy Lewis, our copy editor, for her capable assistance. Finally, we thank the late E. J. O'Brien, who read just about every paper and book we wrote on evolutionary archaeology (and other things) and offered extensive commentary on everything from logic and organization to punctuation and grammar. We grew to depend on his eye for detail, and we sorely miss him.

PART I

Phylogenetic Analysis

ONE

Introduction

Aᴍᴇʀɪᴄᴀɴɪsᴛ anthropology has always had as its primary goal explaining the enormous cultural, linguistic, and biological diversity evident across humanity from its beginning to the present (Boas 1895, 1904; Garbarino 1977; Hallowell 1960; Leaf 1979; Lowie 1937, 1956; Mitra 1933; Radin 1929). One explanatory paradigm long used by many ethnologists and archaeologists rests, to varying degrees, on the notion of evolution, although it is abundantly clear that there are as many anthropological definitions of evolution as there are approaches to its study. In the late nineteenth and early twentieth centuries, cultural evolution typically was termed "development," in large part to keep that process separate from organic evolution. Early models of cultural evolution included those of Edward Burnett Tylor (1871) and Lewis Henry Morgan (1877)—models that were unilinear, progressive, and orthogenetic. This meant that cultural evolution occurred in a straight line; it raised humans from primitive to advanced stages; and it was fueled by some mysterious driving force, often characterized as human need (Dunnell 1980; Freeman 1974; Lyman and O'Brien 1997, 2001b). Some later models (e.g., Kidder 1932; Lowie 1918; Wissler 1917, 1923) had the flavor of Darwinian descent with modification, and although the key mechanism of change was often the same as in the Tylor/Morgan models—human need—submechanisms such as environmental change, population growth, and the like were seen as acting in concert with it to produce change.

Both kinds of models lacked explicit theoretical mechanisms of change. For example, cultural transmission was acknowledged both as *diffusion* (the movement of a culture trait from one culture to another) and as *enculturation* (the process of learning one's culture), but largely ignored was the question of *why* and *how* those mechanisms effected change at particular times and in particular places. Further, diffusion and enculturation as concepts were born out of ethnology. Even though they were not particularly well defined, an ethnologist could at least spot instances of them. But what good did this do prehistorians, who were interested in the *archaeological* implications of these evolutionary mechanisms (Lyman 2001)? Irrespective of the sort of evolutionary model preferred, many anthropologists and archaeologists (e.g., Boas 1911; Lowie 1912) pointed out just how difficult it was to decipher the evolutionary history of cultural lineages—what produced what, what was directly related to what, and so on—often identifying the key problem as sorting out instances of independent invention from instances of diffusion and cultural borrowing (e.g., Goldenweiser 1916; Steward 1929).

Despite such difficulties, archaeologists in particular continued throughout the first half of the twentieth century to attempt to determine the evolutionary histories of cultural lineages and to link various traditions phylogenetically—literally, to reconstruct networks of evolutionary relationships among cultural phenomena. This was in large part what the North American paradigm known as culture history was all about (Lyman et al. 1997; O'Brien and Lyman 1998, 2000) and to a lesser extent what was behind the later paradigm known as processual archaeology. If the unifying goal of archaeology is *not* to explain the historical development of cultural traditions, why would the origins of the use of fire, the emergence of sedentariness and urbanism, the appearance of complex sociopolitical organization, the development of agriculture, the effects of the technological development of pottery, and the like occupy so much of our attention? The answer, of course, is that the explanation of cultural traditions always has been and will be fundamental to archaeology. In fact, it is impossible to imagine an archaeology that does not have that as a central focus.

This book presents our views on how archaeologists can begin to find answers to questions concerning the evolution of cultural phenomena. It is worth pointing out that the book is largely about a particular method for building testable hypotheses regarding cultural evolution. We unabashedly borrow the method from biology and paleontology, two disciplines that have had analytical goals similar to those of anthropology and archaeology, respectively, since the late nineteenth century (O'Brien and Lyman 2000). The method, originally termed *phylogenetic systematics* but now known simply as *cladistics,* was developed explicitly to resolve evolutionary relationships among groups of organisms. Our objective is to show the power of cladistics to assist in the phylogenetic reconstruction of anything that evolves, not simply organisms.

The kind of evolution in which we are interested is Darwinian evolution, which we define as "any net directional change or any cumulative change in the characteristics of . . . populations over many generations—in other words, descent with modification" (Endler 1986:5). What is not explicit in this definition is that transmission results in the replication of ancestral forms by descendant forms. *This* is what makes Darwinian evolution distinct from mere change: fidelity of replication resulting from transmission results in descendant phenomena resembling their ancestors to greater or lesser degrees. There are three minimum requirements for this kind of evolution to occur: (1) variation among individuals (at some scale), (2) inheritance of variant characteristics (requiring transmission), and (3) differential perpetuation (variants are replicated at varying frequencies). The key as far as phylogeny is concerned is transmission. We introduce the topic of cultural transmission below and examine how archaeologists have traditionally addressed it. We return to select aspects of transmission in Chapter 4.

CULTURE HISTORY, CHRONOMETERS, AND CULTURAL TRANSMISSION

Archaeologists have long used artifact change to measure the passage of time. They also have long recognized that change is not bound by a single tempo. Change can occur rapidly, and it can occur slowly—sometimes so slowly that if we are not careful observers we won't even notice that it has occurred. Archaeologists have created myriad scenarios to account for culture change, just as they have tried to account for shifts in the tempo of change. Similarly, they have used perceived shifts in the tempo of change in one part of culture—tools, for example—to monitor change in other parts. Perhaps, for instance, rapid change in artifact form or decoration is a result of outside influence, whereas slow, deliberate change is simply the result of natural forces working from within. This kind of inference, in fact, characterized the thinking of culture historians in the first half of the twentieth century (Lyman et al. 1997). Artifact sequences, especially those sequences comprising artifacts that were very similar in form or decoration, implied that a direct connection existed between artifacts placed next to one another in the sequence. In the rare instances when early archaeologists and anthropologists mentioned that connection, cultural transmission was viewed as the cause (Lyman 2001). Culture historians and ethnologists were seldom more explicit than this, and through the first half of the twentieth century "cause" became ever more obscure as archaeologists in particular spoke of "persistence" of artifact types, "series" of similar artifacts, and "historical continuity" between artifacts arranged in a temporal sequence (Lyman et al. 1997).

Archaeologists took for granted that historical continuity—one thing following another—equaled *heritable continuity*—one thing resembling another as a result of transmission. They forgot (or ignored) that the former does not necessarily imply the latter. Instead of pursuing the issue of what artifact similarity and difference might have to say about various kinds of cultural transmission, archaeologists turned attention to building chronometers (time pieces) from their artifacts, where "a chronometer of history has one, and only one, rigid requirement—something must be found that changes in a recognizable and irreversible way through time, so that each historical moment bears a distinctive signature" (Gould 1987:157). Archaeologists working in the first half of the twentieth century were highly successful in measuring variation in artifacts such that the variation could serve as a historical chronometer (Lyman and O'Brien 2000a; O'Brien and Lyman 1999). Those successes rested ultimately on cultural transmission between generations of artifact makers, although this aspect was seldom mentioned.

Perspectives have shifted radically from the early decades of the twentieth century in terms of how much time is represented in the archaeological records of various locales; but even today, when sophisticated methods exist to assess the absolute age of objects and deposits, change in form, decoration, and other visible aspects of artifacts remains a primary source of chronological information. The logic behind using artifact change as a chronometer is simple: Over time, humans modify the ways in which they do such things as manufacture tools, decorate pots, and construct houses. Not only do the methods of manufacture, decoration, and construction change, but so too do the products in terms of appearance. Changes in appearance can be quite visible or extremely subtle. Many changes can take place at once, or it might be that only one small portion of a kind of object changes.

If we have numerous specimens of a particular category of object—say, cooking pots—that we have reason to suspect were not all manufactured at the same time, we might be able to order them chronologically by examining their form or decoration. Our ordering could be created by noting features that are exactly the same or nearly the same on different specimens and placing those specimens next to each other in the sequence.

If the changes are ordered correctly, a historical sequence of forms is created. If we have not assumed something about the direction of change, such as that the size of ceramic vessels changed from large to small over time, independent evidence such as superposition or radiometric dating is needed to root the sequence. In the absence of an assumption of the direction of change, the ordering itself cannot tell us which end of the order is older and which is younger.

James A. Ford's (1962) illustration of change in the form of three fictional categories of ceramic vessels (Figure 1.1) is a useful heuristic device because it clearly and concisely displays historical continuity. Ford's diagram shows a sequence in which one vessel form follows another, changing ever so slightly from one point in time to the next. We term the technique that Ford used to create the ordering *phyletic seriation* (Lyman et al. 1997; O'Brien and Lyman 1999), which is the development of an ordering using change in appearance as the ordering principle. The subtleness of the change from one form to the next creates the impression of continuity in form over time. If presented with the specimens in one of the categories, an archaeologist would probably have little or no trouble duplicating Ford's historical sequence. Ford intended his graph to show historical continuity; but based on his view that culture could be modeled as a steadily flowing stream as a result of cultural transmission (O'Brien and Lyman 1998), he also meant it to show something else. Although he was not explicit, Ford intended the graph to show heritable continuity (O'Brien and Lyman 1998, 1999) between chronologically adjacent vessel forms, with one form evolving from another. Thus, in addition to producing a historical sequence, Ford also produced a *phylogenetic* sequence, meaning that the sequence captured the evolutionary history of three categories of vessels. Moreover, as shown in Figure 1.1, the three sequences are unrelated *lineages* of vessels, meaning that there is but one evolutionary pathway shown for each of the three. Ford's view of change in vessel shape was *anagenetic*, meaning that there is directional (not meant to imply "progressive") evolution within a lineage without diversification (branching).

Ford was preceded by other prehistorians who, although interested primarily in chronological matters, created orderings that implied heritable continuity between sequent forms. Figure 1.2 shows A. V. Kidder's sequence of designs on pottery from Pecos Pueblo, New Mexico. Kidder constructed the suspected ordering based on his impressions of how the designs had changed over time from earliest (1) to latest (5) (Kidder 1915).

Figure 1.1. James A. Ford's conception of culture change as manifest in artifacts (after Ford 1962). Note the consistent and gradual change in each of the three forms through time. Not only is the passage of time measured by the sequence of forms, but heritable continuity and transmission are implied, indicating that each line of vessels constitutes a lineage.

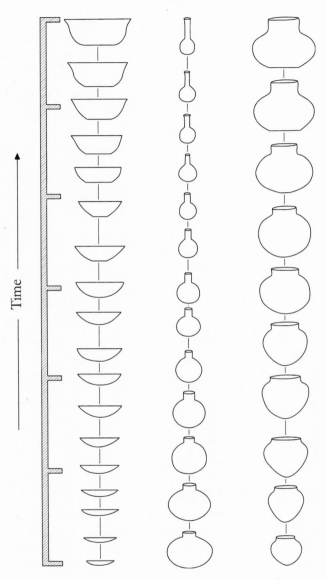

He proposed that through time the pottery design became less intricate, changing from a stepped motif (1) to a pair of stepped motifs (2) and finally to a series of ever-larger white spaces (3–5). He confirmed the ordering two years later (Kidder 1917) through the study of stratigraphically superposed collections. Like Ford's ordering, Kidder's sequence was anagenetic.

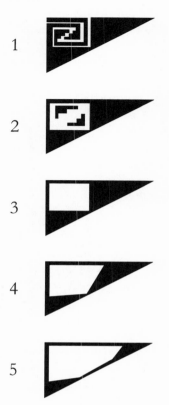

Figure 1.2. A. V. Kidder's illustration of the evolution of a ceramic design on pottery from Pecos Pueblo, New Mexico (after Kidder 1917). The designs are numbered chronologically, with 1 being the earliest. Kidder proposed that through time the pottery design became less intricate, changing from a stepped motif (1), to a pair of stepped motifs (2), and finally to a series of ever-larger white spaces (3–5).

Not all phylogenetic orderings in archaeology have been anagenetic. Consider, for example, W. M. Flinders Petrie's (1899) illustration of his ordering of types of ceramic vessels from predynastic burials north of the Valley of the Kings in Egypt (Figure 1.3). In his final report, Petrie (1899:300) referred to portions of his sequence as "genealogies." Time runs from top to bottom, so that vessel types with smaller numbers are chronologically earlier than those with larger numbers. There are two interesting aspects to that figure. First, Petrie's illustration shows one vessel type producing two offspring. For example, type 48 produced types 54 and 55, and type 70 produced types 72 and 73. This is the evolutionary process of *cladogenesis,* the branching and diversification of lineages during evolution. As opposed to anagenesis, cladogenesis involves the multiplication of taxa, creating multiple related lineages. Second, Petrie's illustration indicates that two types could merge to produce a single later type. Type 38, as shown in Figure 1.3, is a cross between types 34 and 36. This is the evolutionary process of *hybridization*. Petrie did not discuss the

Figure 1.3. W. M. Flinders
Petrie's genealogy of
ceramic-vessel forms
recovered from burials in
three localities in Egypt
(after Petrie 1899). The
numbers refer to periods;
30 is oldest, 80 is youngest.
Lines between vessel forms
imply heritable continuity.

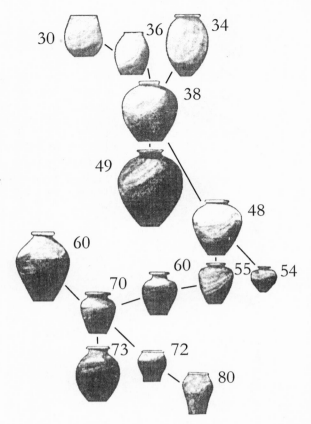

ramifications of either cladogenesis or hybridization; nor did he discuss
the mechanisms by which either might occur, but no other archaeologist
at the time did either.

Petrie was interested in chronological ordering, not in mechanisms of
transmission—how potters learned from other potters and so on—and we
suspect that his use of the word "genealogies" was more metaphorical
than literal. Kidder offered a little more in the way of explanation. He
spoke of successions of Puebloan groups being responsible for the changes
in vessel decoration at Pecos Pueblo and indicated that one pottery type
might "father" another (Kidder 1915:453), but any sense that his ordering had genealogical implications, meaning that there was heritable continuity between designs, was at best an interpretation. Further, such an interpretation contradicted Kidder's view that different Puebloan groups
probably were responsible for the design changes. Thus, Kidder couched
his conclusions in conservative tones.

Neither Kidder nor Petrie was explicit about why these orderings of artifacts should be chronological. Another individual, however, did touch on this matter. A. L. Kroeber invented the technique of *frequency seriation* at the same time that Kidder was discussing the succession of Puebloan groups (Lyman et al. 1997; O'Brien and Lyman 1999). Frequency seriation is a technique for chronologically ordering collections of presumably historical types (for Kroeber it was pottery types) such that each type has a continuous distribution and a unimodal frequency distribution. The significance of Kroeber's seminal frequency seriation of pottery from the countryside around Zuni Pueblo, New Mexico, shown in greatly stylized form in Figure 1.4, resides in his observation that the seriated assemblages "shade into one another," and there is "no gap or marked break between" the prehistoric and historical periods (Kroeber 1916a:44). The two periods might have been "as distinct as oil and water" (Kroeber 1916b:9) when distinguished on the basis of other chronometric data, but these were not the data used in the seriation. Kroeber (1916b:15) indicated that the prehistoric and historical periods "can normally be distinguished without the least uncertainty, and the separateness of the two is fundamental," but his frequency seriation of pottery indicated the two periods "do not represent two different migrations, nationalities, or waves of culture, but rather a steady and continuous development on the soil."

This was the clearest expression to that point in the history of Americanist archaeology of the belief that time could be measured archaeologically as a continuous, linear dimension. As a result of the manner in which artifacts were categorized, ethnic, and thus heritable, continuity could be documented. Kroeber knew this, but he did not develop his insights further. Other archaeologists working in the Southwest a few years later perhaps had the requisite knowledge of biological evolution to understand the significance of cultural transmission and heritable continuity for phylogenetic reconstruction, but they were no more explicit than anyone else at the time in terms of theoretical development.

Two such individuals were Harold S. Colton, a biologist by training, and Lyndon L. Hargrave, who together published a statement on the phylogenetic implications of pottery types that were being described for the Southwest. To Colton and Hargrave (1937:2–3) a *type* was "a group of pottery vessels which are alike in every important characteristic except (possibly) form," and a *series* was "a group of pottery types within a single ware in which each type bears a genetic relation to each other." Colton and Hargrave's use of "series" stemmed directly from Kidder's

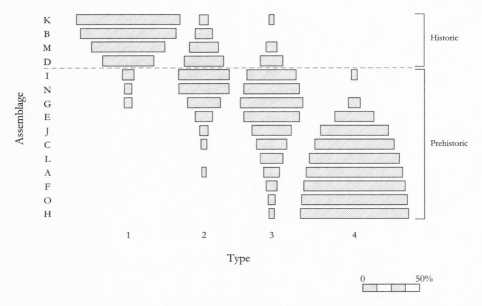

Figure 1.4. Frequency seriation of 15 assemblages and four pottery types based on A. L. Kroeber's (1916b) data from Zuni Pueblo, New Mexico. The assemblages are arranged in such an order that the types exhibit normal distributions. Here Kroeber knew which end of the seriation was early and which was late because of historical evidence.

(1917) earlier use of the term, which was as a synonym for "sequence," but they pushed the biological analogy much further than their predecessors had. Not only did their scheme involve types, but those types carried genealogical-sounding names such as *derived, collateral,* and *ancestral* (Figure 1.5). Anagenetic evolution was an important component of Colton and Hargrave's model—note the straight lines depicting the evolution of one pottery type from another—but the model also shows cladogenesis, or branching and diversification.

Kidder's (1915, 1917) simpler phyletic scheme (Figure 1.2) denoted some of the same sorts of relations between pottery types, but his contemporaries did not heap criticism on him the way they did on Colton and Hargrave. Julian Steward (1941:367) pointed out that "it is apparent from the cultural relationships shown in [Colton and Hargrave's] scheme that strict adherence to a method drawn from biology inevitably fails to take into account the distinctively cultural and unbiological fact of blends and crosses between essentially unlike types. . . . It is true that cultural streams often tend to be distinct, but they are never entirely unmixed and

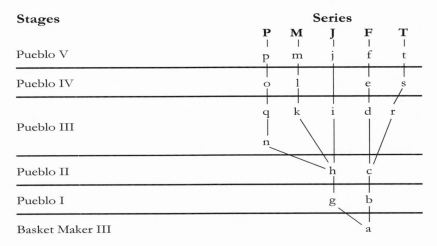

Stages   **Series**

| | | P | M | J | F | T |

Pueblo V   p   m   j   f   t

Pueblo IV   o   l   e   s

                        q   k   i   d   r

Pueblo III   n

Pueblo II   h   c

Pueblo I   g   b

Basket Maker III   a

Figure 1.5. Harold S. Colton and Lyndon L. Hargrave's hypothetical representation of the relation between a pottery series (capital letters) and its types
(lowercase letters) (after Colton and Hargrave 1937). Anagenetic evolution
was an important component of the model—represented by the straight lines
depicting the evolution of one pottery type from another—but the model also
shows cladogenesis, or branching and diversification.

often approach a complete blend." Steward, in other words, was saying
that one could never trace cultural phenomena phylogenetically because
culture was like a braided stream: It ran in channels that would begin to
diverge but then would move back together, then diverge, then move back
together, and so on. This is known as *reticulation*. Without clear and un-
equivocal divergence, how could one hope to trace ancestry? This is still a
commonplace view in anthropology and one to which we devote considerable attention in Chapter 4.

The most stinging criticism was delivered not by Steward but by J. O.
Brew (1946:53), who noted that the evolutionary implications of schemes
such as that presented by Colton and Hargrave were unacceptable for the
simple reason that "phylogenetic relationships do not exist between inanimate objects" such as potsherds. Brew's indictment of Colton and Hargrave's scheme effectively precluded future attempts to view archaeological change in evolutionary terms, and it would be another three decades
before anyone seriously raised the prospect of integrating the biological-
evolution model into archaeology.

WHY ARE TWO THINGS SIMILAR?

Colton's knowledge of biological evolution no doubt underpinned the scheme he and Hargrave used, and the key to the scheme was the supposition that forms were related because they were similar. This is a questionable assumption; but as we discuss in Chapter 2, it was one that long underlay the efforts of biologists to unite the eighteenth-century classificatory efforts of Carolus Linnaeus and the nineteenth-century processual insights of Charles Darwin. Linnaeus placed organisms in the same species because they looked similar. At a high level in his taxonomy, he placed two species in the same genus because they were more similar to each other than either was to a species not placed in that genus. After Darwin provided the theoretical underpinnings for why those two species should be placed in the same genus—descent with modification—the Linnaean taxonomy was no longer simply a means of showing similarity but a means of showing similarity *and* phylogeny.

The notion that formal similarity can be used to indicate heritable continuity between cultural phenomena appears to have originated with the use of the comparative method in linguistic studies of the late eighteenth and early nineteenth centuries (Leaf 1979; Platnick and Cameron 1977). As we pointed out earlier, culture historians of the twentieth century regularly referred to general processes of cultural transmission such as enculturation and diffusion (e.g., Kroeber 1940b; Thompson 1956), but rarely were they explicit about what was transmitted or why this might be important. For example, Gordon Willey (1953:368) remarked that "theories of culture change and continuity are fundamental to [Americanist] archeological studies," but he did not elaborate on what those theories were; nor did he point out that the notion of continuity had to rest on heritability and transmission. Albert Spaulding (1954:14) provided a brief but revealing insight into the theories to which Willey was referring:

> If we view the ultimate task of archeology as the development of the ability to explain the similarity or lack of similarity of any two [archaeological manifestations], the significance of [classifying those manifestations according to their positions in time and space and their formal resemblance] is easy to state. All [three—time, space, and form—] can be related to the proposition that culture change is systematic rather than capricious and to the auxiliary proposition that an important basis for the systematic behavior of culture is its *continuous transmission through the agency of person to person contact.* (emphasis added)

To culture historians, formal similarities between cultural phenomena signified some kind of ethnic relation—a predictable result of using ethnologically documented mechanisms such as diffusion and enculturation to account for typological similarities in the archaeological record. No one realized it, but this was tautological and put the cart before the horse. Thus Willey's (1953:363) statement that "typological similarity is an indicator of cultural relatedness (and this is surely axiomatic to archeology), [and therefore] such relatedness carries with it implications of a common or similar history" caused little or no concern within the discipline. It might have caused considerable concern, because the axiom falls prey to a caution raised by paleontologist George Gaylord Simpson (1961), using monozygotic twins as an example: They are not twins because they are similar; rather, they are similar because they are twins. That is, they are similar because they share a common history.

The root of Simpson's caution was the indiscriminate use of similarity as a measure of relatedness that plagued systematic biology in the 1940s and 1950s (Chapter 2). There the problem was exacerbated because evolutionary taxonomies were intended to reflect not only patterns of ancestry and descent but also the degree of divergence between and among taxa. This was the result of marrying the Linnaean taxonomy to Darwin's descent with modification, the product of which attempts to do two things at once. Evolutionary taxonomy purportedly is based on the same axiom that underlies any approach to understanding evolutionary pathways: Similarity of phylogenetically related organisms is a result of replication through transmission. During organismic reproduction, organisms transmit genetic material, creating either an offspring that is an exact copy of the parent (asexual reproduction) or an offspring that has characteristics of both parents (sexual reproduction). Over time, because of transmission errors, mutation, and/or recombination, the organisms composing a population (or species) change. These changes might not be detectable from one generation to the next; but after sufficient time we notice that the two ends of the lineage are represented by dissimilar individuals, whereas individuals adjacent to one another in the lineage are virtually identical. The same thing is evident in Ford's sequence of vessel forms (Figure 1.1).

Despite close adherence to the axiom that similarity of phylogenetically related organisms is a result of replication through transmission, evolutionary taxonomies were problematic because the two features that were being shown—pattern of descent and degree of divergence—did not always follow the same patterns and rates (e.g., Eldredge and Gould 1972, 1977, 1997; Gould and Eldredge 1977, 1986, 1993). Thus it became difficult, if not impossible, to incorporate into a consistent classification both the relative time of lineage splitting and the rate of change since the split (Brown and Lomolino 1998). The end result was widespread subjectivity, with each systematist arguing for his or her own idiosyncratic taxonomy. Worse, it became evident that the very features the taxonomies were supposed to show—descent and divergence—were being shown incorrectly. Why was this happening, and what did it say about the future of evolutionary taxonomy?

This is a critical issue, but we save further discussion of it for Chapter 2. Here the more important issue is the central axiom that similarity is a result of replication through transmission. Notice that we placed no modifier in front of "transmission." Certainly when we talk about organisms reproducing we are talking about genetic transmission, but is that the only kind of transmission that occurs? Similarly, from an evolutionary perspective, is organismic reproduction the only kind that occurs? The answer to both questions is no. From the standpoint of transmission, considerable work has been done in anthropology relative to understanding cultural transmission, beginning with early studies by Ted Cloak (1973, 1975) and continuing through those by William Durham (1976, 1978, 1982, 1990, 1991), Ronald Pulliam and Christopher Dunford (1980), Luigi Cavalli-Sforza and Marcus Feldman (1981), and Robert Boyd and Peter Richerson (1982, 1983, 1985, 1987; Bettinger et al. 1996; Richerson and Boyd 1992). This work often is referred to collectively as *dual-inheritance theory,* and although there are significant differences in terms of how various authors view the transmission process, there are enough similarities that they can be viewed as complementary (Winterhalder and Smith 2000). In dual-inheritance theory, genes and culture provide separate, though linked, systems of inheritance, variation, and change. The spread of cultural information is affected by several processes such as the strength of the transmitters and receivers, decision making, and natural selection.

Given what was known of cultural transmission throughout the twentieth century, it is apparent that archaeologists believed that more-recent tool forms were modeled on preexisting tool forms. Those later tool forms carried inherited characters that were replicated on the basis of older forms (Leonard and Jones 1987). David Clarke (1978:181) well understood the importance of transmission to maintaining heritable continuity among cultural items when he remarked that "it is the artefact maker who feeds back into the phenotypic constitution of the next generation of artefacts the modified characteristics of the preceding population of artefacts, and it is in this way that the artefact population has continuity in its trajectory and yet is continuously shifting its attribute format and distribution." Continuity is ensured by cultural transmission, leading over time to tool *traditions,* with tradition defined as "(primarily) temporal continuity represented by persistent configurations in single technologies or other systems of related forms" (Willey and Phillips 1958:37). More specifically, and from an evolutionary perspective more explicitly, a cultural tradition "is a socially transmitted form unit (or a series of systematically related form units) which persists in time" (Thompson 1956:38). This definition reflects transmission, persistence by means of replication, and heritable continuity. To us, a tradition is a *clade,* which for our immediate purposes can be defined as a set of related lineages and their common ancestor. The identification of clades and what they tell us about phylogeny is the main topic of this book.

Cultural transmission and genetic transmission operate similarly. From a purely biological standpoint, meaning that we are ignoring the effects of the social and physical environment, organisms within a population begin to look different from their ancestors because of changes in the relative frequencies of alleles (alternate gene expressions) within a population. Selection, drift, and other sorting mechanisms start to move the relative frequencies of different alleles in one or more directions, and the outward expressions of the organisms—their *phenotypes*—respond in kind. For example, selection against light-skinned organisms might cause a rise in the relative frequency of organisms that carry darker skin pigmentation. As a result, the number of alleles that cause light skin decreases in the gene pool relative to alleles that cause dark skin. From a cultural standpoint, projectile points, pots, and houses look different over time because of changes in the relative frequency of different *memes* (or whatever we choose to call the "particles" of culturally transmitted information [Chapter 4]) within a population. Those memes are the constituent parts of recipes used to make projectile points, decorate pots, and construct houses. And those recipes, like languages and species, have evolutionary histories. With the appropriate methods and data, we can begin to explore those histories. Some methods and data are more appropriate than others for particular kinds of phylogenetic research. More importantly, there are significant ontological differences among various approaches that have been used to examine phylogeny. We examine these critical differences in Chapters 2 and 3.

STARTING POINTS

Much of what falls under the general rubric *evolutionary archaeology* has its roots in how archaeologists in the early and mid-twentieth century approached the material record. For overviews of that period of Americanist archaeology, particularly with respect to evolution, you might want to see what we have to say on the subject (Lyman and O'Brien 1997; Lyman et al. 1997). But don't take what we have to say as the final word; read some of the original pieces. A good place to start is with A. L. Kroeber's (1916a, 1916b) work in the countryside around Zuni Pueblo, New Mexico. It was during the analysis of Zuni potsherds that Kroeber invented frequency seriation, which is one basis for showing heritable continuity between archaeological phenomena. You should also look at A. V. Kidder's (1915, 1917) early work at Pecos Pueblo, in which he wrestles with establishing what today we would call pottery lineages. Then look at Harold Colton and Lyndon Hargrave's (1937) statement on the phylogenetic implications of pottery types that were being described for the Southwest. Most archaeologists were not impressed with the evolutionary implications of schemes such as that proposed by Colton and Hargrave. Take a look especially at the criticism provided by J. O. Brew (1946), who failed to see any phylogenetic relationships among inanimate objects such as potsherds. Brew's sentiment was so widespread in the discipline that it would not be until the late 1970s that anyone raised the prospect of integrating the biological-evolution model into archaeology.

This does not mean that Americanist archaeologists were uninterested in such things as cultural transmission. To the contrary, numerous statements appeared as to how cultural transmission could be studied in the archaeological record. What grew out of such studies was the dictum that typological similarity could be used as an indicator of cultural relatedness. Gordon Willey's (1953) efforts in establishing this dictum are worth reading in their entirety. Unremarked was the fact that biologists and paleontologists were viewing the problem differently—that two things are similar because they are related, not that because they are similar they are related. Cultural transmission and how it differs from biological transmission continues to be a focus of anthropological and archaeological interest. Although they were written several years ago, two key works are William

Durham's (1991) *Coevolution: Genes, Culture, and Human Diversity* and Robert Boyd and Peter Richerson's (1985) *Culture and the Evolutionary Process*. The latter contains mathematical sections that might scare off potential readers, but those sections can be skipped if necessary without losing the key points. For a very readable introduction to the cultural-transmission literature, see Stephen Shennan's (2002) *Genes, Memes and Human History: Darwinian Archaeology and Cultural Evolution*.

TWO

Evolutionary Taxonomy and Phenetics

Two Approaches to Classification and Phylogeny

Biologists use three main approaches to understand phylogenetic relationships among organisms, one of which is cladistics, the focus of this book. Each approach differs from the other two both methodologically and ontologically, and it is difficult to discuss why, when phylogeny is the issue, cladistics is superior to the other two methods without discussing, if only briefly, what those other methods entail. The first approach we examine is evolutionary taxonomy, which traces its ancestry directly to the Linnaean taxonomic system of the eighteenth century. Although its roots go back to Linnaeus, evolutionary taxonomy is based in large part on the notion of descent with modification that Darwin advanced in 1859. Linnaeus provided the structure—a hierarchical taxonomy based strictly on degrees of similarity—but Darwin provided the reason *why* two phenomena are similar: They are similar because they are phylogenetically related. Thus, as a classificatory method, evolutionary taxonomy simultaneously addresses phylogeny and similarity.

The second approach we examine is phenetics, which made its appearance in the mid-twentieth century and by roughly 1965 had attracted considerable attention. As opposed to evolutionary taxonomy, phenetics addresses similarity only and makes no *direct* claim about phylogeny. This does not mean that phenetic orderings cannot be interpreted from a phylogenetic perspective, and certainly many pheneticists have done so. There are, however, good reasons to suspect that any ordering produced through the phenetic approach has less chance of reflecting the true phylogeny of the taxa involved than a cladistic ordering does. This is because of the undifferentiated nature of the attributes used to create phenetic orderings. If this were a modern text on biological phylogeny, we would pay scant attention to phenetics, given its general fall from favor, but the method has long been used in archaeology as a method of grouping cultural phenomena. The very reasons that led many biologists to abandon it in favor of cladistics should lead to its abandonment by archaeologists.

Throughout the chapter we employ a number of terms that, although often used by archaeologists in a general or vague sense, need to be defined precisely. The most critical of these are *classification, units, taxonomy,* and *affinity. Classification* involves the creation of new units and the modification and revision of old units by stipulating the necessary and sufficient conditions that something must exhibit to qualify for membership within a particular unit. The necessary and sufficient conditions for membership are the *definitive* criteria of a unit. They define the members of the unit and at least partially describe those members. A *unit* is a conceptual entity that serves as a standard of measurement (Lyman et al. 1997; O'Brien and Lyman 2000). A centimeter is a unit constructed explicitly to measure linear distance; the degrees on a compass are units constructed explicitly to measure direction or orientation. Units can be either *ideational* (centimeters and degrees) or *empirical* (a set of 10-cm-long pencils). Those particular pencils are in that set (an empirical unit) because they meet the necessary and sufficient conditions for membership: their length is 10 cm (an ideational unit), and each is a pencil (another ideational unit with a particular definition). We call that kind of set a *group.*

As conceptual entities, units, regardless of whether they are empirical or ideational, must be explicitly defined to be useful for measuring (characterizing, describing, categorizing, defining) something. Units can be specified at any scale. Things to be classified can occur at different scales. For example, the things we are interested in classifying might be discrete objects such as projectile points or organisms, or they might be sets of discrete objects, such as assemblages of tools or populations of organisms. Things are classified on the basis of the *characters* they display, such as size, shape, color, and material. Each character is a unit. Characters used to classify things occur at a finer, less-inclusive scale than the things themselves. Characters are mutually exclusive properties of things, and each character potentially can take any of several values, termed *character states,* each of which also is a unit. The character "weight," for example, can have the states 1–5 grams, 6–10 grams, 11–15 grams, and so on. Similarly, the character "color" can have the states blue, green, turquoise, and so on.

Taxonomy concerns theories of classification: their bases, principles, procedures, and rules (Simpson 1961). Although the term is often used as a synonym for *systematics,* we prefer to distinguish between the two. Systematics is the study of the diversity exhibited by the phenomena of interest, irrespective of their scale or kind. Systematics involves the sorting of diversity into sets (groups) such that like goes with like according to some principle of sorting. The generic sorting principle is that each set should be internally homogeneous so that within-group variation is analytically meaningless and between-group variation meaningful. Formally similar phenomena are often, but not always, conceived of as being similar in other ways as well, and this constitutes the specific sorting principle— often termed *affinity*—applied in particular classifications. Affinity refers to the particular relationship of analytical interest among formally similar specimens within a group or among groups of formally dissimilar specimens. Multiple kinds of things may be affines because they are close in form, in time, in function, in ancestry, or in terms of something else (Lyman and O'Brien 2002; O'Brien and Lyman 2002b, 2003a). The analyst must choose *which* kind of affinity is to be examined because different kinds of affinity are reflected by different characters.

Measuring a particular kind of affinity is the ultimate goal of classification, irrespective of discipline, but the process does not stop there. In science, classification should be problem oriented, meaning that it should be geared toward some larger goal than simply measuring how similar particular phenomena are to one another. The problem takes the general form: *Why* are phenomena A and B similar to one another and dissimilar to phenomenon C? Answering "why?" questions demands an explanatory theory, or taxonomic principle, concerning a particular kind of affinity. Darwin provided such a theory, at least as it applies to plants and animals, in 1859—the kind of affinity between units of organisms is phylogenetic—but there were still earlier theories behind biological classification, some of which were well reasoned.

BIOLOGICAL CLASSIFICATION BEFORE 1859

Prior to the eighteenth-century work of Carolus Linnaeus and creation of the system of biological classification that carries his name, numerous methods of classifying organisms existed. Linnaeus's *Systema Naturae,* the first edition of which appeared in 1735, completely redefined the study of the living world, putting it on a par with other, more prestigious and mathematically oriented pursuits that can be lumped under the broad term *natural philosophy* (Ritvo 1997). *Natural* is a word with broad usage today, but to Linnaeus it had a very specific meaning, which stemmed from the Aristotelian view that things in nature have an essence. The scientist's job was to identify that essence by deciding which characters defined it. Once those characters were identified, specimens that contained them—for Linnaeus, the specimens were plants and animals—could be divided into appropriate groups, referred to as *taxa*. The lowest taxon was the variety, although Linnaeus focused on the species as the fundamental taxonomic unit. Above it, in ascending order, were genera, orders, classes, and, finally, two kingdoms (plants and animals). Today taxonomists recognize at least twenty different taxonomic units. Linnaeus's classification is a hierarchical arrangement of nested sets such that less-inclusive, lower-rank units are included in more-inclusive, higher-rank units. Taxa of a particular rank can be symbolized as T_j. Each particular taxon comprises one or more taxa of rank T_{j-1} and is itself a member of rank T_{j+1}. Multiple taxa of rank T_j are termed *parallel taxa,* taxa of rank T_{j+1} are *superior taxa,* and taxa of rank T_{j-1} are *subordinate taxa* relative to taxa of rank T_j. The lowest-ranking taxa are called *terminal taxa.* Taxa of rank T_j are said to be *nested* within taxa of ranks T_{j+n} because the latter comprise *all* members of lower ranks. In nested taxonomies no two taxa of rank T_j have any T_{j-1} member in common. The specimens representing the lowest, least-inclusive rank are of rank zero and are themselves not a taxon but a *population,* or aggregate, of individuals. Populations are the operational units of classification (Buck and Hull 1966).

Linnaeus's overarching achievement was to take procedures that his predecessors had used incidentally or on a small scale, to analyze and evaluate them from the standpoint of their usefulness, and then to apply them consistently across the living world as it was then known (Stearn 1959). His proposed system replaced a cumbersome diagnostic polynomial (multiname) system that described taxa with an easily memorized binomial (two-name) system that designated and named taxa. The tenth edition of the *Systema Naturae* was published in 1758 and is generally taken to be the initiation of modern biological taxonomy, because it is in that edition that Linnaeus first applied his taxonomic method consistently and thoroughly throughout the volume.

It has been argued (Mayr 1969; Moore 1993; Stearn 1959) that Linnaeus's system was artificial, but we argue to the contrary. The natural, or correct, system of classification was an expression of divine creation and revealed the exacting order that God had intended his universe to exhibit. The basis for finding this natural order resided in morphological characters exhibited by plants and animals, although other kinds of characters, including those associated with behavior and ontogeny (development), were sometimes used (Brady 1985; Ereshefsky 2001). The closer the morphological resemblance of two taxa, the closer the natural affinity between them. Development and use of the Linnaean taxonomy was enhanced by the notion that taxa were immutable and did not evolve. This was entirely reasonable if species were natural units.

In constructing his hierarchical taxonomy, Linnaeus began not with species but with genera. The genus was a general and collective category, such as "owl," whereas the species designated kinds within the category—"screech owl," "barn owl," "burrowing owl," and the like. Genera were distinct entities with distinct names, and they were natural, so that all naturalists would agree on their limits (Cain 1959). Linnaeus reasoned that it was difficult for a layperson to distinguish among the particular species observed, so the genus category was necessary. He also wanted a readily learned system of classification that made finer-level distinctions between groups of organisms. His binomial system served both functions. Species, like genera, were viewed as distinct entities that eventually would be clearly separable from each other. The word "eventually" is critical, because the criteria used to distinguish among species in a genus could be altered whenever new species belonging to that genus were found.

As modeled in Figure 2.1, the characters that species possess are of several kinds: (1) those that every member of a genus possesses but that are also possessed by members of other genera; (2) those that every species member and only a member of the genus possesses; and (3) those that only a given species member possesses. Thus, the *definition* of a genus includes those characters that a species shares with other member species of its genus. This is implied by giving that species and other member species the same generic name. The characters that distinguish a species from the other members of the genus are its *differentia* (Stearn 1959), or what we term *significata* (Dunnell 1971).

Through the first half of the nineteenth century, each unit in the Linnaean taxonomy, regardless of rank, was seen as an *archetype,* a term that was introduced formally by English naturalist Sir Richard Owen in 1848 (Padian 1997) but had been around in concept well before Linnaeus. An archetype was a model organism, constructed from the sum of morphological characters shared by a group of organisms (Hall 1996). Archetypal

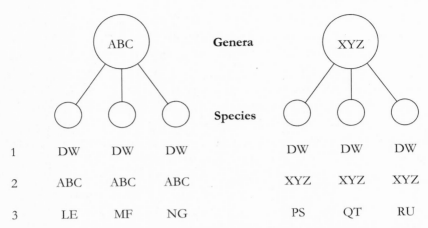

Figure 2.1. A model of the differentia and other characters of two genera (large circles) and six species (small circles) (after Stearn 1959). Each capital letter denotes a particular character and each number a kind of character:
1, characters shared by members of multiple genera;
2, characters shared by species members of one genus (genus differentia);
3, characters shared by members of a single species.

classification, because it commonly is based on morphological characters, is referred to as *morphological classification* or *typological classification.* An archetypal classification has a particular basis for grouping organisms:

> Its basis is the grouping of animals according to the number, and to some extent the kind, of structural characteristics that they have in common. Each grade in a hierarchy corresponds with certain fixed characters possessed by all the animals included under a given rubric at that level. The lower the hierarchic rank, the more characters held in common by the included forms. At one end the highest category is organic creation, with only life common to all its members, and at the other end are minimum units, each including individuals alike in all their hundreds or thousands of characters except for incidental, random fluctuation. Each group of the system has a fixed model, an archetype, consisting of a given set of morphological characteristics, and any animal that agrees, in this set of peculiarities, with the archetype belongs to that group. (Simpson 1945:3)

The archetype as a useful concept in biological classification would meet its demise when Darwin redefined the concept of a species. As opposed to being a static entity that could be captured by an essence, it was now seen as an entity that never held still. Things that don't hold still, but instead are always in the process of becoming something else, cannot possibly have an essence.

BIOLOGICAL CLASSIFICATION AFTER 1859

Organisms in the natural groups produced by Linnaean classification had affinity with other organisms in a particular group, but it was not until Darwin's (1859) *On the Origin of Species* that there was an explicit scientific account of both "natural affinity" and "natural group." In Chapter 13 of the first edition, Darwin specified a reason why various sets of organisms were more, or less, similar to one another. It was not a reflection of some divine plan but rather "propinquity of descent,—the only known cause of the similarity of organic beings" (Darwin 1859:413). In general terms, those "organic beings" that were similar had a recent common ancestor, whereas those that were not so similar had a remote common ancestor. We say "in general terms" because Darwin was well aware that processes such as convergence could produce similar organisms that were not closely related through descent.

As opposed to the use of what were previously viewed as "more essential" characters—the ones that together formed the essence of a species—Darwin's work shifted the focus to those characters that were least likely to be altered in the course of evolution. These were referred to as "primitive" characters and were viewed as providing the necessary phylogenetic clues to link descendant taxa with their ancestral taxa. What was happening, then, was more an attempt to accommodate what was thought to be implied by the Linnaean taxonomy—evolutionary descent with modification—than an attempt to alter how that classification system was implemented. As George Gaylord Simpson (1945) noted, superficial aspects of classification do not necessarily change when the underlying meaning of the classification changes. Similarly, Ernst Mayr (1969) pointed out that accepting evolution did not necessitate any major changes in the classificatory technique. The only real change was in the nature of the taxa themselves. No longer did systematists have to "make" taxa; evolution had done that for them. All a systematist needed to do was discover the groups. The discovery process was, however, far from simple, and rarely were procedures for species recognition made explicit. It would not be until the mid-1940s that the first formal statements on taxonomic protocol were published. This was a direct result of the unification of the three great biological schools of the early twentieth century—

first the merger of paleontology and zoology into what has been labeled
the naturalist school, and second the unification of naturalism and genetics. Julian Huxley (1942) appropriately labeled these collective events the
Modern Synthesis. Shortly thereafter, with the prospect of competition
from two new schools of classification—phenetics and cladistics—taxonomists were forced to explain in even greater detail how their method
worked (e.g., Mayr 1965a, 1969; Simpson 1951, 1959, 1961). This formalized method became known as *evolutionary taxonomy.*

EVOLUTIONARY TAXONOMY

Modern evolutionary taxonomy results in the classification of organisms according to their phylogenetic relationships *and* their subsequent evolutionary divergence. The classification procedure is accomplished in two steps, each involving various substeps. The first step
involves sorting individual specimens into species such that within-group
formal variation is minimal relative to between-group variation. Each
group is "recognizable and internally homogeneous," and there are "constant differences between such groups" (Mayr 1969:9–10). Each resulting
group is termed a *phenon,* which is a sample of phenotypically similar
specimens. Construction of phena is a three-part process: (1) determining,
through comparison, what the unique properties of every species and
higher taxon are; (2) determining what properties certain taxa have in
common and what the biological causes for the differences or shared
characters are; and (3) determining the amount of variation within taxa.

Once these things have been accomplished, the second step is under-
taken. This involves (1) putting the species in order by grouping them into
smaller and larger arrays of related species; (2) placing these into a hierarchy of categories such as families, orders, and so on; and (3) omitting
from group definitions characters that are shared as the result of convergence and parallelism (see below). This is accomplished by considering all
available biological data—morphology, behavior, physiology, genetics,
and biogeography—in an effort to make the classification reflect phylogenetic affinity. The kind of characters used is critical: "Characters that are
shared by most species of a higher taxon *are believed to be* the expression
of a complex genotype, particularly when the given character is not directly correlated with utilization of the adaptive zone of the taxon" (Mayr
1969:80; emphasis added). Darwin (1859:414) had said more or less the
same thing: "the less any part of the organization is concerned with spe-

cial habits, the more important it becomes for classification." What are Mayr and Darwin talking about when they use the terms "adaptive zone" and "special habits"?

Even before Darwin penned *On the Origin of Species,* many naturalists made a distinction between what later would be called *analogous* and *homologous* characters, although the manner in which they used the latter term differed dramatically from how it was later used. Analogous characters (*analogues,* for short) are characters that two or more organisms possess that—although they might serve similar purposes—did not evolve because of any common ancestry. Birds and bats both have wings, and those characters share properties in common, yet we classify birds and bats in two widely separate taxonomic groups because birds and bats are only distantly related phylogenetically. This is because these two large groups diverged from a common vertebrate ancestor long before either one of them developed wings. Therefore wings are of no utility in reconstructing lineages, because they evolved *independently* in the two lineages after they diverged.

In Mayr's terms, wings are directly correlated with the use of a particular adaptive zone—the air—by a taxon (birds or bats). In Darwin's terms, wings are part of the organization concerned with special habits—flying. In the case of birds and bats, wings are features that two unrelated lines developed that provided adaptive advantages in the particular environments in which they found themselves. We might surmise that those particular environments were similar, and hence the adaptive features were common solutions to a common problem, but there is an important point to consider. The presence of wings in the case of birds and bats is an analogous character state (as opposed to the alternate character state, "absence of wings"), but this is a far cry from saying that wings will always and everywhere be analogues. Eagles and sparrows both have wings, but here the presence of wings is homologous, not analogous, meaning that in the distant past the common ancestor of what eventually became eagles and sparrows had wings and passed that character state to its descendants. Homologous characters (*homologues,* for short) are useful for tracking heritable continuity because they are holdovers from the time when two lineages were historically a single lineage. As another example, all mammals have a vertebral column, as do animals placed in other categories. The presence of vertebrae is one criterion that we use to place organisms in the subphylum Vertebrata. The vertebral column is a homologous character shared by mammals, birds, reptiles, and some fishes, and it suggests that at some remote time in the past the organisms in these taxa shared a common ancestor.

Darwin's insight provided a new and logical causal explanation as to *why* there would be formal similarities among organs and organisms and also why the Linnaean taxonomy was hierarchical. Darwin (1859:206) argued that "by unity of type is meant that fundamental agreement in structure, which we see in organic beings of the same class, and which is quite independent of their habits of life. On my theory, unity of type is explained by unity of descent." In two short sentences Darwin clearly distinguished between analogous and homologous characters and provided the first explicitly scientific and theoretical explanation for the existence of homologues: Homologous similarity is the result of heritable continuity.

Darwinian evolutionary theory provides the explanation for homology, but it does not tell us how to identify instances of it. As one should guess from Simpson's (1961) example of monozygous twins cited in Chapter 1, operationalizing the concept in biology does not rest solely on formal similarity. Rather, "homologous structures may be extensively similar or very dissimilar. Therefore similarity is to be considered something quite apart from considerations of homology. . . . Similarity does indeed suggest homology, but dissimilarity is also abundantly evident in homology. The concept of homology cannot logically be tied into any definitions of similarity or dissimilarity" (Smith 1967:101). Or as Mayr (1981:511) put it, "so-called similarity is a complex phenomenon that is not necessarily closely correlated with common descent, since similarity is often due to convergence." These statements do not mean that mere morphological or formal similarity is unimportant. To the contrary, such similarity is what compels us to postulate homology (Cracraft 1981)—a fundamental position in cladistics, as we will see in Chapter 3. Most morphologists would agree with the point that similarity can be factual, whereas homology must usually remain a hypothesis (Patterson 1988: 604). Of course, if it is a hypothesis, then it is testable—another fundamental position in cladistics.

Evolutionary classification produces the familiar taxonomic tree, or *phylogram*, which records both the branching points and the degrees of subsequent divergence of taxa. This is a result of the fact that both classificatory criteria—formal (phenotypic) similarity and shared ancestry—are included in the classification (Bock 1973). Some argue that the former, although measurable, provides an unsatisfactory measure for our intuitive concept of evolutionary divergence (Griffiths 1973). They would argue further that in several respects evolutionary taxonomy is a more or less best-guess enterprise, with the results of those who have been the most deeply immersed in their specimens being favored over the results of neophytes. It is in part for this reason that a more "objective"—so characterized because a mathematical algorithm produces the groups—classification procedure was developed. That procedure is phenetics, referred to originally as *numerical taxonomy*.

PHENETICS

After the Modern Synthesis of the 1930s and 1940s and the emergence of the new taxonomy, there were still those who raised questions about the evolutionary implications of the hierarchical classification system that originated with Linnaeus. R. S. Bigelow (1958:49) highlighted the problem when he noted that it "is not always easy to determine . . . whether a given author means 'similarity' or 'recency of common ancestry' when he uses the term 'affinity.'" He disputed the working assumptions of the evolutionary taxonomist that (1) the degree of similarity denotes the recency of common ancestry and (2) similarity and recency of common ancestry are directly correlated for all characters and character states within a *monophyletic* (natural) group of taxa. By *monophyletic* we mean that a group, of whatever taxonomic rank, contains an ancestor and all, not just some, of its descendants. Another term for monophyletic group is *clade*. Bigelow pointed out that evolutionary taxonomists hold that "nonadaptive," evolutionarily "stable" (conservative) characters are the best ones for determining phylogenetic history, apparently because of the assumption that similarities in stable (nonadaptive) characters are more likely to have been derived from common ancestry, whereas similarities in "plastic" (adaptive) characters are more likely to be convergent and phylogenetically misleading. Bigelow argued further that this belief is fallacious, because it is not adaptive characters but *convergent* characters that should be avoided. This is the distinction we made above when we noted that wings are adaptive characters but not necessarily analogous characters. As Bigelow (1958:54) put it, "to avoid adaptive characters summarily involves passing over most of the best possible taxonomic characters." We agree in general with this statement—a point that will become important in Chapter 5.

Several individuals (e.g., Bader 1958; Cain 1956; Simpson 1951, 1959, 1961) agreed with these criticisms but pointed out that evolutionary taxonomy builds *hypotheses* of phylogenetic relationships that can be tested with independent data such as stratified sequences of fossils. Nevertheless, criticisms such as Bigelow's (e.g., Sokal and Camin 1965) resulted in the formalization of a different method of biological classification during the 1950s and 1960s—a method that had been around in various guises for decades (e.g., Gilmour 1937, 1940, 1951). It was formalized in the 1960s when computer technology became available for analyzing large sets of phenotypic data. Debate over the meaning and significance of homologous characters, in conjunction with a perceived difficulty in recognizing them, was one reason for the development of the method. Another reason was that the exact procedures by which evolutionary taxonomy was implemented seemed to be vague, subjective, and intuitive (Colless 1967; Sokal and Camin 1965). Phenetics was intended to bypass these problems.

In phenetics discrete organisms or sets thereof are grouped together based on their phenotypic similarities. One of the techniques by which the grouping can be implemented is numerical taxonomy (Sokal and Sneath 1963), although it is not the only technique (e.g., DuPraw 1964). The method emerged at the hands of several individuals more or less simultaneously (Cain and Harrison 1958; Michener and Sokal 1957; Sneath 1957; see Hull 1988b for an excellent discussion), with the most prominent center of phenetics being the University of Kansas Museum of Natural History. Early statements on the method and various of its techniques were synthesized and expanded in a single landmark volume (Sokal and Sneath 1963) that later was revised in light of various criticisms (Sneath and Sokal 1973).

The phenetic method considers only formal, or phenotypic, similarity. It begins by recording numerous *unit characters,* defined as those that cannot be subdivided into logically or empirically independent characters. That is, a particular state of a character should not itself have varied states, which Graham Griffiths (1973) pointed out was logically impossible save perhaps at the atomic level. The various techniques of implementing the phenetic method involve an assessment of the phenetic distance (dissimilarity) between the phenomena to be classified, which are termed *operational taxonomic units* (OTUs). OTUs can be individual organisms or aggregates thereof, such as higher taxa. An OTU is simply the lowest-level taxonomic unit employed in a given numerical taxonomic study (Sokal et al. 1965). OTUs are both the units that are classified and the units produced by the classification procedure. They are *polythetic,* meaning that they include multiple characters, although individuals within an OTU will not necessarily share every character of that particular OTU. Pheneticists argue that "adoption of polythetic principles of classification negates the concept of an essence or type of any taxon. No single uniform property is required for the definition of a given group nor will any combination of characters necessarily define it" (Sokal 1974:1117).

Because phenetic classification is based solely on formal resemblance, a pheneticist defines natural classification as yielding taxa in which members of a taxon are in some sense more similar to one another than any of them is to members of any other taxon. The subjective element of measuring similarity that characterizes evolutionary taxonomy is replaced by an operational and objective measure of similarity (Colless 1967). OTU A can be said to be more similar to OTU B than it is to OTU C because A and B share more unit characters than A or B does with C. Clearly, as the number of shared characters decreases, the level of similarity decreases and the more inclusive an OTU is.

Characters are given equal weight in phenetics. In fact, phenetics was a reaction to perceived subjectivity in the weighting of characters that is routine in evolutionary taxonomy. In phenetics characters can be randomly selected, or they can be chosen if they are "taxonomically useful" and represent "OTU characters" (Colless 1971). OTU characters do not vary over the study group and thus cannot indicate intragroup structure. The character of four legs, for example, would not be a good OTU character for distinguishing among different taxa of mammals. Pheneticists argue that evolutionary taxonomy provides no explicit method for measuring the similarity of organisms and taxa or for assessing the correlations of characters. They also argue that not only do evolutionary taxonomists weight characters a priori by selecting some but not others for consideration, but they are not explicit about why some characters are selected and others are not (Sokal and Camin 1965; Sokal et al. 1965). We find this characterization inaccurate. Pheneticists further note that their method is theory free; that classifications having but a single purpose are "useless" with respect to other purposes; and that the purpose or purposes of a classification must be explicit (Sokal et al. 1965:240). We agree with all these statements.

Pheneticists are quick to point out that the classificatory results of their analyses *might* reveal something about phylogeny (e.g., Camin and Sokal 1965; Colless 1970; Sokal and Camin 1965). For example, Robert

Sokal and Peter Sneath (1963:48) defined phenetics as "the numerical evaluation of the affinity or similarity between taxonomic units and the ordering of these units into taxa on the basis of their affinities. The term may include the drawing of phylogenetic inferences from the data by statistical or other mathematical methods to the extent to which this is possible." Pheneticists are much more explicit than many previous commentators about the exact meanings of the terms *affinity* and *relationship,* noting that for a pheneticist they mean phenotypically similar, which in turn might (or might not) be caused by shared heritage.

Evolutionary taxonomists (e.g., Kiriakoff 1965) argue that because phenetics considers all characters to be of equivalent classificatory value, this obscures any phylogenetic signal that might be captured in a character. Further, phenetics can result in the placement of phenotypically similar sister species in the same OTU (Kiriakoff 1965). Pheneticists counter the first point by arguing that phylogeny is not necessarily the goal of their classification (Sokal 1966; Sokal et al. 1965). They counter the second point by arguing that sister taxa grouped within the same OTU are not implied to be the same biological (reproductively isolated) taxon but are only phenotypically identical in terms of the analyzed characters.

The results of various phenetic techniques represent what is called a *phenogram,* which displays the overall degree of phenetic similarity within (and difference between) groups. The structure of the classification is one of hierarchical, nested, and nonoverlapping units (as shown in Figure 2.2). Each branch of a phenogram denotes an OTU of some level of inclusiveness and implies that, within the hyperdimensional area of phenetic space, OTUs of lower scales of inclusiveness will emerge as clusters rather than be randomly or uniformly distributed (Sokal 1974). Such results refer "only to the observed properties of entities, without any reference to inferences that may be drawn *a posteriori* from the patterns displayed. . . . [To] be strictly phenetic [such classifications must] provide nothing more than a summary of observed facts" (Colless 1967:7). Phenetics, then, is a grouping technique for placing morphologically similar specimens together into OTUs of varying levels of inclusiveness. What those groups might signify other than formal similarity is a separate issue.

CLASSIFICATIONS OF CULTURAL PHENOMENA

In evolutionary taxonomic classification, phenotypic similarity is used as a proxy for genetic similarity: The greater the phenotypic similarity

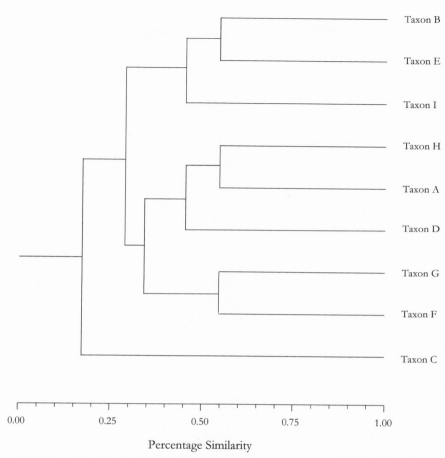

Figure 2.2. A phenogram showing phenetic similarity within (and difference between) groups of taxa. The structure of the classification is one of hierarchical, nested, and nonoverlapping units. Each branch of the phenogram denotes an operational taxonomic unit (OTU) of some level of inclusiveness and implies that, within the hyper-dimensional area of phenetic space, OTUs of lower scales of inclusiveness will emerge as clusters rather than be randomly or uniformly distributed. The scale on many phenograms is inverted from what is shown here so that *dissimilarity* increases to the left. We find it more intelligible to draw and label the scale bar as shown here.

between two organisms or groups of organisms, the closer the inferred genetical relationship between them. Phenotypic similarity/dissimilarity can also be used as a rough gauge of evolutionary distance: The greater the similarity, the less evolutionary modification of a descendant and hence the closer the relationship to its immediate ancestor. Cultural evolutionary taxonomies share these features, but with humans the phenotype can be expanded to include language, artifacts, social forms, and the like. Cultural evolutionary taxonomies of various sorts appeared throughout much of the first half of the twentieth century (Lyman and O'Brien 1997; Lyman et al. 1997; O'Brien and Lyman 1998, 1999), although the warrant for why a biological taxonomy served as the model for classification of archaeological phenomena—the notion of an extended phenotype that included cultural features—was left unstated. These forays into biological classification were met with criticism by archaeologists who saw no connection between biology and artifacts. We will have considerably more to say about the extended phenotype in Chapter 4.

Our brief discussion below does not do justice to the subject of cultural taxonomy, but here our attention is focused on but a single point: that similarity in architecture between the Linnaean system and the phenetic system is not a good indication of analytical purpose. Inattention to this key detail has led not only to inaccurate histories of various cultural classifications (e.g., Kehoe 1990) but to epistemological problems that continue to plague our understanding of the archaeological record.

One classic example of a cultural taxonomy that had clear phylogenetic overtones was a framework developed by Winifred Gladwin and Harold S. Gladwin (1934) for dealing with archaeological remains in the Hohokam area of southern Arizona. The Gladwins believed that all prehistoric groups in the Southwest had passed through the same cultural stages but at different times in different places—classic unilinear cultural evolution in the Tylor and Morgan mold (Chapter 1). The Gladwins' system of nomenclature was taxonomic in structure, and from top (most inclusive level) to bottom the tree consisted of four basic units (Figure 2.3). The *roots* of the tree were the principal recognized cultures in the Southwest: Hohokam, Caddoan (subsequently labeled Mogollon), Basketmaker (subsequently labeled Anasazi), and Yuman (subsequently labeled Patayan and later Hakataya). The four roots are still used as a conceptual framework to classify the prehistory of the Southwest. *Stems* were regional variants of the roots (e.g., San Juan stem of the Basketmaker root), and *branches* were still smaller geographical variants within stems (e.g., Chaco branch of the San Juan stem of the Basketmaker root). Each branch could be divided into time-space-bound cultural variants termed *phases,* which represented distinct developmental stages that were recognized by finely grouped traits of material culture such as pottery and architecture (Russell 1992).

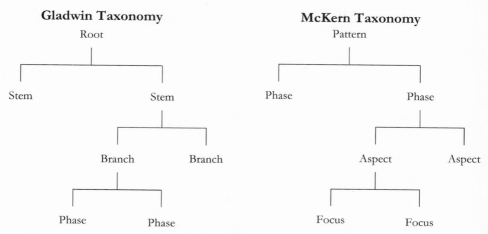

Figure 2.3. Comparison of cultural taxonomic frameworks developed by Winifred Gladwin and Harold S. Gladwin for the Southwest and by W. C. McKern for the Midwest. Despite the similarities in structure, the Gladwin model had clear phylogenetic overtones, whereas the McKern model did not.

Harold Gladwin (1936) saw parallels between the southwestern taxonomy and one that was simultaneously being developed in the Midwest by W. C. McKern (1939), which became known as the *midwestern taxonomic method* (Figure 2.3). McKern had the same motivation for devising a taxonomy that the Gladwins had: the need for a method of keeping track of archaeological variation that was rapidly growing with each passing field season. In outline, the method was simple. The entities arranged—the building blocks of the method—were called *components,* which were assemblages of associated artifacts that represented the occupation of a place by a people. In practice, components were sets of stratigraphically associated artifact types that could be described by a trait list. The similarity of trait lists, in turn, was used to assign components to groups. Five levels of groups were recognized in the method. From least to most inclusive, these were *focus, aspect, phase, pattern,* and *base.* Components belonging to a single focus shared most traits, and the traits (e.g., particular designs on pottery vessels) were specific. Foci that shared many, usually more general, traits (e.g., technique of decoration) than those used to create foci were grouped as an aspect and so on, until one reached the base, where only a few, often inferential, traits (e.g., agriculture) were held in common. Three kinds of traits were distinguished: *linked traits* were common to more than one unit; *diagnostic traits* were limited to a

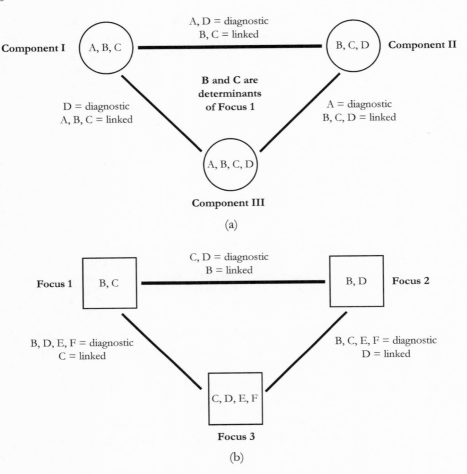

Figure 2.4. Analytical relations among traits (capital letters), components (circles), and foci (squares) in the midwestern taxonomic method (from Lyman et al. 1997). In (a), because components I, II, and III share traits B and C, those traits are linked traits; other traits are diagnostic. In (b) traits B and C are determinants of focus 1; components not containing traits B and C are not members of focus 1.

single unit; and *determinants* were traits that occurred in all members of a unit but in no other unit (Figure 2.4).

Gladwin was correct in noting similarities between the two taxonomic frameworks (Figure 2.3), but it was similarity in architecture only, not in how the results were viewed. Whereas the Gladwins believed their taxonomy had explicit phylogenetic implications, McKern saw no such implications in his taxonomy (Lyman and O'Brien 2003; Lyman et al. 1997). In fact, McKern was explicit that the units in his taxonomy did *not* have any necessary temporal or spatial meaning; such meaning had to be acquired independently of the method. Excluding space and especially time precludes phylogenetic implications (see also Rouse 1955). This is what McKern wanted. He did not deny that perhaps some of the groupings *did* have phylogenetic implications, but this was a separate issue from the taxonomy itself, which was founded purely on formal similarity of units. In modern terms, the method is an application of phenetics without recourse to the actual measurement of similarity (Lyman and O'Brien 2003). Indeed, McKern's contemporaries (e.g., Kroeber 1940a, 1942) were quick to point out that the failure to measure similarity quantitatively was a major flaw of the method.

A FINAL WORD ON PHYLOGENY AND CLASSIFICATION

The Linnaean taxonomy epitomized for many early-twentieth-century biologists "a pure science of relations, unconcerned with time, space, or cause" (Borgmeier 1957:53). That evolutionary descent with modification *might* be reflected in the Linnaean taxonomy was of less importance. Certainly biological taxonomists did not, until the late 1930s, incorporate the growing body of genetic information into their classifications. And although they believed their taxonomies reflected evolutionary descent, they were hesitant to argue strongly in this direction for a number of reasons. These included the lack of a generally accepted and well-understood mechanism for the process of heritability and the fear that convergence would obscure the phylogenetic signal (Mayr 1982). Thus, their taxonomies reflected "relations," as Thomas Borgmeier (1957) put it, but those relations were as much phenetic as they were phylogenetic. The Linnaean biological taxonomy had, after all, been built with no knowledge of evolutionary descent (Ereshefsky 1994, 1997, 2001). Rather, that taxonomy (reflecting pattern) provided independent evidence that Darwin's theory (concerning process) was correct (Brady 1985; Brower 2000).

Marked differences in the goals of evolutionary taxonomy and phenetics should be apparent. Although both approaches to classification are said to be directed toward measuring affinities among taxa, those affinities might be formal (phenetics) or formal and phylogenetic (evolutionary taxonomy). In other words, each method has a different primary analytical goal. We emphasize "primary" because some pheneticists argue that although they are measuring formal affinities directly, those formal affinities might well point to phylogenetic affinity. There can be little question that if phylogeny is our primary goal, then homologous characters are useful, whereas analogous characters—which by definition are unrelated to common ancestry—are not. Most pheneticists would not argue with this, but they *would* argue that the strength of their approach is in its ability to sidestep the issue of having to decide whether a particular character is analogous or homologous. Their point is that although a phenogram will only approximate phylogeny, so too will a phylogram, because of the inevitable inclusion of analogous characters despite the best efforts of evolutionary taxonomists to exclude them. This might be true, but it is odd to credit homologous characters with conceptual superiority and then negate that superiority by using undifferentiated characters. No one ever claimed that distinguishing between homologous and analogous characters was easy; and errors in assignment have been, and will continue to be, made. But why not at least attempt to filter out as many analogous characters as possible and concentrate on only those characters suspected of being homologous? This is the strength of evolutionary taxonomy as practiced from the mid-1940s on (Crowe 1994).

Despite its focus on homologous characters, evolutionary taxonomy has a weakness with respect to phylogenetic reconstruction: its dual emphasis on similarity *and* phylogeny. Descent with modification makes evolution a two-part process because two mechanisms are involved: mutation and natural selection. Note that Darwin used the phrase "descent *with* modification," not "descent *and* modification." Descent has "conceptual priority over modification such that modification is best viewed within the context of descent" (Knox 1998:4). This critical point was largely overlooked by naturalists working after Darwin, who settled on the postulate that "structural similarity is indicative of common phyletic origin, and as a rule its degree is proportional to the nearness of the common ancestry" (Simpson 1945:7). In one stroke *natural affinity* came to denote *common ancestry*, and *natural group* came to mean *related by shared ancestry*. Simply because entities can be classified within a taxonomic architecture does not mean that the results reflect phylogeny.

It should be reasonably clear by now that, despite the emphasis it places on homologous characters, the Linnaean taxonomic system has several drawbacks relative to its ability to demonstrate phylogenetic relationships. One drawback is its duality of purpose: It attempts to show

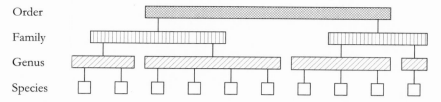

Figure 2.5. Nested (aggregative) structure of the Linnaean taxonomic system (after Valentine and May 1996).

overall similarity of taxa *and* phylogenetic relationships. Sometimes it can do both, and sometimes it can't, but there are many times when we have no objective grounds upon which to make a judgment as to its success. There is another drawback, and this one stems from its architecture. The Linnaean structure is an *aggregative hierarchy,* meaning that it consists of a set of nested units (taxa), with each higher level encompassing greater inclusiveness than the ones below (Figure 2.5). In an aggregative hierarchy "the fundamental units in the structure are species [and] at each successively higher taxonomic rank, new entities are formed by the aggregation of phylogenetically related species. Nestedness in this hierarchy results from the aggregation of units of equal rank" (Valentine and May 1996:26). Individual organisms are the basal units of the Linnaean hierarchy. Sets of individual organisms that are reproductively interactive and isolated from other such sets constitute a local population, or *deme,* of a species; multiple demes that are reproductively isolated from other demes comprise species (the biological species concept). The units of different rank in the Linnaean hierarchy display different properties. Individuals do not evolve, for example. Rather, populations and species evolve as the individual members change over time. Because of these differences in properties displayed by the different ranks, interactions within and between units within a rank are typically the subjects of study. What many systematists are interested in, however, is evolutionary descent and phylogenetic history. These are difficult to get at through an aggregative structure.

An example of evolutionary descent is shown in Figure 2.6. This is a *positional structure,* the basis of which is merely priority of appearance. In positional structures, all positions are occupied by the same sort of entity. There are no ranked collectives, and the position of particular entities is specified by the order of their appearance. Each positional structure "has a founding entity, and subsequent entities may be positioned in a

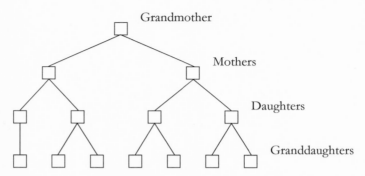

Figure 2.6. A positional-structure hierarchy of descent for four generations of related women (after Valentine and May 1996).

single series or in branches that form a tree-like structure" (Valentine and May 1996:29). In an aggregative hierarchy,

> the units are collected from the bottom up into more inclusive units. In a positional structure they are established from a founding entity and proceed so to speak from the top down. That is, a tree has a trunk first and then branches. [The included entities] are not ranked [so] nesting cannot involve the grouping of entities of equal rank. Rather, nesting involves the inclusion, within a group, of the founder of that group and of subsequent members of the series of entities along its branch and along any branches therefrom. Thus, in principle, each entity has nested within it all the subsequent entities. (Valentine and May 1996:29)

The Linnaean taxonomy does not and cannot trace the phylogenetic tree because it is an aggregative hierarchy rather than a positional-structure hierarchy. Simpson (1961) made a similar point when he noted a common confusion between a phylogenetic tree and taxa of different ranks. Our rendition of his illustration of this confusion is shown in Figure 2.7. Figure 2.7a shows a phylogenetic tree with branches and a stem—incorrectly conceptualized as Linnaean taxa of different rank. Time is implied to pass from bottom to top. Figure 2.7b shows the same phylogenetic tree as in Figure 2.7a, but with the various branches grouped correctly into Linnaean taxa; again, time passes from bottom to top. Figure 2.7c is a dendrogram showing Linnaean taxonomic relationships between terminal species (signified by dots) of Figure 2.7a and 2.7b. The dendrogram is not a phylogeny, and thus time is not included or implied; but note that the horizontal lines connecting vertical lines denote relationships and are topologically like those in Figure 2.7b.

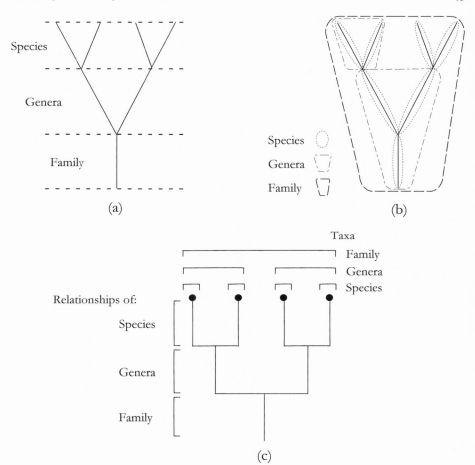

Figure 2.7. Hierarchical structures showing phylogeny and the relationships of higher and lower taxa: (a) a phylogenetic tree with branches and stem incorrectly conceptualized as Linnaean taxa of different rank (if time were included, it would pass from bottom to top); (b) the same phylogenetic tree as in (a) with branches and stem, and sets thereof, correctly conceptualized as Linnaean taxa (time passes from bottom to top); (c) dendrogram showing Linnaean taxonomic relationships among the terminal species (black dots) of (a) and (b). In (c) the lines of relationship are topologically like those in (b), but (c) is not a phylogeny because time is excluded (after Simpson 1961).

The aggregative structure of the Linnaean system, coupled with a dependence on the axiom that similarity is an indicator of relatedness, leads to the creation of nonnatural groups—those that do not include an ancestor and all its descendants. Some Linnaean taxa meet the definition of a

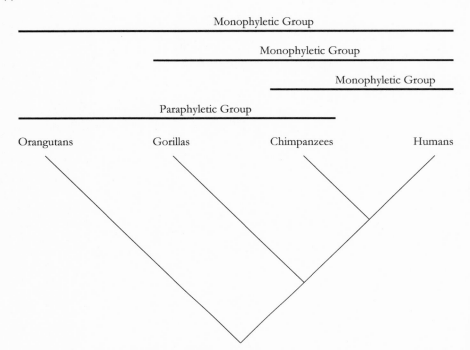

Figure 2.8. Phylogenetic ordering of four taxa, showing the difference between monophyletic and paraphyletic groups. A monophyletic group includes an ancestor and all its descendants; a paraphyletic group contains an ancestor and only some of its descendants. The diagram shows three monophyletic groups (clades) of primates and a paraphyletic group comprising orangutans, gorillas, and chimpanzees but not humans.

natural group, but many others do not. One taxon might include an ancestor and some descendants, whereas other descendants are placed in another taxon. We term these *paraphyletic groups*. For example, some molecular data suggest that humans, chimpanzees, and their common ancestor represent a clade—a natural, or monophyletic, group (Figure 2.8). They do so because the group includes two *sister taxa* and their common ancestor. Humans, chimpanzees, gorillas, and their common ancestors form yet another, more inclusive, clade. Adding orangutans and a common ancestor creates yet another clade. At each level of inclusiveness a monophyletic group is formed because all sister taxa *and* all common ancestors are included. Thus we say clades are "natural" groups. But standard taxonomic practice has long been to group chimpanzees, gorillas, and orangutans together and to refer to them as great apes and to place

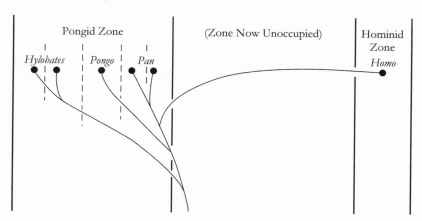

Figure 2.9. Adaptive basis for splitting out hominids from pongids and placing each in a separate grade (after Simpson 1963).

humans (including fossil humans) in a separate group or *grade*. Cladistically the grade "great apes" is a paraphyletic group when humans are excluded (Figure 2.8).

Paraphyly is common, and acceptable, in evolutionary taxonomy. We see four major reasons for this. First, paraphyletic groups are easily recognized (Brummitt 1996), although different researchers might classify the groups differently. Second, tradition and a kind of consensus as to the general arrangement of groups (with some divergence of opinion over precise relationships) contribute to the acceptance of paraphyletic groups (van Welzen 1997). Third, there is a general belief that grouping taxa based on the presence of commonly held morphological characters, regardless of the kind of character (Chapter 3), gives us extra information about the evolutionary history of the taxa. That extra information is considered to be the degree of evolutionary divergence. By keeping humans separate from the great apes, taxonomists emphasize *autapomorphies,* or characters that humans developed that the great apes did not—language, culture, and the like. As the traditional argument goes, the hominid split was so rapid and so pronounced (Figure 2.9) that hominids deserve to be kept in a separate grade. Fourth, paraphyletic groups are considered to be ancestral groupings. For example, reptiles are thought to be ancestral to mammals and birds; thus crocodilians are placed with reptiles even though cladistically they are more closely related to birds than they are to other taxa in the group. Any clade that does not include birds as well as crocodilians is paraphyletic.

If our interest is in phylogeny, then paraphyletic groups are of no help. What we need are monophyletic groups that allow us to track phylogeny from ancestors to descendants in an orderly and repeatable fashion. We should not have to rely on intuition or experience in creating the classification; nor, as the pheneticists argue, should we be forced to include any and all characters in order to generate a phylogenetic signal. The method that meets these criteria is *phylogenetic systematics,* commonly referred to as cladistics. Explaining the theoretical and methodological underpinnings of cladistics is the focus of Chapter 3.

STARTING POINTS

For an overview of units, classification, and systematics, especially as they pertain to archaeology, you might want to read several of our discussions (O'Brien and Lyman 2000, 2002a) as well as Robert Dunnell's (1971) seminal book, *Systematics in Prehistory.* For an excellent discussion of hierarchies in biology and paleobiology, see James Valentine and Cathleen May (1996). One of the best (and most readable) accounts of the Linnaean biological taxonomy is Marc Ereshefsky's (2001) *The Poverty of the Linnaean Hierarchy: A Philosophical Study of Biological Taxonomy.* Ereshefsky, a philosopher of biology, not only places the taxonomic system in historical perspective but points out the fatal flaws in it. He ends up calling for complete abandonment of the Linnaean structure—a call that has been echoed by some biologists and paleobiologists and condemned by others. Currently, considerable tensions exist over efforts to replace the Linnaean structure with one based entirely on phylogeny, termed *PhyloCode* (Cantino 2000; Pleijel and Rouse 2000; see the PhyloCode homepage at http://www.ohiou.edu/phylocode).

The complaint that phylogentically minded biologists and paleobiologists have against the Linnaean biological taxonomy is that, after Darwin introduced the notion of descent with modification, taxonomists tried to categorize organisms simultaneously on the basis of both morphology and phylogeny. This dual-purpose classification became the cornerstone of evolutionary taxonomy, as exemplified in Ernst Mayr's (1969) classic book on the subject, *Principles of Systematic Zoology.* The efforts of evolutionary taxonomists were roundly criticized in the 1950s—see R. S. Bigelow (1958) and A. J. Cain (1959), for example—and by the 1960s numerical taxonomy, or phenetics, rose up as a challenge to evolutionary taxonomy. For an excellent in-depth look at the early development of numerical taxonomy, look at David Hull's (1988b) treatment in his book *Science as a Process: An Evolutionary Account of the Social and Conceptual Development of Science.* Also take a look at Mark Ridley's (1986) *Evolution and Classification: The Reformation of Cladism,* which despite its name is an excellent introduction to evolutionary taxonomy and phenetics as well as to cladistics. For overviews of numerical taxonomy by those who developed it, see Peter Sneath and Robert Sokal's (1973) *Numerical Taxonomy,* Sokal (1966), and Donald Colless (1967, 1970). For an example of an early phenetic approach in archaeology, see W. C. McKern's (1939) efforts to build what became known as the midwestern taxonomic method. McKern never used the terms "numerical taxonomy" or "phenetics" to describe what he did, but his approach was identical to what the numerical taxonomists later did: remove time (hence phylogeny) from the classification and concentrate on any and all phenotypic characters. McKern's method was largely abandoned by the 1940s for that very reason—it ignored time, which is the backbone of archaeology. We cover the history of McKern's method and how it contrasts with Linnaean biological taxonomy in our book *W. C. McKern and the Midwestern Taxonomic Method* (Lyman and O'Brien 2003).

THREE

Cladistics

An Alternative Approach to Phylogeny

Taxonomists have long recognized two distinct kinds of homologous characters, but the manner in which the characters have figured into phylogenetic schemes has depended on the method of classification to which one subscribes. The two kinds are *ancestral,* sometimes referred to as *primitive,* characters and *derived* characters. The easiest way of visualizing the dichotomy is to think of derived characters as evolved novelties and ancestral characters as their lineal precursors. Although taxonomists typically speak of ancestral and derived characters, what they often mean are ancestral and derived character *states.* Consider a taxon comprising five-toed organisms, which over time evolve into four-toed organisms. The character is "number of toes"; the character states are the actual number of toes present—one toe, two toes, and so on. In this example, "five toes" is the ancestral character state, and "four toes" is the derived state. We prefer *ancestral* over *primitive* because the latter term carries the connotation that evolution is progressive—that it is somehow *inherently* better to have four toes than it is to have the primitive condition of five toes.

Until the mid-1950s, phylogenists tended to focus the majority of attention on ancestral characters in order to determine phylogenetic affinity. That preference for using persistent characters was what led Ernst Mayr (1965a:172) to note that the "classical phylogenist looked backward to the common ancestor." Mayr was correct. Taxonomists working in pre–Modern Synthesis days looked backward to ancestors despite acknowledging that evolution consists of descent *with* modification. If modification goes hand in hand with descent, then this should be a clear signal that ancestral characters can be misleading when the goal is detailed phylogenetic analysis.

The presence of a complex structure such as a vertebral column is pretty good evidence that birds, humans, dogs, snakes, and literally thousands of other taxa are somehow related. This relatedness is part of the reason for the identification of a subphylum called Vertebrata. The vertebral column is a homologous character shared by mammals, birds, and other higher taxa, but it is a character that extends so far back in time as to be essentially meaningless in terms of helping us understand how the myriad backboned organisms of the last 400 million years are related phylogenetically. Thus we use other characters such as the presence of hair and a four-chambered heart to segregate mammals from other classes of organisms that have backbones. This segregation, or cut, takes us back to about 200 million years ago. Then we make another cut based on the presence or absence of other characters to subdivide the sample further, then another cut, and another, and so on. The characters that allow us to make the cuts are derived characters. Ancestral characters are indeed homologues, but because they are shared by all members of all groups descended from the first ancestral taxon to have the character, they do not help in the construction of phylogenies. Cladistics relies solely on derived characters—or, to be more precise, on what we *perceive* as being derived characters.

THE BASIC TENETS OF CLADISTICS

The distinction between ancestral and derived characters, together with their roles in phylogenetic analysis, was made explicit by the German entomologist Willi Hennig (1950) in a treatise titled *Grundzüge einer Theorie der Phylogenetischen Systematik* (Fundamentals of a Theory of Phylogenetic Systematics), which was published during the heyday of the Modern Synthesis and the ascendancy of evolutionary taxonomy. Hennig is widely acknowledged as the founder of cladistics, although basic elements of his work occur in scattered earlier publications of other phylogeneticists. Hennig undoubtedly was aware of some of this earlier work, but it was he who laid out in considerable detail a systematic study of phylogeny that was built solely around derived characters. Despite the importance that some systematists would impart to his work a decade-plus later, Hennig's *Grundzüge* had no immediate impact on systematics in the English-speaking world. Neither did it have any impact on the way in which systematics was practiced in Germany. There emphasis continued to be placed on "ideal morphology," which had undergone a post-Darwinian resurgence in the 1930s at the hands of O. H. Schindewolf and others (Reif 1986). Ideal morphology centered on a search for *Baupläne* (pl.; sing. *Bauplan*), a word meaning "the basic organizational plan common to higher taxa at the level of the phylum, order, or class" (Hall 1996:225). Hennig's *Grundzüge* was an attempt to distance himself from typological classification.

In part to overcome the lack of recognition that his book received, Hennig published a summary of it in English in the journal *Annual Review of Entomology* (Hennig 1965). This was followed a year later by a greatly edited translation of the *Grundzüge* (Hennig 1966) by comparative anatomist D. Dwight Davis and paleontologist Rainer Zangeriwas, both of the Field Museum of Natural History in Chicago. At that point cladistics became more than a cottage industry practiced by a German entomologist and a few disciples willing to slog through his dry text. Various centers of cladistic taxonomy—Mayr (1982:226) derisively referred to them collectively as a "cult"—sprang up, one of the more vocal being a collective of individuals working at the American Museum of Natural History in New York. Taxonomists of various persuasion began taking a closer look at what Hennig was doing with his derived characters. Many of them were not amused. Hennig had termed his method *phylogenetic systematics,* but this term tread on the toes of evolutionary taxonomists, who saw themselves as doing phylogenetic work and doing it systematically. Mayr (1965b), drawing on the term *clade,* apparently first used by Julian Huxley in the 1950s to refer to a lineage (Schuh 2000), coined the term *cladistics* for Hennig's approach. Mayr used the term in a pejorative sense, and despite efforts to eradicate it, the name stuck. *Clade* comes from the Greek word *klados,* meaning "to branch," and although it appropriately describes the basic structure that Hennig's method produces, that method has less to do with the creation of individual taxa through branching and more to do with how collections of taxa are related phylogenetically.

Hennig broke with taxonomic tradition on two fronts. First, he claimed that "recency of common ancestry must be considered a criterion of ranking" within a classification (Hull 1970:24). For Hennig this meant total exclusion of ancestral characters from taxonomic consideration. Second, Hennig claimed that phylogeny should be the *only* criterion underpinning taxonomic classification. This is what upset the evolutionary taxonomists: Hennig was advocating that evolutionary pattern be divorced from evolutionary process. Hennig was not saying that evolutionary

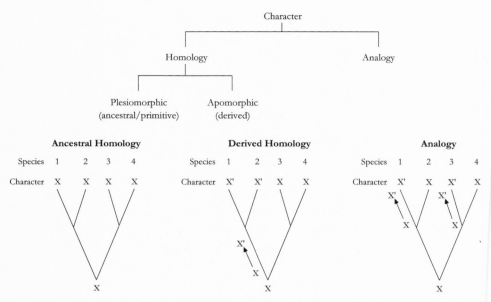

Figure 3.1. A taxonomy of kinds of characters (top) and the differences among them (bottom). Note that analogous characters (or character states) originate in lines not united through an immediate ancestor.

process was unimportant, but he *was* saying that the taxonomic mixing of pattern and process had greatly obscured efforts to understand phylogeny.

Hennig used some rather arcane language in his book, referring to ancestral characters as *plesiomorphies* and to derived characters as *apomorphies*. Where two or more taxa shared a plesiomorphy, Hennig termed that character a *symplesiomorphy*. Apomorphies could be of two kinds. If only a single taxon exhibited the character, he termed that character an *autapomorphy*. Where a character was shared by two or more taxa arising from the same ancestor, he termed it a *synapomorphy*. We say "arising from the same ancestor" because it was the ancestor that first gained the character and then passed it on to its immediate offspring. Figure 3.1 illustrates both a taxonomy of the different kinds of characters discussed here, including analogous characters, and the differences among them.

Mayr, who saw cladistics as the bête noir of systematics, nonetheless provided one of the earliest non-jargon-laden descriptions of the method:

> After a phyletic line has split into two separate lines, the subsequent reten-
> tion of ancestral characters and the acquisition of new, derived characters
> occur independently in the two lines. The basic rationale of all cladistic

methods is that the more recent the common ancestry of two species (or other taxa), the more characters in common they should have. The same thought, expressed in terms of taxonomic characters, is that the occurrence of a relatively new character will be limited to the descendants of the particular species in which the new character originated. A careful study of the distribution of characters in the taxonomic hierarchy should therefore give information on the grouping and ranking of taxa. The determination of the phyletic age of characters is the key operation in this method. (Mayr 1969:213)

Mayr was saying that in its most basic form cladistic phylogeny consists of a sequence of dichotomies, or branching events, each representing the splitting of a parental species into two daughter species. The ancestral species ceases to exist at the time of the dichotomy, and the groups it produces must be given the same categorical rank (as shown in Figure 3.2). Stage I consists of a single taxon, A. Stage II represents the splitting of Taxon A into two taxa, B and C. They are *sister taxa* to each other. As soon as the split occurs, Taxon A ceases to exist. Stage III represents the splitting of Taxon C into two new taxa, D and E, at which point Taxon C ceases to exist. Thus, depending on where one is in time, a taxon can be either a descendant or an ancestor.

The splitting is termed *cladogenesis*, hence the term *cladistics*. Immediately upon splitting, a clade is formed. In Figure 3.2, when Taxon A splits during stage II to form Taxon B and Taxon C, the clade B + C + common ancestor (Taxon A) is created. Another clade is created during stage III with the splitting of Taxon C into taxa D and E. That clade is defined as D + E + common ancestor (Taxon C). Two descendants of a common ancestor, say D and E, exhibit both the characters that their immediate ancestor (C) inherited from its ancestor (A)—plesiomorphies (ancestral characters)—and any characters that their immediate ancestor (C) picked up after its split from its ancestor (A)—apomorphies (derived characters). Cladists, following in the Hennigian tradition, view clades (monophyletic taxa) as "actual historical units" (Eldredge and Novacek 1985:66). This view is not completely at odds with how an evolutionary taxonomist views things, differing mainly in how the term "actual" is interpreted. A cladist would argue that the taxa in an evolutionary taxonomy might be historical, but how would we know, given that many of the taxa are probably paraphyletic (Chapter 2)? As with evolutionary taxonomy, cladistics produces a hypothetical phylogeny that can be tested and

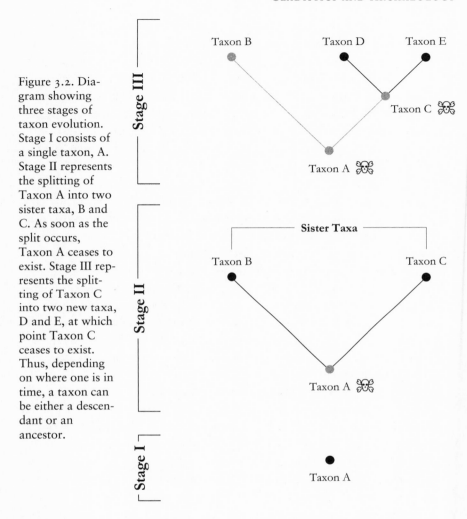

Figure 3.2. Diagram showing three stages of taxon evolution. Stage I consists of a single taxon, A. Stage II represents the splitting of Taxon A into two sister taxa, B and C. As soon as the split occurs, Taxon A ceases to exist. Stage III represents the splitting of Taxon C into two new taxa, D and E, at which point Taxon C ceases to exist. Thus, depending on where one is in time, a taxon can be either a descendant or an ancestor.

evaluated in light of additional data, such as by using additional or different characters than the ones used to create the phylogenetic ordering.

In our view the production of a hypothetical phylogeny *is* the ultimate goal of cladistics, although we have to be careful in how we state that. Technically, what we're seeing when we construct a cladogram (see below) is simply a pattern of character distribution and nothing else. Logically, a cladogram cannot make claims about the process that created the distribution. But the mere creation of synapomorphy patterns was not Hennig's original intent; nor is it the intent of most cladistically inclined biologists and paleobiologists. The intent was and is to understand phylogeny, which demands that the pattern be explained through the invocation of a process. This is done through reference to Darwinian evolutionary theory (descent with modification). Note that this is a far cry from saying that descent with modification provides independent support for any kind of systematics, including cladistics. If we could get away with such epistemological sleight-of-hand, then we would be assured that descent "explains pattern similarity, modification explains pattern differences, and their combination can explain any pattern that might be observed" (Brower 2000:151). Such a notion is both metaphysical and unverifiable (Popper 1974). The very strength of cladistics is its nonreliance on evolutionary theory (or any other theory) as a necessary ontological basis (Brady 1985; Lee and Doughty 1997; Platnick 1979, 1985; Rosen 1982). Some cladists (e.g., Beatty 1982; Kluge 2001) find this unacceptable, denying the possibility that Darwinian theory (process) can ever be strictly divorced from pattern. Such ontological wranglings have been going on in cladistics for some time (see Hull 1988b and Ridley 1986 for early accounts) and are apt to continue in the future.

TREES AND TAXA

Unfortunately, not only does cladistics contain arcane terms (such as *synapomorphy* and *symplesiomorphy*), but some of the more common terms are not used consistently. The biggest problem is in the use of the terms *tree* and *cladogram*. Some authors make a hard and fast distinction between the two, but we take a somewhat more relaxed approach. Let's look at the basic structure of a cladogram. Figure 3.3a is a simple cladogram that classifies three taxa. It tells us that based on a certain character distribution, the precise nature of which is irrelevant here, taxa B and C are more similar to one another than either is to Taxon A. This information, which could easily be written as a Venn diagram (Figure 3.3b) or in parenthetical notation (Figure 3.3c) without changing any of the information, is what is referred to as a *three-taxon statement*. The need for at least three taxa is obvious. If only two taxa are used, there is nothing against which to compare them. We need at least three taxa to make the claim that one taxon is more similar to another taxon than it is to any other taxon.

To us, a cladogram becomes a phylogenetic tree when we root it—meaning we identify a starting point. A cladogram always has a branching appearance, and hence looks like a tree, but without a root we do not

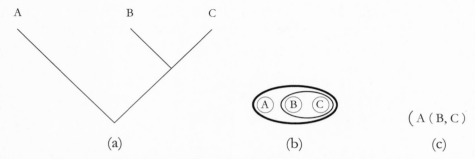

Figure 3.3. Three ways of illustrating the formal relations of three taxa (A–C):
(a) the conceptual underpinnings of cladistics rendered as a cladogram;
(b) a Venn diagram; and
(c) parenthetical notation.

know the precise pattern of branching. It is knowing that pattern that makes a cladogram a rooted tree. A simple cladogram such as the one shown in Figure 3.3a belies the fact that most cladograms can hypothetically be rooted at any number of points, and how we choose that point bears directly on the resulting taxonomic arrangement. We come back to this important topic below, but here there is a more pressing, general idea to be stated: A cladogram that gets turned into a phylogenetic tree is not the same as the phylogenetic tree shown in Figure 2.6 because it does not and cannot show the positioning of *real* ancestors and their descendants. In fact, ancestors play no direct role in cladistics. This seems counterintuitive and at first glance appears to contradict what we said earlier about ancestors ceasing to exist as soon as they produce descendant taxa (Figure 3.2). If they can "cease to exist," then how can they not be real? They must have existed at one time—otherwise they could not cease to exist. We discuss this sticky issue in more detail later; the thing to note here is that, technically, descendant taxa do have ancestors, but can we ever hope to pinpoint which specific taxon gave rise to other specific taxa? Probably not. Hence we refer to ancestors as "hypothetical" ancestors. They are "real" in the sense that for any taxon an ancestor certainly once existed, but whether we have identified the precise one or not is immaterial. Thus, whereas a rooted tree derived from a cladogram is a positional structure, it differs significantly from the positional structure shown in Figure 2.6, where ancestry can be traced through *known* ancestors.

In cladistics the convention is to place *nodes* at the points where *branches* meet and to refer to the nodes as ancestors that produced the *terminal taxa* (those at the branch tips) (Figure 3.4a). In our tree shown in

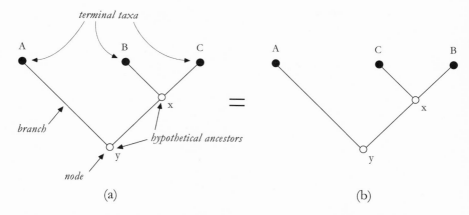

Figure 3.4. Cladogram showing commonly used terminology and landmarks. Notice that the topology of the cladogram (a) is not changed when we rotate taxa B and C at node x (b).

Figure 3.4a, taxa B + C, together with their hypothetical common ancestor (node x), form a monophyletic group, or clade. Taxa A + B + C, together with their common ancestor (node y), form another, more inclusive clade. Relative to the shape of the cladogram, termed its *topology,* we could reverse taxa B and C by rotating them at one ancestral node (x) and not change the topology (Figure 3.4b). Likewise, we could rotate the cladogram at the other ancestral node (y) and not violate the topology.

Recall that cladograms can hypothetically be rooted at a number of points (the precise number is dependent on the number of taxa), and how we choose that point bears directly on the resulting taxonomic arrangement. In the simple example shown in Figure 3.4, we constructed the cladogram purposely to show the intended order of taxa. We produced a *rooted tree,* with the root below the ancestral taxon (y) that produced A and B + C. But rooted trees start their lives as unrooted trees, or cladograms. We cannot stress enough that *unrooted trees are not phylogenetic orderings.* Such orderings, as we discuss below, are based on evidence other than what is contained in a cladogram. Figure 3.5 shows the seven possible rooted trees that can be derived from the unrooted tree at the top. For simplicity, we have excluded the characters that we used to create the unrooted tree, and we are ignoring the 14 other unrooted trees that could have been produced for taxa A–E. The unrooted tree shows several things. For one, taxa A and D are more similar to each other than either is to any other taxon. We can see this because it takes two moves through

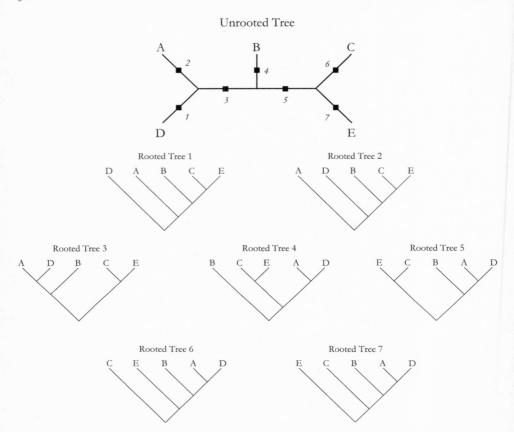

Figure 3.5. An unrooted tree (cladogram) and seven possible rooted trees for the five taxa (A–E) shown in the unrooted tree. The numbered squares on the unrooted tree correspond to the basal nodes on each of the seven rooted trees.

branch joins to get from either A or D to B, whereas it takes only one move through a branch join to get from A to D or vice versa. In like fashion, taxa C and E are more similar to each other than either is to any other taxon. Taxon B is not connected directly with either of those pairs but falls between them. The unrooted tree tells us about formal similarity, but it tells us nothing definitive about phylogenetic affinity.

Think of the unrooted tree in Figure 3.5 as a five-armed string. Notice the seven squares on the branches of the tree. Pick the string up at point 1 and lay it back down so that point 1 is at the vertex. What you will get is a taxonomic arrangement shown in the diagram labeled "Rooted Tree 1." You'll have to bend the thread around to get the nice shape as illustrated, but the taxa will assume the positions as shown. You've now created a tree rooted below the node that produced Taxon D and the ancestor of the other four taxa. You could also pick up the thread at any of the other six points and produce the arrangements shown in the other rooted-tree diagrams. We might be surprised at some of the arrangements. For example, we might have assumed, based on the shape of the unrooted tree, that taxa A and D were related through a common ancestor because they are joined at an apex. We might have assumed the same for taxa C and E. But notice that two rooted trees (1 and 2) do not show taxa A and D as descendants of a common taxon, just as two trees (6 and 7) do not show taxa C and E as descendants of a common taxon. Similarly, we might have expected that Taxon B would be somewhere in the middle of the other taxa in terms of descent, but it is possible that it lies outside the clade containing the other four taxa (Rooted Tree 4). This is why we said that it is difficult to overemphasize the point that unrooted trees tell us nothing definitive about phylogenetic affinity. This means that cladistics is really a three-part process. First, synapomorphic characters (or states) are used to create a similarity tree. Second, theory tells us that taxa are related through ancestors at increasing levels of inclusivity (clades). Third, a cladogram must be rooted in order for phylogeny to be read. Given so many possibilities, how does one decide where to root a tree? It obviously is critical to have some objective means of doing so; otherwise, we are left to guess at the correct phylogenetic ordering. We discuss this topic next.

CHARACTER POLARITY AND OUTGROUPS

The distinction between ancestral and derived characters or character states is clear, but it is perhaps not so clear that, depending on the scale at which a character is viewed, it can be both ancestral and derived. This is a key point and one directly related to the fact that a taxon, depending on the scale at which it is viewed, can be either an ancestor or a descendant (Figure 3.2). The dual nature of characters is implied in Figure 3.1 but is spelled out more clearly in Figure 3.6, which shows the evolution of a collection of avian lineages, beginning with Ancestor A. For simplicity we are tracking only a single character, feathers, for which two character states are possible: unfeathered and feathered. Over time, Ancestor A, which is unfeathered, gives rise to two lines, one of which is unfeathered, like its ancestor, and the other of which is feathered (Figure 3.6a). Thus the character state "feathered" in Taxon 2 is apomorphic, meaning it is derived from the ancestral character state, "unfeathered." In Figure 3.6b, Ancestor B (old Taxon 2) gives rise to two new taxa, 3 and 4, each of which carries the derived character state, "feathered." At this point "feathered" becomes a shared derived character state, or synapomorphy, meaning that it is shared only by sister taxa and their immediate common ancestor. Characters in sister taxa that have been inherited from an ancestor more distant than the common ancestor are ancestral characters. In Figure 3.6c, in which two descendant taxa have been added, feathering is now an ancestral character *relative* to taxa 5 + 6 because it is shared by three taxa and two ancestors. But relative to taxa 3 + 5 + 6, feathering is a derived character state because it is shared by three taxa and their immediate common ancestor, B. Thus depending on where in a lineage we begin, which influences the scale or degree of inclusiveness of the lineage or clade, a trait can be derived or ancestral. Notice that in cladistics shared derived characters "are nested. From the point when a feature first appears in phylogenetic history, it will be passed along in some guise (i.e., in the same or transformed version) to descendant taxa. [By] mapping the distribution of such attributes, monophyletic taxa—branches of the tree of life—are delineated, defined, and recognized" (Eldredge and Novacek 1985:67). Also notice that in the above example we could have substituted "projectile-point lineages" for "avian lineages" and substituted "fluted/unfluted" for "feathered/unfeathered." The presence of both sets of characters in descendent taxa is controlled by transmission, irrespective of the precise transmission mechanism. As such, the characters are ripe for use in cladistics.

The question is, how does one actually distinguish between ancestral and derived character states—termed *character polarity*—in order to plot the course of evolution relative to those taxa? In our examples, we have indicated which character states are ancestral and derived, but in the real world this is seldom obvious. General knowledge might give us clues as to which states are which, but such information might be confined to one or only a few characters. Characters can be thought of in terms of binary opposites—they are either present or absent—but character states are another matter. First, their presence depends on the character itself being present. Thinking in terms of the absent state of an absent character gets us nowhere. Second, more than likely there are more than two states of a character. This is referred to as a *multistate transformation series* (as opposed to a *binary transformation series* if there are only two states). This places an added burden on our analysis, because in terms of character po-

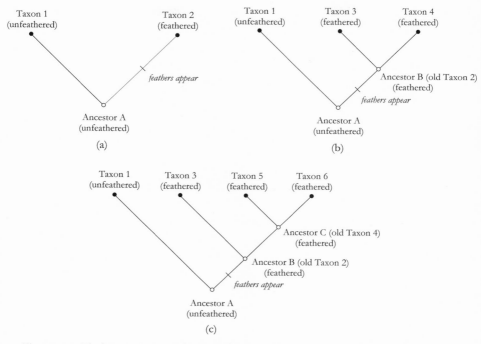

Figure 3.6. Phylogenetic trees showing the evolution of six taxa (after O'Brien et al. 2001). In (a) feathers appear during the evolution of Taxon 2 out of its ancestral taxon. Its appearance in Taxon 2 is as an apomorphy. In (b) Taxon 2 has produced two taxa, 3 and 4, both of which contain feathered specimens. The appearance of feathers in those sister taxa and in their common ancestor (B) makes it a synapomorphy. In (c) one of the taxa that appeared in the previous generation (Taxon 4) gives rise to two new taxa, 5 and 6, both of which contain feathered specimens. If we focus attention only on those two new taxa, having feathers is now an ancestral character state (plesiomorphy) because it is shared by more taxa than just sister taxa 5 and 6 and their immediate common ancestor. But if we include Taxon 3 in our focus, having feathers is a synapomorphy because, following the definition, it occurs only in sister taxa and in their immediate common ancestor.

larity, it is now not simply a one-to-one ratio between ancestral state and derived state but a one-to-some-multiple-of-one ratio. Not only do we have to figure out which is the ancestral versus the derived state, we now have three, four, or more states to consider. How characters are coded is also an integral part of cladistics, but we reserve discussion of this thorny issue for Chapter 5.

The issue of determining character polarity is complex, but one common (and contentious [Nixon and Carpenter 1993]) method involves *outgroup comparison,* with an outgroup defined as a taxon that is outside the taxa being analyzed (the *ingroup* taxa). This is called *character argumentation.* The working assumption is that a character or character state in the outgroup is ancestral relative to the ingroup taxa. Note that we did not say the outgroup taxon was directly ancestral to the ingroup taxa; rather, we said it was ancestral *relative to* those taxa. Technically, any taxon can serve as an outgroup, but the more closely related it is to the ingroup taxa, the greater the number of characters or character states that might be clarified relative to polarity (Wheeler 1990). Conversely, the more distantly related an outgroup is to the ingroup taxa, the greater the potential for an erroneous reconstruction of the relationships among the ingroup taxa. Selecting an outgroup roots the tree below the intersection of the outgroup and ingroup; ingroup taxa are then arranged in terms of their best fit relative to the characters or character states examined. We discuss how to do this below. Before turning to that topic, however, we need to address two related issues, homoplasy and parsimony.

Homoplasy

Although in the simple examples presented thus far all characters and character states evolved only once, such a neat package is rarely encountered in real-world situations. More likely a tree will contain multiple character states that show up in lines not related directly through one common ancestor. These are referred to as *homoplasy*—a condition that acts to distort our picture of phylogeny. One kind of homoplasy results from character-state reversals—meaning, for example, that character state A changed to state A' and then at some later point in the set of related lineages reverted to state A. For organisms we view this kind of homoplasy more as a classification problem (O'Brien et al. 2001, 2002), meaning that rarely if ever will precisely the same character state reemerge after it disappears, especially if it involves complex structures. This is referred to as the law of phylogenetic irreversibility, or simply Dollo's Law, named after Louis Dollo, a vertebrate paleontologist at the Royal Museum of Natural History in Brussels who formulated the principle (Dollo 1893). Far more likely than a reversal are cases in which the classification system—how we are measuring character states—makes it *appear* as if the new character state is an instance of homoplasy. With respect to cultural phenomena, reversals may be much more common than they are in the biological world—a point we examine further in Chapter 7.

Another kind of homoplasy results from either *parallelism* or *convergence*. Parallelism is a case of an identical character state arising in two distantly related taxa as a result of common developmental histories that channel a character in a certain direction. Convergence is a case of an identical character state arising in two unrelated taxa as a result of similar adaptive paths. Perhaps the most classic case of convergence in the animal world is the Tasmanian wolf (tiger), which is astoundingly close in appearance to members of the genus *Canis,* such as the common dog and North American wolf. Despite the suite of characters they share in common, the Tasmanian wolf (*Thylacinus cynocephalus*) actually has more in common phylogenetically with a kangaroo or an opossum than it does with a dog.

Parsimony

All but the simplest cladograms contain instances of homoplasy, and the task of the analyst is to reduce their influence on phylogenetic reconstruction—one of the most difficult problems in cladistics, if not the most difficult. The presence of homoplasy leads to multiple solutions— usually thousands, if not millions—to arranging taxa, and it is up to the analyst to sort through the solutions (there usually will be more than one optimal solution) and defend why one of them is chosen as the working phylogenetic hypothesis. As we discuss in a later section, computer programs simplify this task and produce various indices by which to judge the overall strength of the ordering.

Outgroup comparison works on the assumption of *parsimony,* but there is considerable controversy over what this means. Mark Ridley (1996:476), for example, states that "outgroup comparison works on the assumption that *evolution* is parsimonious" (emphasis added). This means that when faced with the problem of character polarity, we choose the option that requires the fewest evolutionary events. For example, in Figure 3.6 it is more parsimonious to assume that feathers arose once and only once as opposed to having arisen twice in separate lineages. Thus when faced with specimens in taxa 3 and 4, which exhibit feathers (Figure 3.6b), it is more parsimonious to assume that feathers appeared in Ancestor B than it is to see them as having arisen separately in taxa 3 and 4. That would require two evolutionary steps instead of one. Based on that reasoning, we view feathers as a synapomorphy as opposed to a case of homoplasy.

Analytical use of parsimony, however, has nothing to do with whether evolution itself is parsimonious. Rather, it has to do with logical argumentation: It is more parsimonious to make as few ad hoc phylogenetic hypotheses as possible (Platnick 1977; Sober 1983). Evolution itself may or may not be parsimonious in any given situation. And we may or may not ever know whether evolution was or was not parsimonious in a particular situation. As long as we consistently select the most parsimonious pathway, unless evidence suggests otherwise, we have fewer assumptions to make. Steve Farris (1983:13) put it this way: "only characters conflicting with a genealogy lead to requirements for ad hoc hypotheses, and so the only ad hoc hypotheses needed to defend a genealogy are hypotheses of homoplasy." He was simply restating Hennig's (1966) *auxiliary principle,* which says that homology should always be assumed in the absence of contrary evidence.

Other Methods of Optimization

Although we do not go into any great detail on the subject, there are methods other than parsimony for constructing optimal trees. One is maximum likelihood, the roots of which can be traced to the work of A. W. F. Edwards and Luigi Cavalli-Sforza in the 1960s (Edwards and Cavalli-Sforza 1964; Cavalli-Sforza and Edwards 1967). Maximum likelihood infers phylogenetic relationships using a specified model of character evolution. Basically, the tree is constructed, or "chosen," to maximize the probability of observing the data fed into the analysis, and the model of evolutionary change is used to calculate the probability of observing the data (Swofford et al. 1996). The model does this by giving the probability of a character-state change over a specified evolutionary distance (Huelsenbeck and Bollback 2001). In addition to the model, the probability of observing the data depends on several unknown parameters that include tree topology, the tree branch lengths, and potential variation in the rate of character-state change from branch to branch. These parameters are estimated by "finding that combination of parameter values that maximizes the likelihood function" for a given tree (Huelsenbeck and Bollback 2001:426). Maximum likelihood therefore must solve two problems: finding the maximum-likelihood combination of parameters (tree topology, branch lengths, and so on) for distinct trees and finding the tree that has the greatest likelihood for a given set of characters, character states, and taxa (Huelsenbeck and Bollback 2001).

Maximum-likelihood methods have seen considerable use in molecular phylogenetics but little use in reconstructing morphological phylogenies until recently, with Paul Lewis's (2001) study being the most comprehensive morphological application to date. Obviously, the success of maximum likelihood methods for reconstructing phylogenies resides in the appropriateness of both the model of character evolution specified and the estimated parameter values. Still, in some situations maximum likelihood produces more consistent results than does maximum parsimony. One situation involves a phenomenon known as *long-branch attraction* (e.g., Hendy and Penny 1989; Lewis 2001). As Marcel Harmon as his colleagues point out in their comparison of maximum parsimony and maximum likelihood using ceramic data from Arizona and northwestern Mexico (Harmon et al. 2003), long branches can be problematic because the taxa at the ends of the branches often exhibit character states that show similarity because of convergence or parallelism rather than because of homology. Parsimony ignores branch length, whereas maximum likelihood may separate long-branch taxa if the model of evcolutionary change used in the analysis indicates that the evidence for convergence or parallelism is greater than the evidence for homology. For further discussion of bias in phylogenetic estimation and its relevance to the choice between parsimony and likelihood methods, see Swofford et al. (2001). For a method useful in detecting long-branch taxa, see various articles by James Lyons-Weiler and colleagues (e.g., Lyons-Weiler and Hoelzer 1997; Lyons-Weiler et al. 1996). For a discussion of bias in phylogenetic estimation and its relevance to the choice between parsimony and likelihood methods, see Swofford et al. (2001). For a discussion of adapting maximum parsimony to a likelihood framework, see Goldman (1990).

Outgroup Comparison

The success of any parsimony analysis employing outgroup comparison resides in the appropriateness of the outgroup selected. As we noted earlier, the more closely related the outgroup is to the ingroup taxa, the greater the number of characters or character states that might be clarified relative to polarity. Conversely, the more distantly related an outgroup is to the ingroup taxa, the greater the potential for an erroneous reconstruction of the relationships among the ingroup taxa. Let's work through a simple example of how an outgroup can be used to construct a rooted tree. Borrowing an example from Daniel Brooks and Deborah

	Characters and Character States						
	1	2	3	4	5	6	7
A (outgroup)	0	0	0	0	0	0	0
B	1	1	0	0	1	1	1
C	1	1	1	1	1	1	1
D	1	1	1	1	0	0	0

(a)

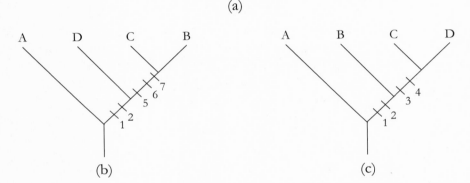

(b)   (c)

Figure 3.7. Character-state matrix (a) used to generate two logically incompatible trees (b and c) for four taxa (A–D) (zero = ancestral state, 1 = derived [apomorphic] state) (adapted from Brooks and McLennan 1991). Tree (b) places taxa B and C in a clade; tree (c) places taxa C and D in a clade. Together (b) and (c) violate Hennig's principle that there is only one correct phylogeny.

McLennan (1991), suppose we have the data matrix shown in Figure 3.7a, which shows the distribution of ancestral (labeled as zero) and derived (labeled as 1) character states for seven characters and three taxa (B, C, and D) plus an outgroup (A). Note that the outgroup character states are all coded as ancestral. The matrix shows us that based on characters 1 and 2, taxa B + C + D form a monophyletic group; but because all three taxa share the same states of characters 1 and 2, we cannot resolve the clade solely on the basis of these two characters. Thus we say that characters 1 and 2 are uninformative. We can resolve things, however, by considering characters 5, 6, and 7. Here taxa B + C form a monophyletic group (together with their ancestor) that does not include Taxon D (Figure 3.7b). Further, based on characters 3 and 4, taxa D + C form a mono-

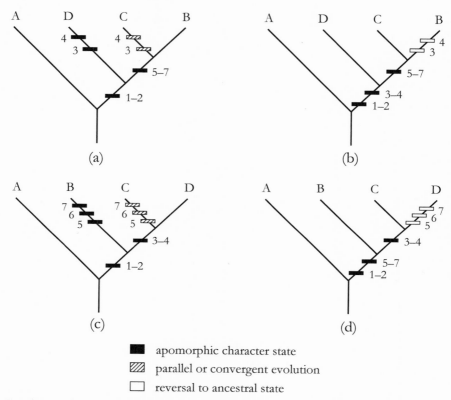

apomorphic character state
parallel or convergent evolution
reversal to ancestral state

Figure 3.8. Alternative hypotheses for the relationships of taxa B–D (see Figure 3.7) that result from homoplasy (adapted from Brooks and McLennan 1991). Characters 3 and 4 could have arisen independently in taxa C and D (a) or in the common ancestor of B + C + D but then reverted to the ancestral states in Taxon B (b). Characters 5–7 could have arisen independently in taxa B and C (c) or in the common ancestor of B + C + D but then reverted to the ancestral states in Taxon D (d).

phyletic group (Figure 3.7c). But here we have run into a problem, in that both statements cannot be correct—either that or we have disproved the first principle of phylogenetic analysis, namely, that there is only one true phylogeny. We immediately suspect that homoplasy is clouding the issue.

Character distributions can be portrayed in sevveral ways: Either the states of characters 3 and 4 arose independently in taxa C and D (Figure 3.8a), or they arose in the common ancestor of B + C + D and were subsequently lost in Taxon B, meaning that they reverted to the ancestral states (Figure 3.8b). The distribution of characters 5–7, which were left

off the tree in Figure 3.7c, shows a similar pattern of homoplasy: Either
the states of characters 5–7 arose independently in taxa B and C (Figure
3.8c), or they arose in the common ancestor of B + C + D and subsequently reverted to the ancestral states in Taxon D (Figure 3.8d). How do
we choose among the various options? One answer is to fall back on Hennig's auxiliary principle that homology should always be assumed in the
absence of contrary evidence. In other words, search for the tree that includes the greatest number of homologies and the fewest number of homoplasies. The trees in Figure 3.8a and 3.8b, which share a common
topology, contain seven derived character states each; the tree in Figure
3.8a also contains two instances of parallelism (or convergence), and the
tree in Figure 3.8b contains two instances of trait reversal. The trees in
Figure 3.8c and 3.8d, which also share a common topology, contain seven
derived character states each; the tree in Figure 3.8c also contains three instances of parallelism (or convergence), and the tree in Figure 3.8d contains three instances of trait reversal. Therefore, we would choose the
trees in Figure 3.8a and 3.8b over the trees in Figure 3.8c and 3.8d. The
trees in Figure 3.8a and 3.8b have a *length* of nine (the sum of derived
character states [= 7] plus homoplasies [= 2]), and the trees in Figure 3.8c
and 3.8d have a length of 10. Importantly, although the trees in Figure
3.8a and 3.8b are more parsimonious accounts of phylogeny than the
trees in 3.8c and 3.8d are, meaning they have shorter lengths, they are by
no means surely correct. They are merely phylogenetic hypotheses.

CONSENSUS TREES

We now have narrowed our choice of trees to those in Figure 3.8a
and 3.8b, but we still have two trees instead of one. Notice that their
topology is identical. This is good news. Some of the character states appear on different branches between the two trees, but at least the ordering
of the terminal taxa is consistent. Most of the time we will not be so for-
tunate. With a larger number of taxa, it would not be surprising to generate hundreds if not thousands of rooted trees of equal length, with a large
number of different topologies. They can't all be correct (and again,
maybe none is), so how do we choose among them? Maybe we decide that
it is more common for a character to be lost than it is for it to arise in separate lineages, so we stake our bet on trees similar to the one in Figure
3.8b. We could claim that we are following Hennig's auxiliary principle—
assume homology over homoplasy—but this is not what he meant. Char-

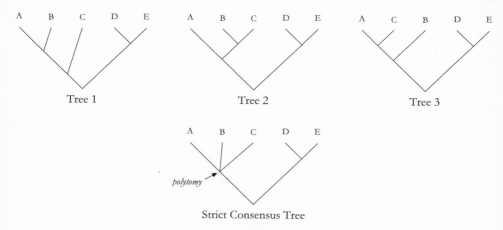

Figure 3.9. Strict consensus tree based on three trees of equal length. A polytomy is created because taxa A–C cannot be resolved further.

acter *loss,* whereby a taxon resembles a taxon not related to it through an immediate common ancestor, is simply another form of homoplasy. We could escape the problem altogether by showing all trees, but this is impractical in most cases. There may be good reasons to reject certain trees—say, based on stratigraphic grounds—but one is still left with too many trees to illustrate. This is where consensus trees come in. Consensus trees are just that: consensus opinions about taxic relationships. They are "best-fit" trees based on certain parameters. There are numerous methods of constructing consensus trees, and we deal with only four. Our discussion is necessarily brief, but you can read more about consensus trees in Ian Kitching et al. (1998:139–150) and Ed Wiley et al. (1991:80–90).

Strict Consensus Tree

Strict consensus trees are the most conservative models, in that they are created by combining only those features that appear in all the trees. Some biologists (e.g., Nixon and Carpenter 1996) refer to any consensus tree other than a strict one as a "compromise" tree. Suppose we had three trees of equal length, as shown in Figure 3.9. The only feature that is common to all three is the clade formed by D + E (for simplicity we refer only to the terminal taxa and ignore the ancestor that produced them). The other three taxa form a clade, but their position relative to each other is ambiguous. Each of the three trees is fully *resolved,* meaning

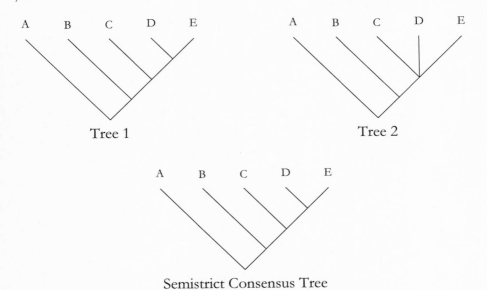

Figure 3.10. Semistrict consensus tree based on two trees of equal length.

that there are two and only two branches coming off each split. But when we calculate a strict consensus tree, we cannot resolve A, B, and C, so we show all three as branching from the ancestor. This branching relationship of unresolved taxa is called a *polytomy*.

Semistrict Consensus Tree

Semistrict consensus trees, sometimes referred to as *combinable component* trees (Bremer 1990), relax the conditions of strict consensus trees and combine those clades that are not contradicted by one of the trees. One of the trees will always contain a polytomy (Tree 2 in Figure 3.10). Semistrict consensus trees often result in better-resolved trees than those produced by the stricter method, although this does not mean a semistrict consensus is more "correct" than a strict consensus tree. The power of a semistrict tree is in its ability to resolve polytomies. This is important in instances where the polytomy is in the minority across the sample of trees. If, for example, nine trees fully resolve a clade in identical fashion and one tree does not, the semistrict consensus tree will ignore that one and show the clade as resolved.

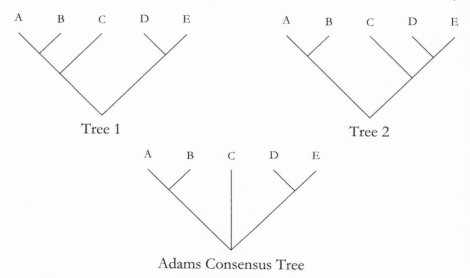

Adams Consensus Tree

Figure 3.11. Adams consensus tree based on two trees of equal length.

Adams Consensus Trees

Adams consensus trees (Adams 1972) take "problem" taxa and relocate them at the nearest node that all of the trees have in common. In Figure 3.11, Taxon C wanders from main branch to main branch across the two trees. The Adams consensus tree places it at the node nearest its occurrence on trees 1 and 2.

Majority-Rule Consensus Trees

Majority-rule consensus trees place taxa in their most common positions across the sample of trees (Swofford 1991). The percentage of trees in which the taxa must occur in the same positions can be varied between 50 percent and 100 percent. Notice in Figure 3.12 that the G + H + I clade has the same arrangement in two out of the three trees; thus that arrangement is the one shown in the 50-percent majority-rule consensus tree. The same is true for the E + F clade. It also holds true for the other four taxa, although it is not as readily apparent.

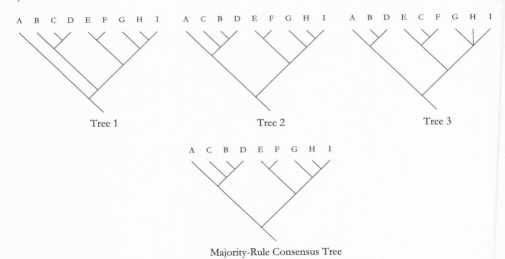

Figure 3.12. Fifty-percent majority-rule consensus tree based on three trees of equal length.

CALCULATIONS OF ROBUSTNESS

How robust are the trees we generate? That is, how well do they show the one true phylogeny that we assume exists? Calculations of robustness are easy to perform when only simple examples are involved, but in complex examples that contain numerous taxa and characters, computers are required. However, the basics are the same. One calculation is the *consistency index* (CI), which measures the amount of homoplasy in a data set (Farris 1989b; Goloboff 1991). The index ranges from zero (complete homoplasy) to 1.0 (no homoplasy) and is calculated by dividing the number of characters in the data matrix by the number of characters on the tree. For example, the CI for trees in Figure 3.8a and 3.8b is 0.78 (7/9), and the CI for trees in Figure 3.8c and 3.8d is 0.70 (7/10) (see Figure 3.7 for the matrix). Even without calculating the CIs we know that the trees in Figure 3.8c and 3.8d will have a lower score than the trees in Figure 3.8a and 3.8b because of the greater number of homoplasies relative to apomorphies.

The consistency index has several potential drawbacks, especially when binary coding is used (Chapter 5). With binary characters, the CI can never reach zero; the individual characters will have a best and worst value that is always above zero. Also, the CI value is not independent of the number of taxa. When the number of taxa increases, the CI value will decrease. To overcome some of the problems with the CI, Farris (1989a, 1989b) developed the rescaled consistency index and the *retention index* (RI), the latter of which measures the fit of characters to a cladogram (the ratio of apparent synapomorphy to actual synapomorphy). By measuring the degree of similarity represented by synapomorphies, the RI provides an indication of how bound together (related) the taxa are. The RI is calculated as

$$\frac{\text{Max. steps in matrix} - \text{No. of characters on tree}}{\text{Max. steps in matrix} - \text{No. of characters in matrix}}$$

Looking again at the data matrix in Figure 3.7, we first calculate the maximum number of steps in the character matrix and sum them. The maximum number of steps for each character is simply the *minimum* number of taxa with either the ancestral or the derived state. In the data matrix, character 1 appears in its ancestral state once in the outgroup and three times in its derived state. One is smaller than three, so we take the one. The same applies to character 2. For the other five characters, the states split evenly between two ancestral and two derived, so we use two. Summing those values together (1 + 1 + 2 + 2 + 2 + 2 + 2) gives us the value of 12 for the maximum number of steps. The other two values—the number of characters on the tree and the number of characters in the matrix—are the same as we used in calculating the CI. Plugging the values into the formula, we get an RI of 0.60—calculated as (12 − 9)/(12 − 7) —for trees in Figure 3.8a and 3.8b and an RI of 0.40—calculated as (12 − 10)/(12 − 7)—for trees in Figure 3.8c and 3.8d. Again, the trees in Figure 3.8a and 3.8b are judged to have better synapomorphic fit, and thus less homoplasy, than those in Figure 3.8c and 3.8d.

COMPUTERS AND CLADISTICS

As the number of taxa and/or the number of characters and character states increases, constructing trees and resolving them becomes impossible to do by hand. The formula for calculating the number of fully resolved (dichotomous branching) unrooted trees is

$$\frac{(2n - 5)!}{2^{n-3}(n - 3)!}$$

where n = number of taxa. With five taxa, the number of possible fully resolved, unrooted trees is 15. With the addition of only two more taxa, the number of possible trees grows to 945. Add just three more taxa, for a total of 10, and the number of possible trees increases to a staggering 2,027,025. But that number simply represents the number of *unrooted* trees. For 10 taxa the number of *rooted* trees climbs to 34,459,425, based on the formula

$$\frac{(2n - 3)!}{2^{n-2}(n - 2)!}$$

where n = number of taxa. Computer assistance obviously is needed, and there are numerous programs available to perform all kinds of calculations and tree building. In fact, there are hundreds. By far the best resource for perusing the various programs and finding out what they can do is on the Web at http://evolution.genetics.washington.edu/phylip/software.html. The site is maintained by Joseph Felsenstein of the Department of Genome Sciences at the University of Washington. Perhaps the most widely used series of programs, and certainly one of the more user-friendly, is PAUP* (Phylogenetic Analysis Using Parsimony *and Other Methods), written by David Swofford (1998) of the Department of Biological Science and the School of Computational Science and Information Technology at Florida State University. It currently is in version 4.0 (beta) and runs on Macintosh, UNIX, and MSDOS machines. Because the Macintosh version offers pulldown menus for all commands and settings, it is by far the simplest to use. Other program packages can be used with tree-generating programs. For example, MacClade (Maddison and Maddison 2001) allows one to study character evolution after trees have been generated by PAUP*. It also provides tools for entering and editing data and phylogenies and for producing tree diagrams and charts. All the trees that we present in subsequent chapters, where we examine archaeological case studies, were generated by PAUP*.

PAUP* and other tree-building programs can use several search methods to generate the shortest possible trees. There are two main kinds of searches: *exact methods* and *heuristic methods*. Which method should we use? That depends in large part on the amount of time available for analysis. Tree building is not a rapid process, especially with a large number of taxa. The bottom line was summed up beautifully by Diana Lipscomb (1998:40): "Balancing the need for precision in finding the shortest tree against a reasonable amount of computation time is one of the most difficult computational problems for systematists."

Exact methods are guaranteed to find all shortest trees—if we have the time and computational equipment. The *exhaustive search* sorts through every possible tree until it finds the shortest one(s). The *branch-and-bound search* works by checking only those trees that are likely to be shorter than the shortest tree already found. It first creates a tree—any tree—and begins creating other trees to compare against it. As soon as it finds a tree of shorter length, that tree becomes the one against which to compare new trees. If a certain partial arrangement of taxa looks as if the trees that it will produce are going to be longer than the comparative tree, the program does not waste time continuing to build trees in that direction. It abandons that direction and takes off in another one. Once it finds a partial solution that looks promising, it continues building in that direction until it finds a shorter solution or decides that it is moving toward a longer tree and abandons that search vector.

If the data set is small, exact searches might be feasible, but with large data sets they often are impossible to do. PAUP* will not run an exhaustive search if more than 12 taxa are included, and even branch-and-bound searches can eat up enormous amounts of time. Thus we might want to turn to one of the heuristic methods. In heuristic searches there are no guarantees that even one shortest possible tree will be found. Mathematicians refer to this kind of problem as *NP complete*—a nondeterministic polynomial. But by using a heuristic strategy, we might get relatively close. One heuristic method is *branch swapping,* of which there are two kinds. In *local swapping,* adjacent branches of a tree are systematically swapped until a shorter length is found. The routine continues swapping branches until no shorter trees are found (or until the operator terminates the search). In *global swapping,* the program slices the trees into "subtrees" and then rearranges the various "subtrees" into new trees and calculates their length.

CLADISTICS VERSUS PHENETICS

Although all rooted cladograms are phylogenetic hypotheses, they should be more realistic hypotheses than trees produced using undifferentiated homologous characters (unless all the characters happen to be derived). That is, rooted cladograms should exhibit more phylogenetic information than either phylograms or phenograms. Pheneticists have long argued that their use of a wide range of characters is preferable to the use of such a restricted set of characters as in cladistics, but this is a red herring. Their claim is based on the unresolved nature of some cladograms,

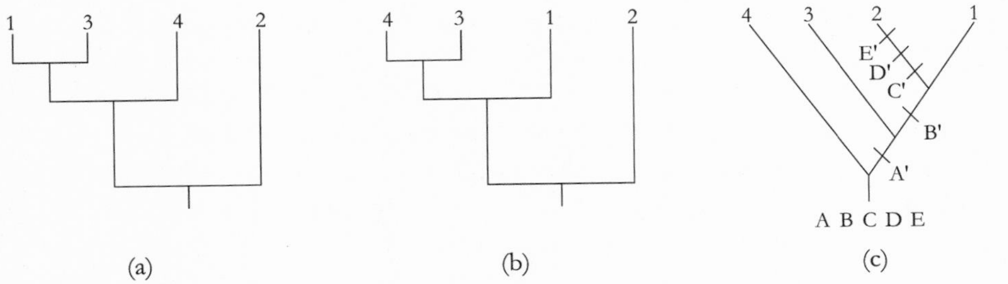

(a)   (b)   (c)

Taxa	Character States				
1	A'	B'	C	D	E
2	A'	B'	C'	D'	E'
3	A'	B	C	D	E
4	A	B	C	D	E

(d)

	1	2	3	4
1	–	2	4	3
2		–	1	0
3			–	4
4				–

(e)

	1	2	3	4
1	–	2	1	0
2		–	1	0
3			–	0
4				–

(f)

Figure 3.13. Comparison of two phenograms (a and b) with a cladogram (c), based on hypothetical states of five characters in four taxa (d) (after Futuyma 1986). Both phenograms can be constructed from the total character states shared by any pair of taxa (e). The cladogram is constructed from only the derived character states (marked by primes) shared by pairs of taxa (f). Note the differences between (a) and (b) compared with (c).

where character distributions just do not provide enough information to allow us to dichotomize the branching sequence. Pheneticists argue that more characters equal better resolution. No one can legitimately argue with the point that more characters might allow better resolution, but at what price if we use any and all traits? Actually, it comes at no price because parsimoniously grouping by synapomorphies rather than by gross similarities will almost always give a more informative classification (Farris 1982, 1983). Two examples illustrate this point.

The first example is illustrated by Figure 3.13, which shows three possible historical patterns—two phenograms constructed using undifferentiated homologous characters (Figure 3.13a and 3.13b) and a cladogram constructed using only derived characteristics (Figure 3.13c)—for four taxa (1–4) and five characters (A–E). As shown in the matrix (Figure 3.13d), for each taxon the five characters are in one of two character states, with derived character states designated by a prime sign and ancestral character states by lack of a prime sign. Figure 3.13e shows the number of shared character states, regardless of whether they are ancestral or derived, between pairs of taxa. Figure 3.13f shows the number of shared derived character states between pairs of taxa. Which pattern best depicts phylogeny? Perhaps the tree in Figure 3.13a is optimal because it denotes a close relationship between taxa 1 and 3, which have four character states in common. But then again, it splits out Taxon 4, which has three states in common with Taxon 1 and four with Taxon 3. Maybe the tree in Figure 3.13b is better in that it minimizes the distance between taxa 4 and 3 and shows that Taxon 1 is closer to taxa 4 and 3 than any of them is to Taxon 2. Taxon 2 shares no character states with Taxon 4—thus we maximize the distance between them; it shares one state with Taxon 3—thus we place 3 closer to 2; and it shares two states with Taxon 1—thus we minimize the distance between them.

On the face of it, the tree in Figure 3.13b is far superior to the tree in Figure 3.13a—a result that we probably would have obtained by plugging the data into most clustering programs. Clustering algorithms search all the data to find the most equitable solution in terms of minimum-maximum distances (similarity rendered as shared character states) between pairs. But does the tree in Figure 3.13b configure the historical evolutionary relationships among the four taxa correctly? Maybe, but we would bet against it, because we made no attempt to discriminate between ancestral characters and derived characters. The tree in Figure 3.13c—the cladogram—illustrates the evolutionary history of the four taxa based solely on an analysis of shared derived character states, shown in Figure 3.13f. Now taxa 1 and 3 share little in common, whereas before they were placed closer together simply because of the total number of character states they had in common. But three of them were ancestral states, not derived states. Analysis of shared derived character states alone indicates that Taxon 3 split off from the ancestral form that produced the ancestor of taxa 1 and 2.

The second example, courtesy of Diana Lipscomb (1998), is built around the five taxa and 10 characters shown in Figure 3.14. The character matrix in Figure 3.14a shows the distribution of characters across the taxa. Each character is in one of two states, signified by plus and minus signs. The matrix in Figure 3.14b shows the similarity between pairs of taxa based on the matrix in Figure 3.14a. The similarity is shown graphically in Figure 3.14c. The scale tells us how similar taxa are to each other. The phenogram in Figure 3.14c is a best fit of the taxa, given the character-state distribution at hand. In a simple example such as this one, a phenogram can be eyeballed, but if the data set is large, any number of cluster programs are available for computer-assisted computation. Regardless of

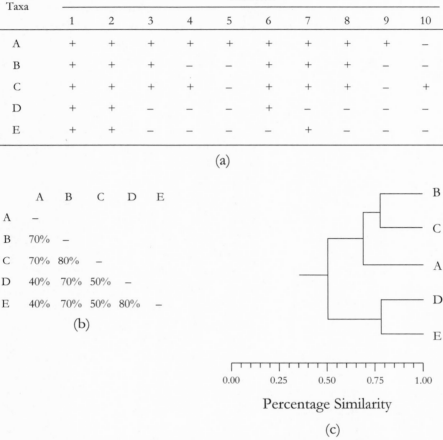

Figure 3.14. Character matrices (a and b) and phenogram (c) for five taxa and 10 characters (after Lipscomb 1998). Each character is in one of two states, signified by plus and minus signs. The matrix in (b) shows the similarity between pairs of taxa based on the matrix in (a). The similarity is shown graphically in (c). The phenogram is a best fit of the taxa, given the character-state distribution at hand.

how the clustering is done, the analyst (you or the program) has decisions to make regarding the placement of taxa. Notice that in the similarity matrix, taxa B and C are 80 percent similar, as are taxa D and E. This is the highest percentage similarity, so we maximize the strength of those similarities by grouping taxa B and C and taxa D and E and drawing their unions at 0.80 on the scale. Taxon A shares 70 percent of its character

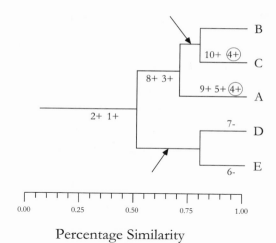

Percentage Similarity

Figure 3.15. Phenogram reproduced from Figure 3.14, showing character states in their correct positions (after Lipscomb 1998). All taxa share the same character states for characters 1 and 2 (see the matrix table in Figure 3.14a), and this creates the basal grouping. Taxa in the A + B + C group share the same states for characters 3 and 8, whereas D and E do not. That difference defines the next split. Characters 5, 6, 7, 9, and 10 help further in the placement of the taxa. But notice that character 4 is homoplasious in taxa C and A. Notice also that two of the branches—the B + C group and the D + E group (arrows)—are not defined by any characters.

states with B and C and only 40 percent with D and E, so we probably should place A with the B + C group rather than with the D + E group and unite A with B + C at 0.70 on the scale. But now we see that Taxon B, which we grouped with C based on its 80 percent similarity, has 70 percent in common each with D and E. Taxon C, however, has less in common each with D and E (50 percent). Finally, Taxon A has even less than that in common (40 percent) with D and E. Trying to balance all these relationships, we finally come up with the phenogram shown in Figure 3.14c. Our clustering program (Hintze 1999) produces the same phenogram and similarity values, so we feel fairly confident that our arrangement is either the best fit or one of several equal best fits.

But what information does our phenogram convey? To examine this, we can place the character states on the phenogram in their correct positions (Figure 3.15). All taxa share the same character states for characters 1 and 2 (plus signs), and this creates the basal grouping. Taxa in the A + B + C group share the same states for characters 3 and 8, whereas D and E

Taxa	Characters									
	1	2	3	4	5	6	7	8	9	10
A	+	+	+	+	+	+	+	+	+	−
B	+	+	+	−	−	+	+	+	−	−
C	+	+	+	+	−	+	+	+	−	+
D	+	+	−	−	−	+	−	−	−	−
E	+	+	−	−	−	−	+	−	−	−
Outgroup	−	−	−	−	−	−	+	−	−	−

(a)

Taxa	Characters									
	1	2	3	4	5	6	7	8	9	10
A	1	1	1	1	1	1	0	1	1	0
B	1	1	1	0	0	1	0	1	0	0
C	1	1	1	1	0	1	0	1	0	1
D	1	1	0	0	0	1	1	0	0	0
E	1	1	0	0	0	0	0	0	0	0
Outgroup	0	0	0	0	0	0	0	0	0	0

(b)

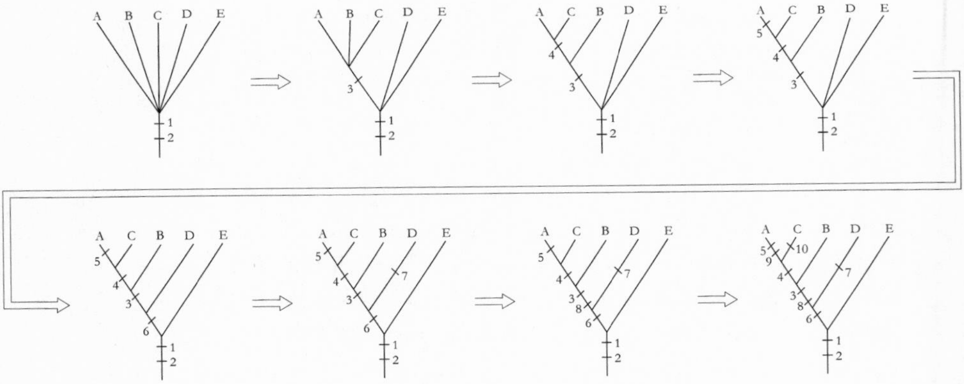

(c)

Figure 3.16. Result of adding an outgroup to resolve character polarity. The matrix (a) is the same one shown in Figure 3.14a but with the addition of an outgroup. Data are recoded (b), using zero for the ancestral state and 1 for the derived state. The recoded data are then used to start building a cladogram, resolving it one step at a time by adding characters (c). Characters 1 and 2 do nothing to resolve it, in that they are shared by all the ingroup taxa; but the addition of the other characters, taken one at a time, allows complete resolution. Notice that, unlike in the phenogram (Figure 3.15), none of the characters show convergence or reversal and all branches are defined by at least one character. The branching pattern of the cladogram deviates from the character-state distributions less in the phenogram and therefore describes more of the character-state changes (after Lipscomb 1998).

do not. That difference defines the next split. Characters 5, 6, 7, 9, and 10 help further in the placement of the taxa. But notice that character 4 is homoplasious in taxa C and A. In and of itself this is not too surprising; nor by itself is it enough to make us abandon phenetics as a taxonomic method. All but the simplest cladograms contain homoplasy, and if we are going to discount phenetics on that ground, we would have to discount cladistics as well. This is one of the rebuttals made by pheneticists when they are criticized by cladists. But notice one other thing in Figure 3.15: Two of the branches—the B + C group and the D + E group—are not defined by any characters (arrows in Figure 3.15). This is problematic, but the clustering program made a dichotomous branching anyway, resolving the phenogram to the best of its ability.

What would happen if we added an outgroup so that we could determine character polarity? The matrix in Figure 3.16a is the same one shown in Figure 3.14a but with the addition of an outgroup. In Figure 3.16b we have recoded the data, using zero for the plesiomorphic state and one for the apomorphic state. We can use those data to start building our cladogram, resolving it one step at a time by adding characters (Figure 3.16c). Characters 1 and 2 do nothing to resolve it, in that they are shared by all the ingroup taxa, but the addition of the other characters, taken one at a time, allows complete resolution. Notice that none of the characters show convergence or reversal, which appears in the phenogram (Figure 3.15). Also, all branches are defined by at least one character, which is not the case in the phenogram. Unlike in the phenogram, the cladogram's branching pattern is the pattern that maximizes the character-state distributions such that homoplasies and character-state changes are both minimized. This means that its information content is higher. In short, cladistics seeks the most parsimonious tree, which phenetics does not. Thus "cladograms should always have higher (or at least equal, if the cladogram and phenogram are identical) information content than a phenogram" (Lipscomb 1998:71).

WHAT HAPPENS TO ANCESTORS IN A CLADOGRAM?

As its name implies, cladistics views speciation as a branching event (even though technically anagenesis could occur after a split), with every speciation event producing at least two daughter species. We have used the term *ancestor* or *ancestral taxon* throughout the chapter, making it sound as if ancestors are real. For reasons noted earlier, the term

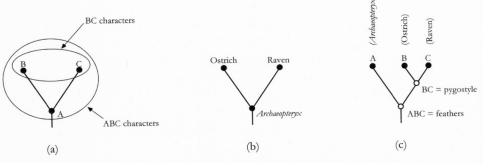

(a)   (b)   (c)

Figure 3.17. Diagram showing the logical inconsistency involved in treating ancestors as individual taxa and how cladists have solved the problem (after Kitching et al. 1998). In (a) three taxa (A–C) form a group because they share three character states (also A–C). B and C are sister groups because they share BC character states, which, logically, A must lack. If A is considered to be an ancestor of B and C, it can be placed at the origin point *only* if it lacks any distinguishing character states of its own; otherwise, it would be placed as a sister group to B + C. As an example (b), *Archaeopteryx,* the traditional ancestor of birds (ignoring more recent findings), has synapomorphies found in all birds, such as the ostrich and raven, but lacks synapomorphies found in the ostrich + raven. Thus in terms of character distribution, the *Archaeopteryx* does not exist. But we know it *did* exist. To get around this problem, cladists do what is shown in (c): They place ancestors as a sister group to their putative descendants and accept that they must be nominal paraphyletic taxa.

hypothetical ancestor is more appropriate. Technically, this hypothetical ancestor is not a taxon but a collection of characters or character states represented at a node.

To examine the implications of treating a taxonomic unit as a real ancestor, we borrow an example from Ian Kitching et al. (1998). Consider Figure 3.17a, in which Taxon A is ancestral to taxa B and C. The three taxa are grouped because they share ABC characters, but B and C are *sister taxa*—they are more closely related to each other than either is to A—because they share BC characters. If A is considered to be the ancestor of B and C, it can be placed at the speciation node only if it lacks any distinguishing characters of its own. Otherwise, it would be placed as the sister taxon of the clade comprising B and C. To state it differently, an ancestor cannot exhibit an apomorphy (a derived character) that is not also present in its immediate descendant. We are left with the illogical position that ancestor A can be recognized only because it possesses ABC characters but lacks BC characters. In Figure 3.17b three avian taxa have been substituted for the letters in Figure 3.17a, with *Archaeopteryx* shown as the ancestor of ostriches and ravens. *Archaeopteryx* has the synapomorphies (e.g., feathers) that are found in all birds but lacks the synapomorphies of the ostrich and raven, such as a pygostyle. In terms of unique characters, *Archaeopteryx* simply does not exist—an odd notion given that its remains have been found. In related fashion, Elliott Sober (1988) points out that parents do not necessarily cease to exist when their children are born. To circumvent this illogical position, *likely ancestors are placed on a rooted tree as terminal taxa as opposed to internal nodes* (Figure 3.17c). We emphasize this point to underscore its importance. In later chapters, where a terminal taxon is shown as having the same character states as an ancestor, you will not be confused by what sounds like an impossibility. Ancestors must, by definition, be totally primitive with respect to their descendants and thus cannot logically be distinguished as individual taxa. Although it is rarely phrased this way, paraphyletic groups, because they are based on shared ancestral characters, can be recognized only by the characters they do not have, not by the characters they do have. Cladists simply accept that in many cases their trees contain nominal paraphyletic taxa because of homoplasy, and they work to reduce it.

STRATOCLADISTICS

One unique attribute that putative ancestors have is their time of existence, and it is at this point that knowledge gained independently from cladistical analysis, perhaps from stratigraphic observations, makes its entrance. But there are potential dangers in using stratigraphic information to construct phylogenetic orderings, the first of which is forgetting that stratigraphic position is no sure indicator of relative age. The law of superposition tells us only that fossils and sediments in lower strata were deposited before those in higher strata. It does not tell us directly that fossils in lower strata are necessarily older than those in higher strata. Second, there may be large gaps in a fossil assemblage as a result of poor preservation or destruction subsequent to deposition. Third, we might easily misread the duration of taxa. Suppose, as is illustrated in Figure 3.18, that a fossil taxon (A) in the most recent of five strata was the first to diverge from a basal group. It also happened to be the most long-lived of the five taxa under investigation. The other four taxa (B, C, D, and E) whose relative branching is shown in Figure 3.18 were short-lived in terms of geological time and thus are preserved only in the older strata. In

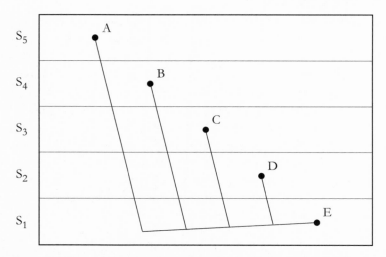

Figure 3.18. Diagram showing the potential hazard of equating stratigraphic position of taxa with their relative age. Taxon A, found in the most recent of five strata, was the first to diverge from a basal group. It also happened to be the most long-lived of the five taxa. The other four taxa (B, C, D, and E) whose relative branching is shown were short-lived in terms of geological time and thus are preserved only in the older strata. Using stratigraphic position to determine the sequence of branching would reverse the order.

terms of superposed taxa, however, it appears that Taxon A is the youngest and Taxon E the oldest. Why Taxon A was not found in the lowermost four strata is a separate issue. Maybe it is a result of our sampling procedure, or maybe it is a result of taphonomic history—older fossils are not as well preserved as younger ones. Regardless, our phylogenetic ordering would be completely wrong if we relied solely on stratigraphic evidence.

All paleobiologists attempt to overcome these problems in their efforts to plot the history of fossil taxa. In the 1990s a subset of paleobiologists began to link stratigraphic information to character-based cladograms to produce phylogenetic orderings (e.g., Clyde and Fisher 1997; Fisher 1991, 1992, 1994; Fox et al. 1999; Polly 1997; Wills 1999). That approach became known as *stratocladistics*. It involves the use of stratigraphic information to help construct a cladogram of evolutionary divergence rather than constructing one based solely on intrinsic formal attributes. Stratocladists calculate what is termed *stratigraphic debt* to determine how much of the record of a particular suite of fossils might be missing—a calculation viewed as being similar to tree length. In Figure 3.18, the stratigraphic debt for the five taxa is 10. This is calculated by counting the number of strata a taxon passes through that contain no evidence of that taxon. Thus the stratigraphic debt borne by Taxon A is 4 (strata 1–4), the debt for Taxon B is 3 (strata 1–3), and so on. The stratigraphic debt for each taxon is treated as a coding character and is added to the morphological-character matrix to produce the final data set used to generate the phylogenetic trees.

Cladists have pointed out what they see as epistemological flaws in the stratocladistical approach. First, cladists place little stock in stratigraphic debt, arguing that using stratigraphic positioning as a character in a data matrix is tantamount to assuming that the order of appearance of the taxa has already been determined. If so, why do cladistics in the first place? Second, cladists point out that the temporal polarity of two apparently related characters—such as might be suggested by their order of appearance in a stratigraphic column—might be misleading as a result of the way in which the fossil record was formed or sampled. Thus cladists argue that one should completely ignore the apparent temporal positions of characters and instead focus solely on the distribution of the characters in question across different taxa. Third, cladists (e.g., Engelmann and Wiley 1977; Norell and Novacek 1997) point out that stratocladists view their faunal successions in terms of ancestors and descendants. Stratocladists counter that this is not necessarily a weakness of the approach. Some very large percentage of species in the past *must* have been ancestral to at least one other species. If so, then it makes no sense to continue to treat all taxa as sister taxa—that is, as end points on branches. We find this argument unconvincing in terms of method. It undoubtedly is true that a large percentage of species in the past must have been ancestral to at least one other species, but to repeat a point we made earlier, how would we know that the correct ancestor of a given taxon or set of related taxa has been found? The answer is that we would not know. There simply is no way of ever knowing. That's why on cladograms internal nodes are labeled as "hypothetical ancestors." Technically, they are nothing more than collections of character states.

Despite the potential problems in using stratigraphic evidence in phylogenetic studies, we are not inclined to disregard it completely (Darwent and O'Brien 2003). What we would do is use stratigraphic evidence as a check on our hypotheses of phylogeny that have been constructed from morphological characters. Such evidence might be useful when we have several competing trees of equal length and want to find an external means of choosing one over the others. There are various means of doing that (e.g., Benton 1994; Benton and Hitchin 1996; Norell and Novacek 1992a, 1992b; Siddall 1996, 1997), but they are beyond the scope of discussion here. The important point is that stratigraphic evidence is properly used as a check of cladistically derived trees (and vice versa). By incorporating such data into the trees we are trying to construct, however, we have negated this usefulness (Rieppel 1997).

DISCUSSION

Cladistics is a method that produces nested series of synapomorphies. Those synapomorphies, or derived characters (or character states), are carried by taxa that we wish to place in phylogenetic order. But it is important to realize that the nested pattern created by cladistics is of characters and not of the taxa themselves. Taxa, being composites of the characters used in a cladistical analysis, are assumed to be represented at terminal nodes of branches. Internal nodes, the vertices of the branches that contain the terminal taxa, are also collections of characters. They are referred to as hypothetical ancestors to underscore that they are not viewed as *the* direct ancestors of terminal taxa.

Cladograms, or unrooted trees, tell us nothing about phylogeny because they make no claims about which character states are ancestral and which are derived. To root a cladogram—to turn it into a phylogenetic tree—means to make an argument for a character being in either the ancestral state or a derived state. One method of doing this, but certainly not the only method, is through the use of an outgroup. We assume that character states in the outgroup are ancestral, and we use that assumption to determine the polarity of character states in the ingroup taxa. In instances where multiple trees are obtained from our polarity-determining analysis—character argumentation—we choose the most parsimonious tree, meaning the tree with the fewest number of instances of parallel or convergent development. The rooted tree that finally is accepted is our hypothesis of phylogeny.

Cladistics has enjoyed wide success in biology and paleobiology. In paleobiology analysis has centered almost exclusively around morphological characters—it would be difficult to find any other kind of characters—but in biology cladistics has included a wide variety of characters, including behavioral, ontogenetic (developmental), and molecular characters. This pluralism should not be surprising, given that cladistics is ap-

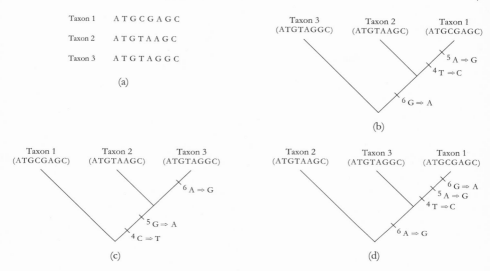

Figure 3.19. Phylogenetic orderings of three taxa using nucleotide sequences. The same genomic region in three taxa (1–3) was sampled and the sequences of nucleotide bases (A, T, G, and C) were read (a). Those sequences then were used to align the taxa (b–d). Using the law of parsimony—just as if we were analyzing trees constructed using morphological characters—the tree in (d), which has a length of four, would be discarded.

plicable to anything that has characters that change from one state to another as a result of transmission. Behavioral characters are as readily classified as morphological characters and thus can be examined from the standpoint of whether they are ancestral or derived. Similarly, molecular sequences can be read as historical statements. Suppose we sampled the same genomic region in three taxa and found the sequences of bases shown in Figure 3.19a. We could then use those sequences to align the taxa, as shown in Figure 3.19b–d. Using the law of parsimony—the same as if we were analyzing trees constructed using morphological characters—we would discard the tree in Figure 3.19d, which has a length of four, and concentrate on the other two. At this point we do not know the placement of the three taxa, but at least we have only two trees and not three to worry about.

So far, we have concentrated solely on somatic features of organisms, but cladistics is applicable to anything that has characters that change from one state to another as a result of transmission. The important point is that transmission is not limited solely to genetic transmission. No one would argue that the number of toes an animal possesses is not genetically determined, as are molecular sequences, but what about behavioral characters? Undoubtedly, genetic transmission plays a large—in some cases overwhelming—role in behavior, but extragenetic transmission can be involved as well. What is important from a phylogenetic standpoint is that changes are inherited. If, for example, a chimpanzee changes its foraging habits and does not pass those changes on to other chimps, then that change is irrelevant from a phylogenetic standpoint. Also important is the relative frequency with which a character state is expressed within a breeding population. If, for example, a behavioral change was limited over time to a small number of individuals, its phylogenetic signal may well be too weak to be noticeable, even if it persists in unaltered form.

The relative frequency of character states is an important issue, but we should not confuse it with the mode of transmission. Again, from the standpoint of phylogeny it is irrelevant how a change is transmitted—whether a molecular change in coding sequence leads to behavioral change in one group of chimpanzees (genetic transmission resulting in behavioral change) or whether chimpanzees in another group teach their young, who in turn teach their young (nongenetic transmission resulting in behavioral change). The important thing is that change takes place and that it is inherited. That makes it fair game for cladistical analysis. Behaviors leave traces, which are also fair game for cladistics. If we can use molecular data and morphological characters to examine, for example, the phylogeny of mud daubers, there is no reason that we cannot also use behavioral by-products. Those material items—mud-dauber nests in this case—are really no different than the hard parts of phenotypes that paleobiologists use to examine phylogeny. With no stretch of the imagination we can extend the method to the study of humans and the cultural phenomena that are part of their phenotypes. We examine this topic further in Chapter 4.

STARTING POINTS

Finding a primer on cladistics that covers all aspects of the approach is wishing for too much. No single book could possibly contain everything that we might need in order to understand the epistemology, let alone the methodological nuances, of an approach as detailed as cladistics. The last place to look for an initial entry point into the literature is Willi Hennig's (1950) seminal book on the subject or the English translation (Hennig 1966) from the original German. Hennig's writing is too arcane and dense for a beginner's purposes. If you are dying to read something by Hennig, try his abbreviated article (Hennig 1965), which contains the basics of his approach to phylogenetic ordering. He wrote it expressly for an English-speaking audience not familiar with his work.

A much better place to start, though, is a good, basic evolutionary-biology textbook that treats phylogeny in depth. The best we have seen is Mark Ridley's (1996) *Evolution*. Another book by Ridley that is well worth reading is *Evolution and Classification: The Reformation of Cladism* (1986). It provides an excellent overview of phylogenetic approaches in general. Then you can move on to one or more cladistics handbooks. One of the earliest of these, and somewhat difficult to find, is Ed Wiley et al.'s (1991) *The Compleat Cladist: A Primer of Phylogenetic Procedures*, published by the Museum of Natural History at the University of Kansas. This book contains a wealth of information on how to construct trees, how to deal with homoplasy, and numerous other topics. It also has problem sets that you can work through. We would not recommend that beginners read Wiley's earlier book, *Phylogenetics: The Theory and Practice of Phylogenetic Systematics* (1981). Go back to it at a later point, once you have gained competence in cladistics. Three other primers stand out, and we recommend them highly: *Phylogeny, Ecology, and Behavior: A Research Program in Comparative Biology* by Daniel Brooks and Deborah McLennan (1991); *Cladistics: The Theory and Practice of Parsimony Analysis* by Ian Kitching et al. (1998); and *Phylogenetic Trees Made Easy: A How-To Manual for Molecular Biologists* by Barry Hall (2001). You should at least skim all three and pick out parts that appear interesting. There is some redundancy in topics, but each text takes a slightly different tack in terms of how the material is presented. Don't let the title of Hall's book throw you: His coverage of trees and tree construction is as fundamental to phylogenetic ordering using morphological characters as it is to ordering using molecular sequences. One nice feature of his book is that he uses actual screen captures to illustrate various PAUP* options.

Another excellent introduction to cladistics—from the epistemological as opposed to the methodological side—is Elliott Sober's (1988) *Reconstructing the Past: Parsimony, Evolution, and Inference*. We also recommend two articles on the philosophical side of cladistics—one by Sober (1983) and one by Steve Farris (1983). Both of them treat the topic of parsimony extensively. For an interesting exchange on parsimony and its reliance/nonreliance on evolutionary theory as a necessary ontological basis, see Andrew Brower (2000) and Arnold Kluge (2001). For excellent overviews of outgroups, including some of the contentious issues surrounding the use of them, see Farris (1982) and Kevin Nixon and James Carpenter (1993). You might also enjoy Joseph Felsenstein's (2001) brief but colorful review of the history of phylogenetics.

For a discussion of stratocladistics and expressions of various viewpoints pro and con, see Andrew Smith (2000), comments by Dan Fisher et al. (2002) and John Alroy (2002), and Smith's (2002) response.

PART II

Cladistics in Archaeology

FOUR

Constructing Cultural Phylogenies

As we discussed briefly in Chapters 1 and 2, phylogeny in various guises has long been a topic of anthropological and archaeological interest. Various methods aimed at constructing cultural phylogenies appeared during the nineteenth and twentieth centuries, including seriation in archaeology (e.g., Evans 1850; Kroeber 1916b; Petrie 1899, 1901), the comparative method in ethnology (e.g., Eggan 1954; Goodenough 1957; Romney 1957; Vogt 1964), and the direct historical approach, which made use of both archaeological and ethnological data (Sapir 1916; Strong 1935, 1953; Wedel 1938). All these methods had as at least an implicit assumption the notion of descent with modification, although it was far from clear how much of a parallel there was between biological and cultural evolution.

For a variety of reasons, the last half of the twentieth century witnessed less emphasis on history in anthropology and archaeology, and phylogenetic studies were eclipsed by other pursuits (Kirch and Green 2001). In archaeology, the emergence of the processual paradigm in the 1960s brought with it a heightened interest in functional aspects of the material record (e.g., Binford 1962, 1965) and a deemphasis of history and thus of homology. The situation changed in the 1980s when a series of phylogenetically centered papers and monographs appeared in both anthropology and archaeology. Our impression is that this renewed interest in phylogeny can be attributed to three factors: (1) an exponential increase in linguistic and especially genetic data (e.g., Cann et al. 1987; Cavalli-Sforza et al. 1988, 1994; Stoneking 1993) compared with what was available earlier; (2) advances in analytical and computing methods that allowed the integration of large data sets; and, most importantly, (3) a heightened awareness among anthropologists of issues in evolutionary biology and a willingness to see human culture as a phenotypic phenomenon and cultural transmission not only as an inheritance system but as a significant source of cultural variation.

Phylogenetic studies conducted in anthropology and archaeology during the last 20 years are difficult to characterize, but they tend to fall into one of two categories: (1) analyses that trace lines of descent back to a common ancestor (a prototype) and then examine the processes that underlie the geographic distribution and cultural development of descendants (e.g., Flannery and Marcus 1983; Gamkrelidze and Ivanov 1990; Green 1991; Kirch and Green 1987, 2001; Moore and Romney 1994; Renfrew 1987, 1992, 1998, 1999, 2000a, 2000b; Renfrew and Boyle 2000; Renfrew et al. 2000; Ross 1989; Rushforth and Chisolm 1991; Sahlins 1958; Vansina 1990) and (2) comparative studies that rely on understanding patterns of descent in order to examine the distribution of adaptive (functional) features (e.g., Borgerhoff Mulder et al. 2001; Holden and Mace 1997, 1999; Mace and Pagel 1994; Sellen and Mace 1997). The modern comparative method (see Harvey and Pagel [1991] for its use in biology) is designed to escape what Francis Galton pointed out in 1889: Comparative studies of adaptation, irrespective of whether the adaptation is a product of convergence or parallelism, are irrelevant if we cannot rule out the possibility of a common origin of the adaptive features under examination (Naroll 1970). To escape Galton's problem requires a working knowledge of the phylogeny of taxa included in the analysis.

Both categories of studies described above can involve numerous lines of evidence, including archaeological and genetic information, but one feature shared by both is a heavy reliance on linguistic analysis to create the basic cultural phylogeny. Language phylogenies form the hypothesized patterns of cultural descent, with subsequent analysis dependent on the correctness of the linguistic trees. Why, of all cultural features, should language be singled out as the basis for cultural phylogeny? Most studies adopting this approach employ reasoning similar to that of Monique Borgerhoff Mulder (2001): (1) linguistic phylogenies offer better resolution of sister groups than do genetic phylogenies; (2) linguistic data are available for more groups than are genetic data; (3) language is more sensitive to horizontal movement (e.g., borrowing) than are genes, which can "leak" over the boundaries of cultural groups with minimal cultural exchange; and (4) language is relatively easy to analyze because it evolves in a cladogenetic manner (Ruhlen 1987).

Figure 4.1 illustrates a tree developed by Ruth Mace and Mark Pagel (1994) in their analysis of camel herding by East African pastoralists. They were interested in testing the proposition that camel herding is adopted in dry climates (camel herding is indicated in Figure 4.1 by the

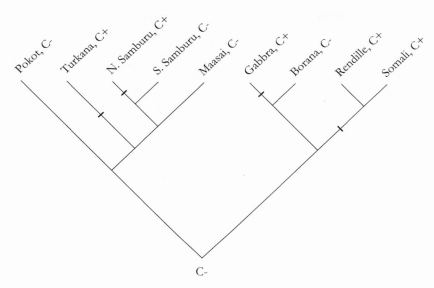

Figure 4.1. Phylogeny of nine Kenyan pastoralist cultures based on linguistic similarity, showing camel-keeping cultures (C+) and cultures without camels (C–). Bars represent the point of camel introduction (simplified from Mace and Pagel 1994).

symbol C+; lack of camel herding is indicated by the symbol C–). To determine whether camel herding was analogous or homologous—Galton's problem—they relied on linguistic data. Based on the phylogenetic tree, camel herding apparently arose independently in three branch-tip groups (Turkana, northern Samburu, and Gabbra) as well as in the ancestor that produced the Rendille and the Somali. As Mace and Pagel point out, their tree is only one of several most parsimonious trees. An alternative pattern—one that is equally parsimonious—is that the common ancestor of the four Eastern Cushitic cultures (Gabbra, Borana, Rendille, and Somali) herded camels and the Borana then lost the trait. Regardless of which tree is more correct, Mace and Pagel found a positive correlation between camel herding and a dry environment, including one case—the northern Samburu—in which the practice was adopted in the 1980s as a result of drought.

Phylogeny, irrespective of the phenomena under investigation, implies transmission, and several anthropological studies have explicitly considered modes of cultural transmission in their models. Cultural transmission can be vertical in the sense of parent to offspring, analogous to genetic transmission, but it can also occur in the opposite direction—from off-spring to parent. Also, unlike genetic transmission, cultural transmission can be horizontal—between people of the same generation (Boyd and Richerson 1985). Mace and Pagel (1994:552) sum up the possibilities: "Unlike biological phylogenies, in which a true pattern of vertical descent exists, cultural phylogenies, even if predominantly vertical, will contain many instances of populations interbreeding and the horizontal transmission . . . of cultural elements . . . [regardless of] the mechanism of or motivation for the adoption of the element." As they point out, horizontal transmission has been referred to variously as diffusion, copying, and borrowing. Those mechanisms have long been "explanatory" mainstays in anthropology and archaeology (Lyman et al. 1997), although in and of themselves they explain nothing. Only when explicitly made part of theory do they have any explanatory power.

One important issue in cultural phylogenetics, as in biological phylogenetics, is the structure of the trees produced: Are they aggregative, similar to the Linnaean taxonomic system, or positional, similar to the one shown in Figure 4.1? Few positional trees have been constructed in anthropology relative to aggregative trees. Even in paleoanthropology, despite the penetration of cladistics (e.g., Strait and Grine 1999; Tattersall 1995), "one cannot avoid the impression that its underlying philosophy has been less thoroughly absorbed" (Tattersall 2000:7). This comment by Ian Tattersall is critical. On the few occasions when the term *cladistic* is used in the archaeological and anthropological literature, the author usually is referring to any classificatory architecture that branches. This leads us to suspect that the differences between evolutionary taxonomy and cladistics are not well understood, which in turn leads us to suspect that there is a lack of appreciation of the difference between evolutionary pattern and evolutionary process. As we stress throughout the book, evolutionary taxonomy and cladistics offer different ways of looking at the world. The former addresses both pattern and process—it tracks "genealogical actors in ecological roles" (Hull 1987:44)—whereas the latter, strictly speaking, addresses pattern only (process comes from the theory chosen to explain the pattern; typically the theory is Darwinian evolution). So which is more useful for cultural studies? As in biology, the answer depends on what is being examined. Are we interested in examining pattern or process? Or are we interested in examining both? And even more important, will we use one method that incorporates both pattern and process simultaneously, or will we have the patience to use separate methods?

OBJECTIONS TO CULTURAL PHYLOGENY

Objections to cultural phylogenetic studies take several forms, four of which are of interest here because together they provide a vehicle for exploring several key issues. The objections have been raised in various quarters and apply generally to any kind of cultural phylogenetic study, irrespective of the structure of the approach used. If we are seriously interested in demonstrating the power of phylogenetic methods, especially cladistics, for understanding cultural phenomena, then we need to make a reasonable attempt to answer specific objections. Our job here is more complicated than it would be, say, for a biological cladist trying to persuade an evolutionary taxonomist that cladistics is a more appropriate method for understanding biological phylogeny than evolutionary taxonomy is. Both at least believe that phylogenetic construction is possible. Many anthropologists, however, maintain that phylogenetic construction is impossible, irrespective of approach. This belief is based on two tenets. First, because artifacts do not interbreed, they cannot convey phylogenetic information. Second, because cultural evolution sometimes involves reticulation, any potential phylogenetic signal is muted to the point of being invisible. Two additional objections have been raised: Phylogenists view cultural taxonomies as statements about process rather than mere pattern, and they assume a concordance among language, culture, and biology, so that if we can reconstruct one, the others tag along in lockstep fashion. We treat each of these objections below.

Artifacts Do Not Carry Phylogenetic Information

When it comes to humans as subjects of study, anthropologists and archaeologists have no problem viewing them in more or less the same light in which they view other organisms—as long as the topic of conversation is oriented toward skeletal biology, comparative anatomy, or genetics. But when the topic turns to what might be termed *nonsomatic* features—those not connected with the body—all bets are off. The reason given is that because humans are culture-bearing animals, they are qualitatively different from all other organisms. Under this view, the evolutionary processes that work on other organisms—selection, drift, and the like—have little or no effect on humans. Whatever small effect they might have does not constitute evolution in a biological sense (e.g., Bamforth 2002). Thus, whereas we might speak of human features such as language as "evolving," it is evolution only in the metaphorical sense of change over time, not in the Darwinian sense. The problem with this perspective, as Robert Leonard and Tom Jones (1987) note, is that by setting humans apart from other kinds of organisms we face considerable difficulties in, among other things, coming to grips with the historical transition from predominantly genetic to predominantly cultural modes of information transmission. Critics might well go along with this argument, but they also would claim that once that transition was made, cultural transmission freed us from the biological processes that fuel evolution.

Recall from Chapter 1 J. O. Brew's dismissal of Harold Colton and Lyndon Hargrave's (1937) work on the phylogenetic implications of pottery types from the Southwest. Brew saw an immediate problem with their scheme, stating that the "only defense there can be for a classification of [artifacts] based upon phylogenetic theory is that the individual objects were made and used by man" (Brew 1946:55). To Brew, evolution involves only the processes of genetic transmission and genetic change. There is, then, only a weak correlation between an organism and the "artifacts" that it might produce, such as birds and eggshells or molluscs and mollusc shells, and no connection at all between people and their artifacts. Given Brew's view that artifacts are not phenotypic phenomena, they cannot be subject to evolutionary processes. And if they cannot be subject to evolutionary processes, then why would anyone think they could be used for phylogenetic purposes? In his review, Brew quoted a single biologist—a geneticist—who argued that a phylogenetic history did not explain organisms. Hence, to Brew (1946:56) it could hardly explain artifacts: "This is a most important point, and I wish to emphasize it here." Of course a phylogenetic history is not an explanation, but knowing that particular history *is* a requirement of using Darwinian theory to explain the diversity of forms of organisms and their distributions in time and space (O'Hara 1988; Szalay and Bock 1991). That point is unassailable.

The general lack of enthusiasm on the part of archaeologists over biological issues is traceable to a deep-rooted belief that, despite some superficial similarities, biological evolution and cultural evolution are just too different to treat under the same umbrella. Cultural historians who had an interest in evolution evidently believed it was possible to solve "the problems of cultural evolution," as A. V. Kidder (1932:8) put it, but they could not reconcile their rudimentary knowledge of how evolution worked relative to somatic features with how it might work with artifacts.

Thus, despite their view that variation was variation, regardless of the "laws" (Kidder 1932:8) that regulated its production, it was too great a leap to make from the evolution of organic features, governed in large part by genetic laws, to the evolution of inorganic features, which were "unregulated" (Kidder 1932:8) by those or similar laws. Some modern evolutionary biologists—Stephen J. Gould (1996) and Ernst Mayr (1982; Angier 1997) being cases in point—also have had problems incorporating human culture under the Darwinian umbrella. Skin and bones, it appears, are appropriate subjects for Darwinism, but not such things as stone tools and ceramic vessels. Those are best covered under a separate kind of process such as the cultural evolutionism of Leslie White (1949, 1959a, 1959b) and Julian Steward (1955).

Yet it is exactly such extrasomatic features that we view as being as subject to evolutionary processes as is any somatic feature (O'Brien and Holland 1992, 1995; O'Brien and Lyman 2000; O'Brien et al. 2003). Put more properly, the *individuals* who made and used stone tools and ceramic vessels were subject to evolutionary processes. Products of technology are not simply adaptive reflections but rather active components of the adaptive process. Variants represent alternative solutions to adaptive problems and have different reproductive consequences for their makers and users and thus for their own replication (Leonard and Jones 1987). Things in the archaeological record are parts of human phenotypes in the same way that skin and bones are, and as such they are capable of yielding data relevant to understanding both the process of evolution and the specific evolutionary histories of their possessors. This is a profoundly different way of viewing archaeological objects than the traditional one of "material culture," although it should not be unduly troubling. Biologists (e.g., Bonner 1980, 1988; Dawkins 1990; Turner 2000; von Frisch and von Frisch 1974) routinely view such things as a bird's nest as part of its phenotype in the same way that they view its beak and feathers. Why shouldn't pots, projectile points, and the like be thought of in the same manner as hair, skin, and other human somatic features? Certainly we should have no trouble accepting that the behaviors that lead to creation of a ceramic vessel or a stone tool are phenotypic. Accepting the *results* of behaviors as phenotypic, then, requires only another small step. Once we make that step, we can begin to talk about such things as selection and drift in terms of how they shaped the variation that shows up in the archaeological record—variation that provides the phylogenetic clues that one looks for to construct evolutionary history.

Biologists have no trouble accepting bird nests, beaver dams, spider-webs, and the like as phenotypic because the behaviors that lead to these end products are at least in part genetically controlled. As far as we know, no one has ever found a gene or series of genes that controls how a beaver builds a dam or how a spider spins a web, but never having found such genes does not destroy the logical proposition that such activities are controlled or at least conditioned by them. As such, behaviors, or at least the genetic basis for certain behaviors, are inherited. If we accept the rather noncontroversial notion that one of the functions of an organism as an interactor with its environment is to act as a vehicle for the replicative units it carries—the genes—then it stands to reason that the vehicle has to do its job of protecting the germ-line *replicators* (Hull 1988a, 1988b) so that information is passed to the succeeding generation. If the vehicle does not do its job, or if it is prevented from doing its job, the germ line dies. Nature has shaped an almost infinite number of vehicles, some of which perform their jobs better than others do in a given environment. The evolutionist's job is to figure out how and why under a given set of circumstances some individuals are more successful—more fit—than others in passing their genes on to succeeding generations. Lest this sound as if it is the most narrow reading of what an evolutionist's job is, we point out that the investigation of the myriad pathways to success that organisms, including humans, have taken is anything but narrow and uninteresting. It brings us into direct contact with all of the complex features produced by the evolutionary process, whether those features are somatic or not, that potentially affect an organism's fitness.

The point we are making is with respect to the genotype-phenotype distinction. If the genotype dictates the formation of "bodily" portions of the phenotype—the somatic features—and those portions protect the germ-line replicators, then the genes that control nest-building behavior can be viewed as producing a further protection for the germ line. The logic is identical. Richard Dawkins (1990:198) makes the same argument:

> The house of a caddis is strictly not a part of its cellular body, but it does fit snugly round the body. If the body is regarded as a gene vehicle, or survival machine, it is easy to see the stone house as a kind of extra protective wall, in a functional sense the outer portion of the vehicle. It just happens to be made of stone rather than chitin. Now consider a spider sitting at the centre of her web. If she is regarded as a gene vehicle, her web is not a part of that vehicle in quite the same obvious sense as a caddis house, since when

she turns round the web does not turn with her. But the distinction is clearly a frivolous one. In a very real sense her web is a temporary functional extension of her body, a huge extension of the effective catchment area of her predatory organs.

We can extend this argument by considering the remains of a mud-dauber's nest and a fragment of daub from a Mississippian-period wall-trench house from the southeastern United States—both recovered from identical archaeological contexts (O'Brien and Holland 1995). Modern biologists would have no difficulty in dealing with both the dauber's nest and the nest-building behaviors within the framework of the extended phenotype. Neither would they have trouble seeing nest-building behaviors as historical features—that is, as features that change over time. Yet many archaeologists will feel compelled to introduce a *behavioral analogue*—one perhaps derived from the ethnographic or ethnohistorical literature—to explain the human-constructed house remains. If, however, the step from a genetic basis for morphological development to a genetic basis for behavior is conceptually negligible, then the step from behavior to extended phenotype—here mud-dauber nests and Mississippian-period wall-trench houses or caddis stone houses and spiderwebs—also is negligible. One result of making this step is that artifacts can be used in phylogenetic orderings, just as can other sets of characters unique to humans, including language and manuscripts.

With respect to language and evolution, anthropologist Franz Boas (1904:518) observed, "Owing to the rapid change of language, the historical treatment of the linguistic problem had developed long before the historic aspect of the natural sciences was understood. The genetic relationship of languages was clearly recognized when the genetic relationship of species was hardly thought of. . . . No other manifestation of the mental life of man can be classified so minutely and definitely as language. In none are the genetic relations more clearly established." Boas's point was solid: Linguistic similarity is the result of cultural transmission and heritable continuity. It is during the transmission process that change occurs, such as in the gain or loss of words or changes in sound and meaning. These are not mere metaphorical analogues of biological features; they are products of the same kinds of mechanisms that create and maintain genetically based variation in organisms.

Not surprisingly, similarities between the goals of systematic biology and historical linguistics have long been noted, dating back at least to the nineteenth century (Wells 1987). Darwin (1859:422), for example, noted the similarity in the *Origin of Species:*

> If we possessed a perfect pedigree of mankind, a genealogical arrangement of the races of man would afford the best classification of the various languages now spoken throughout the world; and if all extinct languages, and all intermediate and slowly changing dialects, had to be included, such an arrangement would, I think, be the only possible one. Yet it might be that some very ancient language had altered little, and had given rise to few new languages, whilst others (owing to the spreading and subsequent isolation and states of civilisation of the several races, descended from a common race) had altered much, and had given rise to many new languages and dialects. The various degrees of difference in the languages from the same stock, would have to be expressed by groups subordinate to groups; but the proper or even only possible arrangement would still be genealogical; and this would be strictly natural, as it would connect together all languages, extinct and modern, by the closest affinities, and would give the filiation and origin of each tongue.

Darwin was speaking of a language taxonomy that resembles that produced by the Linnaean taxonomic system, but it need not take that shape. Linguistic characters are as amenable to division along plesiomorphic/apomorphic lines as biological characters are. Thus they can be used in cladistical analysis to produce unrooted cladograms. Once the polarity of various characters is ascertained, the trees become rooted.

In similar fashion, manuscripts evolve through the addition or deletion of words and punctuation, changes in spelling, and so on. Similarities between biological systematics and *stemmatics* (the study of the history of related sets of manuscripts) were brought to light primarily through an influential paper written by Norman I. Platnick, an arachnologist, and Don Cameron, a classicist (Platnick and Cameron 1977; see also Cameron 1987; Lee 1989; Robinson and O'Hara 1996). Platnick and Cameron pointed out that stemmatists had long used the same principles that underlie cladistics—the identification of changes in manuscripts that, once created, showed up in succeeding copies. Changes from manuscript to manuscript as they are copied by hand create nested series of synapomorphies. It is not synapomorphies, however, that interest historical linguists and stemmatists, who have as one of their goals the identification (reconstruction) of an actual ancestor—in linguistics, the "stem group" (Wiener 1987:221). To meet this goal they rely on symplesiomorphies. Why focus on shared ancestral as opposed to shared derived characters? Because historical linguists view ancestors as real as opposed to hypothetical: "The fact that a set of languages can be shown to be genetically related entails that there was a real protolanguage, spoken by a particular group of people, in a particular region, at a particular time period" (Kaufman 1990:21). If we believe we can identify an actual ancestor, it can be done only on the basis of ancestral characters. No derived character could possibly occur in the true ancestor of a given group of related languages; otherwise it could not be identified as the ancestor (Chapter 3). Platnick and Cameron (1977:383) put it this way: "Although admitting that in most cases possibly ancestral languages do turn out to have autapomorphies 'disproving' such a relationship, linguists consider the failure to find such a character sufficient evidence of actual ancestry." There is, of course, an alternative to labeling specific languages as ancestors: Related languages can be viewed as sister taxa—an approach that illustrates genealogical relationships without recourse to a "real" ancestor.

Before leaving the topic of the extended phenotype and the use of cultural characters in cladistical analyses, we need to clarify one point. Technically, the appropriateness of cladistics for anthropology does not hinge on the acceptance of artifacts or languages or manuscripts as phenotypic. Cladistics works on any set of features that change in nonrandom fashion over time, regardless of the mechanism or process. Even the most conservative-minded archaeologist would not accept that artifact change is random—witness the long-standing support in the discipline for such concepts as *traditions,* defined as temporal continua represented by persistent configurations of related forms (Rouse 1954; Willey and Phillips 1958). Archaeologists believe that traditions are products of cultural transmission (Chapter 1); as such, they should be amenable to phylogenetic analysis. Although we bring this up merely to show that cladistics can become part of the archaeological tool kit regardless of how artifacts are viewed, the next step—asking *why* a phylogenetic ordering assumes the shape it does—can only be taken by linking the ordering to theory. The theory we use to explain the pattern is the same one that biologists and paleobiologists use to explain their phylogenetic patterns—descent with modification. For archaeology, this requires that projectile points, pottery, and the like be viewed in the same manner as hair, beaks, and shells—that is, as phenotypic characters.

Culture Is Reticulate

Some critics of cultural phylogenetic studies have argued that cultural phylogeny is impossible to reconstruct because of the nature of cultural evolution (e.g., Dewar 1995; Moore 1994a, 1994b; Terrell 1988, 2001a, 2001b; Terrell and Stewart 1996; Terrell et al. 1997; Welsch and Terrell 1994; Welsch et al. 1992). They view cultural evolution as a vastly different kind of process than biological evolution, with a faster tempo and often a different mode: reticulation (Chapter 1). Critics argue that the faster tempo and different mode act in concert to swamp all traces of phylogenetic history and thus reduce the cultural landscape to little more than a blur of interrelated forms. This line of reasoning is not new. Since late in the nineteenth century, anthropologists and archaeologists have recognized that cultural evolution includes reticulation (references in Lyman 2001). Julian Steward (1944) used that recognition to criticize W. C. McKern's (1939) midwestern taxonomic method (Chapter 2), and A. L. Kroeber (1948) used it in his comparison of the two trees shown in Figure 4.2, one (Figure 4.2a) representing biological evolution and the other (Figure 4.2b) representing cultural evolution.

Two groups of archaeologists met in the 1950s to deal with culture change, its mode and tempo, and the kinds of archaeological signatures that were left by different modes of change (Lathrap 1956; Thompson 1958). The key criterion they used to distinguish between intralineage change and extralineage change—the difference being whether the source was internal or external to the lineage—was the order of magnitude evident in the change: The greater the magnitude, the more probable the source of change was external (Chapter 1). This same criterion is used today by archaeologists attempting to separate instances of what typically is referred to as "phylogenesis," or internal change, from "ethnogenesis," or change caused by external stimulus. Rarely is "magnitude" quantified, with most investigators relying instead on qualitative assessments such as how strongly one tradition resembles a previously unrelated one. This line of reasoning is circular: How does one know that the two traditions are unrelated (a manifestation of Galton's problem)?

We agree that cultural evolution probably is, in most respects, faster than biological evolution, and we agree that cultural evolution can involve reticulation, but we do not view these aspects as being necessarily problematic. For one thing, biological evolution often involves reticulation in the form of hybridization (Arnold 1997; Doolittle 1999; Endler

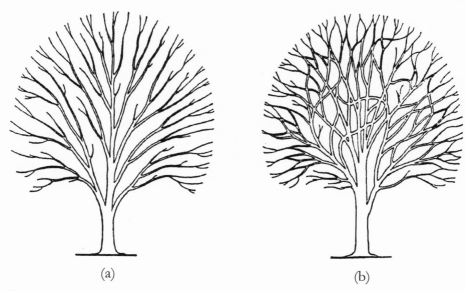

Figure 4.2. A. L. Kroeber's depiction of (a) organic evolution and (b) cultural evolution (after Kroeber 1948). Notice how the branches in the tree on the left constantly diverge, whereas those in the tree on the right diverge and then converge, creating a reticulate structure.

1998), especially in the plant kingdom (Rhymer and Simberloff 1996), where "botanists believe that hybridization between species happens in 6 to 16 percent of plant species" (Levin 2002:254). Although hybridization is less common in animals, it seems that "9 percent of all bird species hybridize" (Levin 2002:254). But the presence of populations of hybrids, or *complex taxa* (Skála and Zrzavý 1994), has not precluded phylogenetic analysis (Nelson 1983; Wagner 1983), despite claims to the contrary (Hedberg 1995; Sosef 1997). In anthropology, critics of cultural phylogenetic analyses (e.g., Moore 1994a, 1994b) have used the term *hybridization* to denote *any* instance of horizontal transmission, thus confusing process (hybridization) with mode (reticulation). In this naive view, only two processes are possible: total divergence (cladogenesis) or total convergence (ethnogenesis). But hybridization and reticulation are clearly not the same. Hybridization involves "successful matings in nature between individuals from two populations . . . which are distinguishable on the basis of one or more heritable characters" (Arnold 1997:4). Note that the two populations need not be of two distinct species; thus hybridization can represent "interbreeding of individuals from what are believed to be genetically distinct populations, regardless of the taxonomic status of such populations" (Rhymer and Simberloff 1996:84).

The equation of hybridization and horizontal cultural transmission is specious. Consider units of three different scales: parental units, offspring units, and units of transmission. The mating of two parental organisms will produce an offspring with 50 percent of its genes originating with each parent, what we will call a 50/50-F1. Thus the offspring unit is an even mixture of its parents in terms of the units of transmission (replicators). Presuming for the sake of argument that there are units of cultural transmission—whether they are termed memes (Aunger 2002; Blackmore 1999; Dawkins 1976), culturgens (Lumsden and Wilson 1981), instructions (Cloak 1973, 1975), mnemotypes (Blum 1963), or something else—horizontal cultural transmission may produce an offspring composed of equal parts of those replicators. But the odds are great that it will not. Whether or not transmission always produces a 50/50-F1 offspring is not an issue in biology because we know the scale of the (genetic) replicators that are transmitted. This is a critically important issue for understanding cultural lineages, even though the precise scale of the replicators is unknown. That horizontal transmission of cultural replicators will rarely result in a 50/50-F1 offspring is known from a wealth of ethnographic and linguistic data. If, for example, you consider that ceramic technology can consist of a lineage or a set of closely related lineages, then it should be clear that the horizontal transmission from another lineage of a replicator concerning how to shape a vessel does not result in a 50/50-F1. This is because the replicators for paste preparation, preparation and addition of temper, firing, surface treatment, surface manipulation, and a host of other phenotypic features in the recipient lineage may be unaffected.

Given the central role of hybridization and reticulation in the arguments of several critics of cultural phylogeny, we need to elaborate on points made in the preceding paragraph. In hybridization, not only must something akin to a 50/50-F1 offspring be produced, but that hybrid must then transfer its mixture of genes into at least one of the parent species in a process termed *introgression* (Anderson 1949). Subsequent generations must next include the extralineage genes, and they must spread throughout the population in order to effect "mongrelization" (Levin 2002). If those extralineage genes do not spread in such a manner, then no hybrid mongrel species will be produced. Figure 4.3 illustrates these processes and outcomes: An individual from species A mates with one from species B to produce a 50/50-F1 hybrid offspring. That offspring then mates with

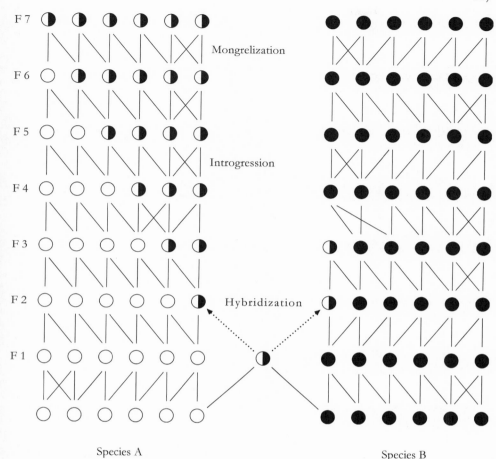

Figure 4.3. A simplified model of hybridization, introgression, and mongrelization. Each circle represents an individual organism;, each row of circles represents a separate generation; and time passes from bottom to top. White circles
represent individuals in species A; black circles represent individuals in species
B; and circles that are half white and half black represent hybrid individuals.
Vertical and diagonal lines represent genetic transmission.

cohorts (individuals of its own generation) to produce hybrid (F2) offspring in each parent species. On the one hand, in species B the second-
generation (F3) hybrid individual fails to reproduce, so hybridization in
this lineage ceases, introgression does not take place, and reticulate evolution has no effect on the lineage. In species A, on the other hand, the F2
hybrid interacts with members of its cohort, as does each succeeding gen-

eration of hybrids, resulting in introgression and eventually mongrelization of the entire species lineage such that no "purebred" individuals of the original species exist. Species A is effectively extinct by generation F7 (Levin 2002; Rhymer and Simberloff 1996).

The model in Figure 4.3 illustrates basic concepts and processes of hybridization, and the history of species A reflects the manner in which hybridization and reticulate evolution of cultural lineages are implicitly viewed by critics of cultural phylogeny. But Figure 4.3 is simplistic with respect to the units of transmission, whether biological (genes) or cultural (memes or the like). To illustrate this point, we begin with a cultural phenomenon, say pottery, that has eight "memes" in its "memotype" (Figure 4.4). The memotype is equivalent to a "cultural recipe" (Neff 1992) for producing an instance of the phenomenon, in this case a ceramic vessel. Every meme is expressed as a cultural character, each of which has four possible character states that occur within the pottery lineage in question during the time span under consideration. We designate each character with a unique capital letter, A–H, and each state of a character with a unique number, 1–4. One kind of change is shown in Figure 4.4a, where over time the states of various characters change as a result of innovation (mutation). Presuming that the characters are independent of one another, they will not all change states simultaneously as a result of being linked in some manner and thus will reflect what is known as *mosaic evolution,* or the independent change of characters. Over time a temporal, and in this case a phyletic, ordering of pottery may look like that shown in Figure 4.4a, where randomly chosen characters change states at random times. We have circled character states when they change to highlight the process; time is presumed to run from bottom to top. Note that heritable continuity between generations of character states is reflected by the sharing (overlapping) of many character states by adjacent generations.

What happens when a new character state (allele) is introduced from an extralineage source? If we designate any such character state with the number 5, and replace one or more character-state changes in Figure 4.4a with a 5 instead of a 1, 2, 3, or 4, we can begin to appreciate not only the importance of the scale of units used in phylogenetic analysis but the fallacious nature of the argument that, because cultural evolution can be reticulate, phylogenetic analysis is impossible. Consider first Figure 4.4b, where a single extralineage character state appears (why it appears and from where are separate analytical issues). Note that the phylogenetic signal provided by overlapping of character states has not been muted at all.

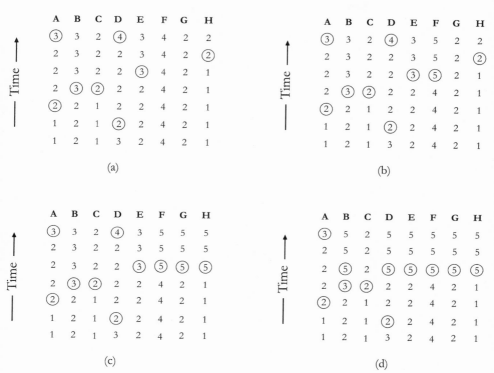

Figure 4.4. Four models of the evolution of states (numbers) of eight characters (letters): (a) no extralineage influence; (b) one character (F) changes as a result of extralineage influence; (c) three characters (F, G, H) change as a result of extralineage influence; (d) six characters (B, D, E, F, G, H) change as a result of extralineage influence. Each character has four possible states internal to the lineage, denoted by 1–4. Character state 5 originates from an extralineage source. Time passes from bottom to top in all the models. Seminal character-state changes are circled.

In this case, even if three characters (37.5 percent) simultaneously change to state 5, as in Figure 4.4c, the phylogenetic signal is still relatively strong. When six characters (75 percent) simultaneously change to state 5, as in Figure 4.4d, then the phylogenetic signal is somewhat obscure because the degree of overlapping, which signifies heritable continuity, has been significantly reduced. Although we acknowledge that such swamping of the phylogenetic signal can and does occur in both biological and cultural lineages, we underscore that the frequency of cultural cases exemplified in Figure 4.4d relative to the frequency of cultural cases exemplified in Figure 4.4b is unknown. Nor do we know the parameters under which one or the other scale—for that is all that Figure 4.4 shows—of cultural "hybridization" is likely to occur. Given its detection of homoplasy, cladistics is one way in which we might begin to determine these frequencies and parameters.

Ward Goodenough (1997:178) makes an excellent point with respect to language: "Contact between Japan and the United States has resulted in considerable borrowing in language and culture by Japan and some reverse borrowing by the United States, but their languages and cultures retain their respectively distinct phylogenetic identities." Borrowing has not created a "hybrid" culture or language. Further, linguists do not flip a coin to determine whether two or more languages share a phylogenetic history. Innumerable case studies have provided the basis for deciding which linguistic characters might be derived characters—bound morphemes and vocabulary, for example—and which might be something else—syntax, for example (see Nichols 1996).

The preceding paragraphs concern the ontology of hybridization, but there are also empirical precedents for not discarding the baby with the bath water. Paleobiologists who examine the phylogenetic history of fossils must assume that the units of analysis—sets of morphometrically similar fossils termed species (or more inclusive taxa)—in fact represent species and thus do not interbreed. Genetic transmission, in other words, is assumed to occur *only* within a lineage of some taxonomic scale—species, genera, families, and so on. Phylogenetic analysis of cultural lineages requires the same assumption—that transmission is primarily within either a lineage or a series of closely related lineages rather than between distantly related lineages. In neither paleobiology nor archaeology can it be *demonstrated* that such is in fact the case, yet the assumption has not put paleobiologists out of business.

We reject the blanket assumption that reticulation precludes cultural phylogenetic analysis. It might make it more difficult than if transmission were strictly vertical, but this is a methodological problem, not a theoretical one (Bellwood 1996). The methodological challenge is to carefully remove the vines from Kroeber's cultural tree (Figure 4.2) so that the branches—lineages—can be seen (Boyd et al. 1997). The key question with respect to cultural phylogeny is the same as it is in biology: Are the taxa arising from a cladistic analysis monophyletic? Importantly, monophyly is not necessarily an evolutionary concept—a feature of an evolutionary lineage possessing only a single ancestor. Rather, monophyly is a concept built around a taxon possessing but *a single root on a cladogram*

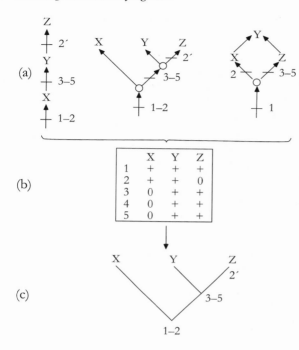

Figure 4.5. Three different phylogenetic scenarios (a), producing a single character matrix (b) and, correspondingly, a single cladogram (c) (X–Z, taxa; 1–5, characters; 2', character reversal) (after Skála and Zrzavý 1994).

(Skála and Zrzavý 1994). This is a key distinction. The branching topology of a cladogram does *not* mean that phylogeny is necessarily always a divergent process. Take the example in Figure 4.5, which shows three different phylogenetic scenarios that can produce the same character matrix and, correspondingly, the same cladogram. Thus, as Zdeněk Skála and Jan Zrzavý (1994:311–312) point out: "The treatment of all taxa should be rooted in the method itself, not in our belief about what the result of an analysis should represent. A cladogram is either *useful or useless* (in terms of reflecting the character patterns), rather than *true or false* (in terms of reflecting the course of phylogeny). Complex taxa are good subjects for examining this important problem."

Taxonomy Is Causal Ordering

John Terrell, a vocal critic of cultural phylogenetic analysis, has stated that phylogenists routinely view taxonomy as a theory of causal ordering. Terrell (1988:648) cites Stephen Jay Gould (1986) as the source of that view and then proceeds to criticize it: "even when we can picture biological speciation as a temporal pattern of descent with modification resulting in reproductive isolation (true 'branching' in an evolutionary sense), the pictured fact of speciation alone tells us little, if anything, about causes and processes leading up to speciation." This is true; a hierarchical taxonomy does not tell us about the "causes and processes leading up to speciation." It is not designed to. Similarly, a cultural taxonomy cannot tell us anything about processes that result in the evolution of cultures. Gould was referring to the fact that Darwinian evolution provides a theoretical warrant for the Linnaean taxonomic system; thus the system and the theory, at least after Darwin's insight, became interconnected (Mayr 1969; Padian 1999; Simpson 1961). Terrell conflates pattern and process—aspects of evolution that biologists since the 1940s have recognized as distinct. As we pointed out earlier, J. O. Brew made this same mistake in his criticism of Colton and Hargrave's (1937) classification of southwestern pottery.

The pattern revealed by the Linnaean taxonomy was, after 1859, explained by the *processes* composing Darwin's theory. The pattern consists of nested taxa of various ranks; groups are constructed on the basis of the formal similarity of each taxon's members, and that is all. Formal similarity results from shared ancestry, parallelism, convergence, and divergence, all of which are in turn driven by natural selection and drift. Darwin (1859) laid this out (minus drift) in Chapter 13 of the *Origin of Species*. It took biologists nearly a century to work out the details in such a manner that we now understand that a set of historical processes provides a *theoretical* explanation for an observed taxonomic pattern. Critics of efforts to build cultural phylogenies seem unaware of this history.

We find it interesting that the critics castigate phylogenists for arguing for the primacy of history as a "source of law and similarity" (Terrell 1988:649). Critics charge that instead of worrying about history, phylogenists should be using the ethnographic record as an inspiration for their explanations. This attitude shows a misunderstanding of history because it conflates it with chronology. The latter is merely a temporal ordering of events, whereas the former includes not only ordering but also cause-and-effect explanations for those events. Darwinism is a historical explanatory theory that includes nomothetic processes (laws) that operate within the historical contingencies of particular spatial and temporal coordinates (Beatty 1995) to produce not only similarities but *differences* between phenomena (Gould 2002).

What about using the ethnographic record as a source of explanation? John Moore (1994b:931) is emphatic about the necessity of referring to the ethnographic record for interpretive inspiration: "Without the inductive discipline imposed by uniformitarianism, theorists are free to construct whatever bizarre theories they might find agreeable, on whatever basis. . . . With no confirmation in the ethnographic record, they invite elaboration into even more confusing interpretations unless they are brought back into contact with reality by the requirement of ethnographic analogy." We take sharp exception to Moore's statement. Why should the ethnographic record be viewed as a source of phylogenetic information for anything other than the cultural phenomena it documents? First, that record is limited even for specific phylogenies—for example, using early-twentieth-century ethnography for a specific cultural group as a guide to the prehistoric ancestry of that group. Second, given his use of the term "uniformitarianism," Moore seems to suggest that we can use the ethnographic record to create analogies. We find that position untenable for several reasons (Lyman and O'Brien 2001a; O'Brien et al. 1998; Wolverton and Lyman 2000), not the least of which is that the ethnographic and ethnohistoric literature offers us "*small-scale* observations on societies already under the influence, whether beneficial or malignant, of colonial authorities" (Bellwood 1996:883; see also Dunnell 1991).

We do not deny the importance of ethnographic research to archaeological endeavors. Such research has over many years produced a wealth of insights that must be considered in efforts to write evolutionary theory in archaeological terms and to adapt phylogenetic models built by biologists to archaeological concerns. We do deny, however, that the ethnographic record is a source of uniformitarian laws that govern cultural evolution. That record is by and large synchronic and at best captures the equivalent of what a paleobiologist would term *microevolution* (Gould 2002 and references therein; see also Simpson 1944). As we have argued elsewhere (Lyman and O'Brien 1998, 2001b; O'Brien et al. 2003), archaeology, because of its resolution of the spatial and temporal continua, is largely constrained to study macroevolution. This is not a flaw but rather a true benefit, because no other discipline has access to the full depth and breadth of cultural evolution. The unique and large spatial and, particularly, temporal scales at which the archaeological record is perceived demand a unique historical theory written at an appropriate macroevolutionary scale rather than at the microevolutionary scale of ethnography. Further, the theory has to be written in archaeological terms (O'Brien and Lyman 2000). This in no way implies that careful analysis cannot lead to understanding complex phylogenetic histories of tools and the people who made them, just as similar analysis in paleobiology can lead to phylogenetic ordering of extinct organisms. It simply means that evolution needs to be studied at both the macro and micro scales. Above all it means that there is no reason to suspect a priori that phylogenetic histories constructed from the ethnographic record have any bearing on those constructed from the archaeological record.

Language, Biology, and Culture Are Not Concordant

The fourth criticism—the claim that phylogenists uncritically assume a close correspondence of language, culture, and biology—raises interesting points, but at the same time it paints a distorted picture of the comparative phylogenetic method. Terrell (2001a:6), for example, states that the comparative method assumes that "language history ought to parallel culture history and the history of human populations"—a statement more or less echoed by Moore (2001:31–32):

> In cladistic theory, genes, language, and culture are said to evolve as a "package," so that all three aspects of human life tend to experience congruent or parallel changes. A biological taxonomy of human populations showing their overall genetic relatedness should be compatible with a taxonomy of their languages, technology, or other aspects of culture. By knowing a group's genetic structure, we should be able to predict such traits as their linguistic affiliations, their social structure, and their religion.

Not only does Moore mischaracterize "cladistic theory"—using it as a synonym for any phylogenetic investigation—but he and Terrell mischaracterize what the comparativists have said. In an early programmatic statement on the comparative method, Kimball Romney (1957:36) made it clear that

> [t]he genetic model takes as its segment of cultural history a group of tribes which are set off from other groups by sharing a common physical type, possessing common systemic patterns, and speaking genetically related languages. It is *assumed* that correspondence among these three factors indicates a common historical tradition at some time in the past for these tribes. We shall designate this segment of cultural history the "genetic unit" and it includes the ancestral group and all intermediate groups, as well as the tribes in the ethnographic present. (emphasis added)

Romney was not claiming an isomorphism among language, genes, and culture. Rather, he was pointing out that a cultural-historical "genetic unit" needs to be defined on independent grounds. *If* there is a high correspondence among the three variables, then perhaps the genetic unit is an analytically useful device. Importantly, "usefulness" is testable. The key point "is not to presuppose the nature of the relationship, but to establish the pattern in order to consider what factors might affect whether there is a positive, neutral or negative relationship" (Foley and Lahr 1997:10). This same reasoning espoused by Romney was used by Evan Vogt (1964) for the Maya, Kent Flannery and Joyce Marcus (1983) for the Zapotec and Mixtec, and Patrick Kirch and Roger Green (1987, 2001) for South Pacific islanders. Kirch and Green (2001) refer to the method as "triangulation"—using independent lines of evidence (linguistic, genetic, ethnohistoric, and archaeological) in phylogenetic reconstruction.

UNITS OF CULTURAL EVOLUTION

What are the units typically used in cultural phylogenetic analysis? In some cases, a distinct minority, individual characters are examined. More commonly, bundles of characters are examined—bundles that "can be transmitted as independent units (i.e., even when other aspects of the culture are not passed on)" (Mace and Pagel 1994:549). Sometimes whole cultures are examined. Here is where Terrell and other critics (e.g., Moore 1994a, 1994b) raise important points. Terrell (2001a:5) points out that the comparativists' claims are grounded in several key assumptions, including "(1) human populations, ethnic groups, cultures, and languages are real things—actual empirical phenomena—and not just convenient analytical fictions; (2) despite births and deaths—and people coming and going—these corporate entities are also historically enduring phenomena . . . (3) like individuals, such corporate things have ancestors, descendants, relatives, and 'patterns of hierarchical descent.'" To Terrell, these are problematic assumptions, and for some scales of analysis we would agree. But comparativists understand the problem of units and scale. Mace and Pagel (1994:552), for example, state that "we shall have to accept, then, that a cultural phylogeny represents only broadly the cultural path that most of the ancestors of the majority of members of that culture followed." The key word is "broadly"; no comparativist would view a cultural phylogeny using "cultures" as taxonomic units as anything but a broad picture of ancestry. For Mace and Pagel's purposes, linguistically defined groups appear to be reasonable units.

Terrell makes an excellent point about the nonempirical nature of units such as human populations, ethnic groups, and cultures, but he errs in calling them "analytical fictions." The real issue is the difference between empirical units and ideational units (Chapter 2). If explicitly defined, units such as "cultures" can have considerable import *for particular kinds of analysis*. As a corollary, "cultures" can be defined differently for different analyses. Similarly, in biology the "species" can be a useful analytical unit, despite the existence of up to two dozen different species definitions (Howard and Berlocher 1998; Mayden 1997; Wheeler and Meier 2000). Is there a correct definition of a species? Maybe, but in our opinion there is not. Rather, we side with a few biologists, paleobiologists (e.g., Cracraft 2000), and philosophers of biology who have come to recognize that a species is a unit constructed for a specific analytical or applied biological purpose. Those purposes might be for managing biodiversity or for studying the phylogenetic history of a group of organisms. Our analytical goal dictates which one of the several available species concepts, and thus which kind of unit, is the most appropriate. This approach sidesteps the issue of whether species are "real."

This perspective has significant connotations for anthropology and archaeology—an issue that we have explored in detail elsewhere (Lyman and O'Brien 2002; O'Brien and Lyman 2000, 2002a) and only summarize here. As with species, it is not difficult to conceive of cultures and the like as empirical entities. We can, after all, *see* them—at least we can see the people supposedly participating in a culture—and thus we can describe them. Similarly, it is not difficult to view cultural groups as natural units. Individual humans within a group do many of the same things intraspecific organisms do: They coexist, they communicate, and they interbreed. They also assist one another in various ways as well as compete with one another. As with other organisms, if we view these human interactions as group-maintaining activities, it is a simple matter to take the next step and elevate the natural group to the level of an Individual—capitalized to denote an aggregate of discrete phenomena as opposed to a single discrete phenomenon (lowercased).

What could be more real than an individual or an Individual, especially given that neither remains static? An individual, whether an organism or a cultural phenomenon such as a ceramic vessel or a ritual, has a developmental history, usually referred to as *ontogeny*. Similarly, an Individual has a developmental history. It can add and shed pieces continually—individuals can come and go through birth, death, immigration, and so on—but for some period the Individual looks very much like it did the last time we saw it. Robert Boyd et al. (1997) refer to the conservative part of the Individual (our word, not theirs) as the *core tradition*. After a time, however, the Individual changes enough in terms of phenotypic characters—language, customs, technology, and so on—that it seems reasonable to label it as a different Individual. This is anagenetic evolution—the result of a slow buildup of change that gradually turns Individual A into Individual A'. Alternatively, for whatever reason, part of group A fissions and the daughter part moves some distance away from the parental part. After a time, the two Individuals develop different tool traditions, customs, and the like, and after more time they have difficulty communicating with each other. This is cladogenetic, or branching, evolution.

Regardless of the mode of evolution, are the units—the Individuals—real? We would argue, as Terrell (2001a) does, that units such as cultures are not real. Rather, they are ideational units created for specific analytical purposes. As such, they should be defined on the basis of some explicit criteria. The specimens, whether individuals or Individuals, placed in a particular kind of ideational unit—a *class* (Chapter 5)—are empirical. We can refer to the collection of actual specimens as the corresponding *group*. This is, however, different than simply placing specimens in a unit because they "seem to go together." Groups that are extracted from classes are not "convenient analytical fictions," despite claims to the contrary (Terrell 2001a:5). As long as theoretically informed definitions are employed, such groups can be used in cultural phylogeny, just as species are used in biological phylogeny. Or, as we discuss below, specific parts of cultures can be examined from a phylogenetic standpoint.

One way of answering the question of the scale at which it is possible to trace cultural phylogeny is presented by Boyd et al. (1997:364), who note that tracing "cultural phylogenies is possible to the extent that there are genealogical entities that have sufficient coherence, relative to the amount of mixing and independent evolution among entities, to create recognizable history." In other words, tracing phylogenetic history depends on there being a phylogenetic signal strong enough to be detected. Further, they point out that if culture is defined as information transmitted from individual to individual through a variety of means, it is not unreasonable to posit the existence of a hierarchy of genealogical entities analogous to the genealogical hierarchy of organic evolution. Thus small elements (particular words, specific innovations, components of ritual practice) are linked together in larger, potentially transmittable entities (technological systems, myth, religion), which themselves are collected into "cultures" that characterize human groups of different scales (kin groups, villages, ethnic groups, and so on). These units can crosscut one another, and thus the analyst must be explicit in defining the unit being used.

Without considerable care, these units can take on a reality—a naturalness—and when classified create the same paraphyly seen in the Linnaean taxonomic system. This result is predictable if we confuse pattern with process and attempt to mix phenotypic similarity and descent. Or worse yet, if we use intuitive knowledge, perhaps gained from ethnography, not only to create the units but to arrange them hierarchically. If we can define the units intensionally, however, meaning that we impose a theoretically informed classification *on* the phenomena being classified as opposed to extracting it *from* the phenomena (Dunnell 1986; O'Brien and Lyman 2000, 2002a), then we have a much better chance of avoiding the construction of paraphyletic groups. What we have in mind is a taxonomy similar to what is shown in Figure 4.6, which in terms of *structure* is no different than the Linnaean system. The difference lies in how the units are created, a topic that we treat in considerable detail in Chapter 5.

As alternatives to the hierarchical model of cultures, Boyd et al. (1997) offer three other models: cultures as species, cultures as assemblages of many coherent units, and cultures as collections of ephemeral entities. Like Boyd et al., we find no support for the culture-as-species model, although the anthropological and archaeological literature is replete with vague references to this culture or that culture, as if they were indeed natural units. Archaeologists (e.g., Cullen 1993; Gladwin 1936; Willey and Phillips 1958) routinely equate "cultures" with species (see also Gould 1987, 1997), despite the fact there is no explicit, generally accepted definition of "a culture" (Lyman et al. 1997; Sackett 1981) that even remotely incorporates the notion of transmission. As a result, any equation of a biological species with a culture is fallacious. We think this is what Terrell (2001a) was reacting to when he labeled such units "convenient analytical fictions." Likewise we reject the cultures-as-collections-of-ephemeral-entities model, which rests on the nihilistic premise that "observable aspects of culture could be the result of units that are beneath the resolution of current methods to observe" (Boyd et al. 1997:366). One reason for this lack of resolution might be the high turnover in cultural elements. That is, change is so rapid that only a weak phylogenetic signal is transmitted— one we would never be able to discern. We reject this model based on our experience and that of others in detecting phylogenetic signals in the ar-

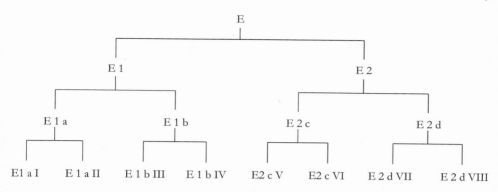

Figure 4.6. A symmetrical taxonomy producing eight classes (after Dunnell 1971).

chaeological record (Collard and Shennan 2000; Foley 1987; Foley and Lahr 1997; Harmon et al. 2000, 2003; Kirch and Green 2001; Leonard 2001; Lyman and O'Brien 2000a; O'Brien et al. 2001, 2002; O'Brien and Lyman 1999, 2000). The third model proposed by Boyd et al. (1997: 376)—cultures as assemblages of many coherent units—views the components as "collections of memes that are transmitted as units with little recombination and slow change, and their phylogenies can be reliably reconstructed to some depth." How deep we can go in the reconstruction hinges on the strength of the "glue" that holds the units together and the degree of openness of cultural systems. In other words, if we think of the components in terms of memes, how cohesive is a set of memes and how freely can memes from the outside enter a set and in what frequency?

The two models that hold the most promise—cultures as hierarchical systems and cultures as assemblages of many coherent units—are not mutually exclusive, and in fact Boyd et al. (1997) view them as modes within a continuum. As they point out, it is difficult to put upper and lower bounds on the modes, and perhaps because of that we should view them as nonexclusive, overlapping modes, especially if the models are applied to cultures in general. Central to their model of cultures as hierarchical systems is the existence of a conservative "core tradition," which is rarely affected by diffusion of units from other groups. New core traditions arise mainly "by the fissioning of populations and subsequent divergence of daughter cultures. Isolation and integration protect the core from the effects of diffusion, although peripheral elements are much more heavily subject to cross-cultural borrowing" (Boyd et al. 1997:365). As for constructing phylogenetic hypotheses, "reasonably deep core-cultural phylogenies can still be inferred, but this requires disentangling the effects of borrowing by distinguishing core and peripheral elements, and especially by methods to identify elements that 'introgressed' into the core" (Boyd et al. 1997:365).

How do we accomplish this? We agree that most cultures probably have a conservative "core tradition"—similar to Morris Swadesh's (1964) "morphological kernel" of a language—and perhaps it can be identified in modern cultures, but what about in archaeological situations? We might start by examining how archaeologists have long viewed traditions, going back to Gordon Willey's (1945:53) definition, which, although it contains reference to pottery, applies to other categories of materials: "a line, or a number of lines, of pottery development through time within the confines of a certain technique or decorative constant." This implies that tradition was being defined at the scale of an attribute of a discrete object, but Willey expanded his definition to include the scales of discrete object and aggregates thereof: "A pottery tradition includes broad descriptive categories of ceramic decoration which undoubtedly have value in expressing historical relationships when the relationships are confined to the geographic boundaries of" what Willey (1945:53) described as "a unified culture area [wherein] important cultural developments were essentially local and basically interrelated for at least a thousand years [thereby demonstrating a] fundamental cultural unity." A pottery tradition "lacks the specific quality of the localized pottery style. . . . In successive time periods through which the history of ceramic development can be traced, certain styles arose within the tradition" (Willey 1945:53).

Hector Neff (1992:152–153) places the archaeological concept of tradition squarely in a Darwinian framework:

> Inter-individual transfer of pottery-making knowledge must produce historical phenomena that [can be referred] to as "ceramic traditions." Shared information dictates where to find clay, how to prepare clay, how to form and decorate pots, how to fire pots, and other aspects of behavior related to pottery-making. Just as the techniques employed by an individual to produce his/her distinctive pots are determined by pottery-making information that individual carries, so the distinctive, collective phenotypic expressions recognizable in particular regions, during particular time intervals, are determined by information shared among individuals working within a tradition. The importance of ceramic traditions to ceramic evolution is that traditions, like individuals, are partitions of information concerning how to produce pot-

tery-making aspects of potters' phenotypes; because evolution results from any disruption of information flow through time, ceramic evolution will result both from disruptions of inter-individual transmission of pottery-making knowledge and from disruptions that simultaneously affect the ability to transmit pottery-making knowledge of all individuals working within a ceramic tradition.

It is at the scale of traditions of artifact kinds—ceramic vessels, projectile points, and the like—that archaeologists can begin to construct testable hypotheses of cultural phylogeny. We view traditions as sets of lineages, defined as single lines of ancestry and descent. Lineages can exist at several scales, as Willey (1945) suggested for archaeological traditions. As in biology, genes, cells, and organisms all replicate or reproduce to form lineages; at a higher level, cell lineages make up organisms; and at a higher level organismic lineages form populations. Lineages are not clades; they are single lines of descent that can be represented on a phylogenetic tree as a set of branches that form pathways from the root of the tree (or an internal node) to a terminal (Figure 4.7). Clades comprise multiple, related lineages at different scales. Whereas clades are by definition monophyletic, lineages can be paraphyletic or even polyphyletic in terms of their lower-level components. In biology, "organisms making up the later part of a population lineage may share a more recent common ancestor with organisms in a recently diverged but now separate lineage than with the earlier organisms of their own lineage" (de Queiroz 1998:60). This is true. Consider that on average we share 25 percent of our genotype with our nieces and nephews, who are not in our lineage, and only 12.5 percent with our great-grandchildren, who are in our lineage (Figure 4.8). Some biologists (e.g., Mayr 1995) have used this point to underscore a logical flaw in cladistics, but they are confusing two entirely separate things: descent and genetic relatedness. Lineages are patterns of genealogical descent; clades are patterns of phylogenetic relationship.

DISCUSSION

The growing interest in cultural phylogenies evident over the last two decades marks a return to the questions on which the founding of archaeology (e.g., Lyman et al. 1997) and much of anthropology (e.g., Harris 1968; Leaf 1979; Stocking 1987) rests. We view this return as critically important to the growth and continued health of anthropology and

Clades   Lineages

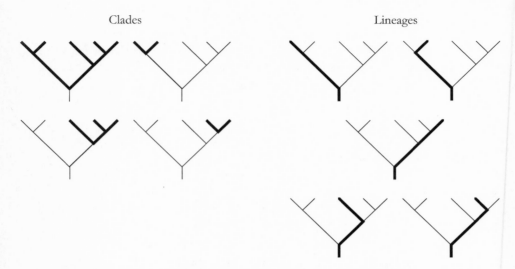

Figure 4.7. Diagrams showing the difference between clades and lineages (after de Queiroz 1998). All nine diagrams represent the same phylogeny, with clades highlighted on the left and lineages on the right. Additional lineages can be counted from various internal nodes to the branch tips.

archaeology, particularly for the latter, given its unique access to the full time depth of cultural development and change. Data for answering phylogenetic questions are now much more numerous and more specific and detailed, and the epistemological nuances and pitfalls are much better known than they were five or six decades ago. Ontological matters are, however, another issue, and until they are cleared up, wrangling over epistemology will continue to consume much effort.

Critics of phylogenetic analysis of cultural phenomena raise some important points, but a large number of specific criticisms display a marked misunderstanding of ontological and epistemological aspects of Darwinian evolution—particularly as implemented by paleobiologists—and cladistics. Many of the critics' arguments can be dispensed with by thoughtful consideration of the scale at which one seeks to monitor phylogeny. Many of Franz Boas's early anthropological efforts (reprinted collectively in Boas 1940) were explicitly directed toward demonstrating that human biology, language, and culture evolved independently of one another. It is not difficult to reduce the scale further and note that individual aspects (some might say subsystems) of culture also evolve independently of one another. For example, as archaeologists we tend to think in terms

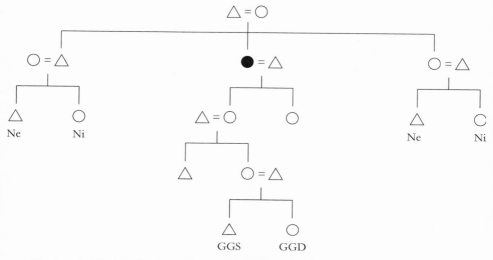

Figure 4.8. Kinship diagram showing five generations. The blackened circle is the person doing the kinship reckoning. That person on average shares 25 percent of her genotype with her nieces (Ni) and nephews (Ne), who are not in her lineage, and only 12.5 percent with her great-grandchildren (GGD and GGS), who are in her lineage.

of empirical units—ceramic pots, stone implements, and the like. Given their technological independence, we believe it is reasonable to think that such tools evolved independently of one another. Reducing the scale still further, we think it is likely that the preparation of the temper and paste along with the forming of a vessel and its ultimate firing are often independent of the colors and elements of design motifs applied to the vessel. Thus, the choice of units, including their scale, for the application of cladistic methods is critical because it should help avoid many of the problems attending phylogenetic analyses. We explore these issues in Chapters 5 and 6.

STARTING POINTS

There are numerous examples of comparative studies that rely on understanding patterns of descent in order to examine the distribution of adaptive, or functional, cultural features. Two we recommend are by Monique Borgerhoff Mulder et al. (2001) and Ruth Mace and Mark Pagel (1994). You also might want to skim Paul Harvey and Mark Pagel's (1991) *The Comparative Method in Evolutionary Biology* to see how biologists use the approach. For an excellent discussion of how the phenotype can be extended to include by-products of behavior, read Richard Dawkins's (1990) *The Extended Phenotype: The Long Reach of the Gene*. A similar argument for extending the human phenotype is made by Robert Leonard and Tom Jones (1987) and by Michael O'Brien and Thomas Holland (1995).

We highly recommend that those interested in applying cladistics to nonorganismic phenomena read the short paper by Norman Platnick and Don Cameron (1977), which points out similarities between what cladists do and what stemmatists do in studying ancient manuscripts from a historical perspective. Their paper was one of the first, if not the first, to point out that the cladistic approach works on anything whose evolutionary development is linked to transmission, including things outside the organic realm.

On the contentious issue of whether cultural evolution is so reticulate that we cannot detect phylogenetic signals, see various chapters in John Terrell's (2001b) *Archaeology, Language, and History: Essays on Culture and Ethnicity* for a pessimistic view. You might also read Terrell et al. (1997). One point that arises in these and similar works is that there is no reason not to assume that human biology, language, and culture evolved independently of one another. Thus, human "cultures" cannot serve as units of phylogenetic analysis because such units do not really exist. Some authors who take a dim view of cultural-phylogenetic efforts appear to think that this perspective is new, but it is not. See what Franz Boas (1940) had to say on the subject. No one, certainly not those who believe cultural phylogenies are obtainable, would argue against the independence of biology, culture, and language, but phylogenists would argue that there are basic patterns of overlap among those variables that under certain controlled circumstances can serve as useful units. This perspective is expressed in excellent detail in Patrick Kirch and Roger Green's (2001) *Hawaiki, Ancestral Polynesia: An Essay in Historical Anthropology*.

For one of the best overviews of phylogenetic reticulation and cladistics, see Zdeněk Skála and Jan Zrzavý (1994). On the question of what kind of units might be applicable in cultural-phylogenetic studies, you definitely should read Robert Boyd et al. (1997). This is a detailed examination of four different scales of units and a thoughtful review of their strong and weak points. Finally, for an excellent discussion of the relationships (and differences) between clades and lineages, see Kevin de Queiroz (1998).

FIVE

Taxa, Characters, and Outgroups

Michael J. O'Brien, R. Lee Lyman, John Darwent,
and Daniel S. Glover

Cladistics can be used to examine phylogeny at various scales, irrespective of whether the taxa house organisms or some other set of phenomena that evolve. In terms of scale, it makes no difference whether the taxa are genera or species or whether they are pottery types or varieties of pottery types. What does make a difference is the nature of the analytical units used: Can they do the work that is being asked of them? The ability of cladistics to produce a phylogenetic ordering of taxa—we assume there is only one true phylogeny—depends on the strength of the phylogenetic signal emitted by character states and our ability to decode that signal. Cladistics, like phenetics, will always produce an ordering. But as the adage goes, if you put garbage into a computer, you'll get garbage out. In cladistics the consistency index helps us decide how much of our output is messy, but that messiness refers only to homoplasy. No index can tell us how much of the messy output is attributable to problems of our own making. Cladistics is difficult enough without having to face problems that could have been overcome had a little more thought gone into the early stages of analysis. Did we, for example, pay enough attention to the scale at which analysis was to be conducted. Just as importantly, did we exercise good judgment in selecting the units to be used? Were the units— both the taxa and the characters and character states used— appropriate for reconstructing phylogeny at that particular scale?

We examine these critical issues through reference to a study that we conducted of projectile points from the southeastern United States that date roughly 11,500–10,000 radiocarbon years before the present (RCYBP), or what is known as the Paleoindian period. The preliminary results of that study have been presented at conferences (Darwent et al. 2000; O'Brien 2001; O'Brien et al. 2000) and published in abbreviated form (O'Brien and Lyman 2002b, 2003a; O'Brien et al. 2001, 2002). Here we expand the study and place the new results in a broad context that allows us to build on topics raised in Chapters 3 and 4. Some readers might be disappointed that we focus on one small segment of culture instead of on cultures themselves. They also might wonder why we do not employ archaeological or ethnohistorical cultures as taxa and then develop trait lists that can be used as characters and character states in a phylogenetic analysis. This certainly could be done, as Mace and Pagel (1994) demonstrated for modern African groups; but by starting at the level of specific artifact taxa we believe we can do better than present general cultural phylogenies. We are focusing on bundles of characters that "can be transmitted as independent units" (Mace and Pagel 1994:549), but we are doing it at a very fine scale. Later, perhaps, those bundles of characters can be combined with other bundles to examine what effect the addition of those new characters has on the phylogenetic ordering of larger-scale taxa. Moreover, using small-scale units initially not only allows later lumping, if deemed pertinent, but also potentially allows the detection and tracking of fine-scale evolution. By this we mean tracking intellectual traditions, such as how to make a projectile point or design a pot, as opposed to tracking the larger cultural complex of which they are a part.

PALEOINDIAN PROJECTILE POINTS IN THE SOUTHEAST

The archaeological literature contains a plethora of type names used to partition the tremendous variety of projectile points from the United States that date 11,500–10,000 RCYBP. In terms of how the types are used by archaeologists, some are restricted to localized areas, whereas others are used to refer to points that occur over wide areas. The type Clovis, for example, is used to refer to projectile points from the Rocky Mountains to the Atlantic Coast. For the southeastern United States— roughly the area bounded on the west by the Mississippi River and on the north by the Ohio River—there are over two dozen Paleoindian-period projectile-point types in common use today.

The type name *Clovis* comes from the town of the same name in eastern New Mexico, near which the type specimen was identified (Cotter 1937). That find was sensational because of the occurrence of projectile

Figure 5.1. Clovis points from New Mexico and Arizona. All but the third specimen from the left (from the Lehner site, Arizona) are from the Blackwater Draw locality, New Mexico. Specimen on the left is 9.5 cm long.

points in association with mammoth bones. In addition, the points were extremely well made (Figure 5.1)—from an aesthetic point of view much more pleasing than many of those known to date to later periods. The points are large and well flaked, and they exhibit longitudinal thinning from the basal edge. The removal of thinning flakes gives Clovis points the unmistakable "flutes" on both faces. After the finds near Clovis, investigations carried out at other locales in the Southwest confirmed the widespread occurrence of Clovis points in association with late Quaternary–age mammals. In large part because of these finds, archaeologists assumed that Clovis points occurred first in the West and then later moved eastward. This assumption was bolstered in the 1950s with the advent of radiocarbon dating. Clovis-age contexts were rare in the East—although eastern Clovis points were abundant as surface finds—but this was not the case in the West and Southwest. Suites of radiocarbon dates obtained from Clovis deposits there set boundaries around the age of Clovis points (ca. 11,500–10,900 RCYBP). Archaeologists became familiar with the

western chronology, and the region began to be looked upon as the home-
land of Clovis.

The first comprehensive study of eastern Paleoindian artifacts was an
article in *Current Anthropology* by Ronald Mason (1962). After survey-
ing the distribution of fluted points in the East and adjacent portions of
the Midwest, he concluded that fluted points were not a western invention
that had diffused to eastern parts of the country, perhaps as Plains and
southwestern groups escaped the drying effects of the terminal Pleistocene. Rather, in Mason's view, it was the other way around:

> [T]he distributional and some of the typological evidence, as currently
> understood, would not seem to favor the proposed western origin for the de-
> velopment of Clovis points and the Llano complex. On the contrary, fluted
> points of every description except Folsom are far more numerous in the East,
> particularly in the southeastern United States, than they are in the Southwest
> or on the High Plains; and this area also has produced the greatest diversifi-
> cation in fluted point styles. On these grounds, then, it is defensible to sug-
> gest the southeastern United States, and not the West, as a possible "home-
> land" of the Clovis complex. (Mason 1962:234–235)

Mason's proposal subsequently was endorsed, either tentatively or whole-
heartedly, by numerous investigators (e.g., Bryan 1991; Meltzer 1988;
Stanford 1991), and the work of David Anderson and colleagues (Anderson 1990, 1991; Anderson and Faught 1998, 2000; Anderson and Gillam
2000; Faught et al. 1994) empirically demonstrated that Paleoindian
points are indeed found in greater numbers in the East than in the West.

The diversity of Paleoindian points from the Southeast is remarkable.
Cumberland points (Lewis 1954), so named because of their occurrence in
significant numbers in and around the Cumberland and Tennessee
drainages of Tennessee, occur across most of the eastern United States.
These points (Figure 5.2) are distinguished by their narrowness and
greater thickness relative to Clovis points and by the presence of recurved
blade edges and often flaring "ears" at the basal corners that are accentu-
ated by incurving blade edges. They frequently exhibit fluting, usually
produced by removal of a single, deep flake that on many specimens extends from the concave base almost to the tip. Some point-type guides
(e.g., Perino 1985:94) state that "not all [Cumberland points] are fluted."
Other Paleoindian projectile-point types in the Southeast include Suwannee (Bullen 1968), Simpson (Bullen 1968), and Hazel (Van Buren 1974),
all of which have indented bases and basal thinning, which often takes the

Figure 5.2. Representative specimens of some Paleoindian projectile-point types (from left): Cumberland (Tennessee), Suwannee (Florida), Simpson (Florida), Hazel (Oklahoma). Specimen on the left is 9.4 cm long (photographs courtesy Alex Thornburn [Cumberland], Lawrence Tully and Steven Tully [Suwannee and Simpson], and Lonnie and Sherry Hartline [Hazel]).

form of fluting (Figure 5.2). Specimens of all these types share morphological characteristics with Clovis points, and one hypothesis would be that they are sister taxa with Clovis or descendants of that taxon.

The Clovis-Dalton Connection

Any number of proposed chronological sequences of projectile-point forms have been proposed for the Southeast, such as the one shown in Figure 5.3, which begins approximately 11,500 RCYBP with Clovis points, proceeds to Cumberland, Suwannee, and Simpson forms, then to Beaver Lake and Quad forms, and finally to Dalton forms at approximately 10,000 RCYBP. The rooting of the sequence in Clovis points is

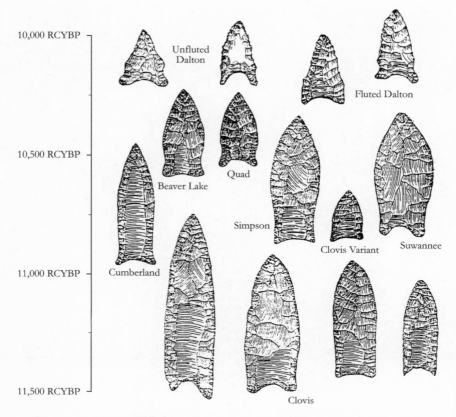

Figure 5.3. One possible historical sequence of Paleoindian projectile-point types in the southeastern United States (after Anderson et al. 1996).

traditional in North American archaeology, but that tradition is based entirely on radiocarbon dates and stratigraphic evidence from the Plains and Southwest. There is no a priori reason to believe that the rooting is correct for the Southeast (Anderson et al. 1996). Dennis Stanford (1991), in fact, speculated that Simpson/Suwannee points are slightly older than Clovis points. Ignoring for a moment the rooting of the chronological sequence, several hints suggest that other aspects of the sequence might be incorrect, one of which comes from closer examination of specimens placed in the Dalton type (Figure 5.4). Specimens assigned to this type exhibit such wide variation that a host of type names and subtype names have been used, such as Holland (Perino 1971), Colbert (DeJarnette et al. 1962),

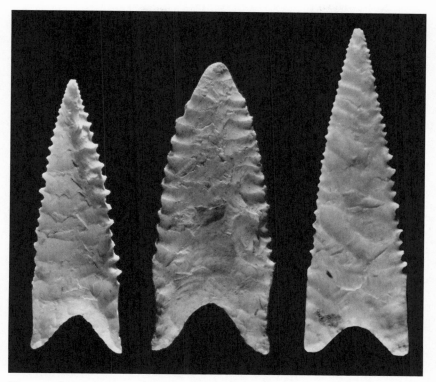

Figure 5.4. Dalton points from the Midwest. Specimen on the left is 7.4 cm long.

Greenbrier (Lewis and Kneberg 1958), Meserve (Bell and Hall 1953), and Hardaway-Dalton (Coe 1964).

The dating of Dalton points has long been problematic because of the almost total absence of secure radiocarbon-dated contexts (Goodyear 1982; O'Brien and Wood 1998). This is a problem that plagues the Southeast in general relative to all the projectile points discussed here. The overall shape, flaking characteristics, and presence of haft-area grinding—features that many Dalton points share to greater or lesser degrees with other Paleoindian points such as Clovis (concave and thinned base; ground base and blade edges in the haft area)—previously led some archaeologists (e.g., Chapman 1948; Mason 1962; Wormington 1957) to argue in favor of a cultural continuity between early Paleoindian tool complexes and Dalton. If the points were technologically similar, so they reasoned, then they should be fairly closely related temporally. This plausible proposition received support from the fact that many of the other tools—wedges, gravers, end scrapers, and bone needles—found in Clovis and Dalton tool kits are similar.

The proposal of a cultural continuity between Clovis and Dalton, however, was not universally accepted. The general reluctance to place Dalton on the heels of Clovis, even by archaeologists who noted similarities (e.g., Chapman 1975), was based on the assumption that the western chronology is applicable to the Southeast. Clovis points were followed chronologically on the Plains and in the Southwest by Folsom points (Figure 5.5)—which are smaller on average than Clovis points but resemble them in several key ways. The Folsom point, like Clovis, has a concave base, fluting on both faces, and grinding along the distal third or so of the edges. Folsom points have been found stratigraphically above Clovis points, the former associated with bison remains and the latter with mammoth remains. The reported occurrence of stratigraphic separation (Cotter 1937) was at the site outside Clovis, New Mexico, that produced the eponymous type specimens. This finding set the stage for the two-part subdivision that became archaeological canon: first Clovis, then Folsom. Subsequent chronometric dating of contexts producing Folsom points has demonstrated that they indeed are younger than Clovis points. After closely examining stratochronological data from widely distributed sites in the Plains and Southwest, R. E. Taylor and his colleagues stated that the "latest North American Clovis occupation predates the earliest occurrence of Folsom" (Taylor et al. 1996:523). They also noted that the chronological transition from Clovis to Folsom could have occurred within a period of 100 years or less. Folsom points ceased to be manufactured by about 10,550 RCYBP.

Despite the established sequence of Clovis followed by Folsom in the Southwest and Plains, it is not of much help in the Midwest (where Folsom points are rare occurrences) or in the Southeast (where Folsom points are even rarer). For years the near absence of Folsom points in those regions was difficult to explain, as was the apparent radiocarbon gap of several hundred years up to a thousand years between the terminal date for Clovis-point manufacture and the beginning date for the manufacture of Dalton points and a host of similar lanceolate points placed in other types. The absence of Folsom points in the region was accommodated by substituting another fluted point—Cumberland—for it. Cumberland then became the southeastern equivalent of Folsom simply because it more or less looked like Folsom in terms of the long single flute on each face. Notably, Cumberland was assumed to be a *homologue* of Folsom, not an analogue.

Figure 5.5. Folsom points from New Mexico. Specimen on the left (4.6 cm long) is from the Folsom locality; others are from the Blackwater Draw locality.

In other words, archaeologists assumed that the two forms were related because they were similar. But recall from Chapter 2 that this inverts the real relationship: Two things are similar because they are related. No one had ever established that Cumberland and Folsom are sister taxa, and without doing so we cannot assume that they are anything but distantly related types that happened to converge on fluting as a character.

The "gap" between Clovis and Dalton is more apparent than real. In fact, it is not real at all, despite the presence of what appears to be a gap in radiocarbon dates. It is clear to us (O'Brien and Wood 1998), as it was to Albert Goodyear (1982), that radiocarbon dates for Dalton contexts are not dating Dalton points at all but rather carbonized wood that post-dates the manufacture of Dalton points by up to a millennium or more. Even so, the phylogenetic relation between Clovis and Dalton points had been staring archaeologists in the face for years, but few recognized it, tenaciously holding to the belief that the western chronology—Clovis followed by Folsom (or a Folsom look-alike, Cumberland, in the East)—is applicable to the Southeast. Based on morphological criteria, it now is apparent that Dalton points evolved directly out of Clovis points (Anderson

et al. 1996; O'Brien and Wood 1998). Empirical evidence for this proposition comes from Bruce Bradley's (1997) examination of 146 complete
Dalton specimens from the Sloan site in northeastern Arkansas. Bradley
made an important distinction between what he termed technological fluting and morphological fluting:

> Technological fluting is where basal thinning is done by the removal of one
> or more flakes that proportionally reduce the longitudinal thickness of the
> biface. This involves the removal of flakes that travel past the point of max-
> imum longitudinal thickness. It makes no difference whatsoever if the result-
> ing flake scars are retained in subsequent flaking. Morphological flutes, on
> the other hand, are simply basal flake scars that extend past the point of the
> hafting element and are visible on the finished object [evident on specimens
> in Figure 5.1].
>
> With these definitions, it is possible to have points that were technologi-
> cally fluted but are not morphologically fluted, if the channel scars are re-
> moved by subsequent flaking. It is also possible to have points that are mor-
> phologically fluted but whose basal flakes did not extend past the point of
> maximum longitudinal thickness. These did not technically thin the preform.
>
> Most Sloan Dalton points, and probably most other Dalton points, are
> not morphologically fluted [Figure 5.4]. I suspect, however, that the major-
> ity were technologically fluted at some stage in their manufacture and prob-
> ably more than once. (Bradley 1997:54–55)

In a few short paragraphs Bradley reduced the archaeological mys-
tique surrounding fluting, which is nothing more than the removal of longitudinal flakes from the base of a point to thin it. Both Clovis points and
Dalton points were fluted, although the visual effect on each might differ—as is evident by comparing specimens in Figures 5.1 and 5.4. But
does the visual effect always differ? Perhaps it does with respect to fluting,
but what about other characters? Look at the point on the left in Figure
5.6. Although the photograph does not show it, this 13-centimeter-long
specimen is less than 5 millimeters thick at its widest point—thinner than
the majority of "typical" Clovis points but well within the range of "typical" Dalton points. The specimen also has the deeply concave base found
on Dalton points, but it has morphological fluting (Bradley's term), identical to what is found on Clovis points. (Compare the point at the left in
Figure 5.6 to the point in the lower left of Figure 5.3, which Anderson et
al. [1996] place in the Clovis type. They are almost identical.) What does
one do with such a specimen in terms of categorizing it? One option is to

Figure 5.6. "Transitional" Dalton-Clovis point from Missouri on the left (13.0 cm long); Dalton point from the Blackwater Draw locality, eastern New Mexico, on the right. The point on the right was found in a level containing mammoth bones and Clovis points, all of which were stratigraphically beneath a level containing Folsom points and bison bones.

create a new type in which to place it (say, "fluted Dalton"); another option is simply to place it in one of the two existing types—Clovis or Dalton—and note that it shares character states with points in the other type. A third option, which we discuss in the following section, is to do away with existing types and create *classes*.

Regardless of what kind of units we employ, a specimen such as the one in Figure 5.6 emits a strong signal that it is morphologically—and thus *potentially* phylogenetically—located between two types, here Clovis and Dalton. Suppose we were to line up three points—one that all archaeologists agree belongs in the Clovis type, one that all agree belongs in the

Dalton type, and the point on the left in Figure 5.6, which we will call "transitional"—and show them to a group of nonarchaeologists. We should not have much trouble getting general agreement that the temporal—and perhaps phylogenetic—sequence went either Clovis $\rightarrow$ "transitional" $\rightarrow$ Dalton or Dalton $\rightarrow$ "transitional" $\rightarrow$ Clovis. We might guess, and we would be correct, that the evolution was fairly rapid—on the order, we suspect, of only a hundred years or so. "Transitional" specimens are important not only as chronological markers but for what they can tell us about evolutionary change within a clade; here the clade that we propose includes Clovis and Dalton points.

Recall from Chapter 1 that the kind of ordering illustrated by our Clovis $\rightarrow$ "transitional" $\rightarrow$ Dalton example is termed *phyletic seriation* (Figure 1.3). As we examine in more detail in Chapter 6, no seriation technique can detect cladogenesis, but seriation does provide a means of making an initial pass at ordering taxa in gross phylogenetic sequence. Large chunks might be missing between the units in the seriation, and seriation might not show this, but perhaps we can augment the strength of our seriation through superpositional evidence. In the case of Clovis and Dalton, however, to the best of our knowledge no site in the Southeast or Midwest—the heartland of Dalton points—has produced such data. Interestingly, a site in the Southwest has.

Take a close look at the small technologically fluted point shown on the right in Figure 5.6. Now compare it to the specimens shown in Figure 5.4. The point in Figure 5.6 could have come from Missouri, Arkansas, or any of a half-dozen other midwestern states, and from a morphological standpoint no archaeologist would find it the slightest bit odd. In all respects it looks like a Dalton point. But the point did not come from the Midwest. Instead, it came from Blackwater Draw, the Clovis-point type site in eastern New Mexico. More importantly, it came from a level that produced Clovis points and mammoth remains (Cotter 1937:9, 12). The presence of a Dalton point in eastern New Mexico suggests that either (1) technological innovations spread fairly rapidly during the Paleoindian period, whether as a result of word of mouth, trade, and/or population movement (see Boyd and Richerson 1985, Cavalli-Sforza and Feldman 1981, and Guglielmino et al. 1995 for rates of spread under different kinds of transmission) or (2) unrelated groups more or less simultaneously "invented" the Dalton point. The second scenario strains credulity, given the bundle of character states that are identical between the Blackwater Draw specimen and many eastern specimens.

In our view the context in which the Blackwater Draw Dalton point occurred provides independent support for Bradley's (1997:57) conclusion that "the data currently point to an in situ technological development of Dalton points directly out of a Clovis technology." Note that his statement is written in clear evolutionary language. Bradley is not speaking metaphorically when he says that Dalton points developed out of a Clovis technology any more than we are speaking metaphorically when we say that one biological species developed out of another species or that the Pentium® computer chip developed out of the 486 processor. Clades of projectile points or computer chips, and at a lower scale the lineages that make up the clades, are the products of cultural rather than genetic transmission, but this does not make them less real than biological clades or lineages. Bradley's language is the result of careful examination of technological variation as manifest in morphological characters—the features that provide the basis for a cladistical analysis of projectile points from the Southeast.

CONSTRUCTING ARCHAEOLOGICAL TAXA

Granting that cladistics can be used to construct archaeological phylogenies, how do we go about creating the units that will be used? In archaeology we are faced with two problems: We have to select not only appropriate characters and character states but also appropriate taxonomic units. In biology, the problem ordinarily reduces to deciding which characters and character states to use. Despite the theoretical issues surrounding the species concept (e.g., Howard and Berlocher 1998; Wheeler and Meier 2000), species have always assumed primacy as analytical taxa in phylogenetic systematics. In archaeology there is no unit equivalent to a species, nor should we ever expect to find one (Chapter 4). Hence we must create our own taxa. Maybe we could use existing projectile-point types, which are, after all, the discipline's "basic unit[s] of classification [used] to make sense of past material culture" (Thomas 1998:235). Archaeologists create types because in dealing with large sets of materials it is impractical to describe each specimen in excruciating detail. Nor is there necessarily any reason to do so if we can somehow construct groups of things and describe each group in a way that does justice to the things placed in the groups. By this we mean that the description of the group becomes a legitimate proxy for individual specimens in the group. Types are idealized categories, often formed around central tendencies evident in a set of objects. When we state that a particular object is of Type A, what we really are saying is that there is a category known as Type A into which are placed certain objects that share a suite of particular character states (O'Brien and Lyman 1999, 2002a). There is nothing "real" about the types, although archaeologists tend to forget this caveat, as was noted over half a century ago (Phillips et al. 1951).

Implicit in the creation and use of archaeological types is the acknowledgment that specimens placed in a type are more like each other than are specimens not placed in that type. Rarely will the specimens in Type A be clones, meaning that they will differ in terms of certain character states. This is not too important if those character states are not the *distinguishing* character states that together act as the basis for the type. Often we read a type description that says something like "objects placed in Type A exhibit traits 1, 2, and 3. Further, length usually varies from w to x centimeters and width from a to b centimeters." Based on this description, traits 1–3 should be present for an object to be placed in Type A, but length and width are not too important in making an assignment. This does not mean that variations in length and width are unimportant; all it means is that they are unimportant when deciding whether or not an object falls in a particular type.

All of this would be well and good if existing archaeological types were objective formulations, meaning that they were redundant in terms of the characters and character states used to create the types. We then perhaps could use existing types—Clovis, Dalton, Cumberland, and so on—and abstract characters and character states from the specimens in each type. But existing types are *not* redundant in terms of the characters used in the definitions. One type might be defined by base shape and degree of shouldering, whereas another type might be defined by base shape and angle of notching. It might be argued that in biology species are nonredundant in terms of definition, especially in cases where morphological characters are used as sorting criteria, and yet they constitute the taxa often used in cladistics. We agree with this assessment, but the lack of redundancy in species definitions is no warrant for introducing the problem into archaeological systematics (O'Brien and Lyman 2000).

Another feature of artifact types that mitigates against their use in cladistics is that in most cases they are *extensionally* defined (Dunnell 1986)—the definitions are derived by sorting through a pile of specimens, placing similar specimens together, and using average properties of the specimens in each pile as the basis of the definitions (O'Brien and Lyman

2000, 2002a). When more specimens are introduced, type definitions must be reconfigured to account for the new variation. At some point the analyst may decide too much variation is being introduced and create another type. Types formed in such a manner are often fuzzy amalgams of character states—another problem that was raised in archaeology over a half-century ago (Phillips et al. 1951). The problem reduces to this: Extensionally derived units (types) conflate the taxon and the specimens in it. Some biologists (e.g., Jardine 1969) have recognized this problem with respect to organisms and taxa. This should not be read as saying that there is no analytical role for traditional units such as named projectile-point types, because some of those traditional units are excellent at what they are supposed to do, such as tracking the passage of time (O'Brien and Lyman 1999). But even the most useful types are not multipurpose units. Neither are the kinds of units—paradigmatic classes—that we discuss below. Rather, they are useful for specific analytical purposes.

Analytical units, regardless of whether they represent organisms or projectile points, are *classes*—conceptual (as opposed to empirical) units of measurement (Chapter 2). Because they are not empirical, they cannot be discovered. They can only be created. To do that, the analyst specifies which characters and character states to use. The intersection of character states defines the classes (see below). Classes can be univariate or multivariate. One advantage of multivariate classes is that they allow, if constructed in a particular way, simultaneous consideration of the values taken by "state, meristic, and metric variables" (Gould 1991:420) within a set of specimens. This means that by using classes we perhaps can simultaneously monitor shape (state variables), frequency (meristic variables), and size (metric variables). The alternative to using multivariate classes is to track first one character, then another, and so on. Artifacts, however, like organisms, are multivariate entities. Thus we should be interested in tracking not simply single characters but bundles of characters simultaneously. Classes formed in the manner discussed below allow us to do this. We might not know before analysis begins which specific combinations of characters will be of interest, but with multivariate classes we don't need to worry too much about this, in that characters can later be combined in any number of ways. If, conversely, our interest does happen to shift to a single character, the classes allow us to track that character easily and objectively through its various states (e.g., Beck 1995).

The procedure for constructing multivariate classes was spelled out independently by Alan Shaw (1969) in paleontology and Robert Dunnell

(1971) in archaeology and termed *paradigmatic classification* by the latter. Paradigmatic classification maps *morphospace*—the multidimensional space encompassing the range of morphological variation of a specific set of taxa. Morphospace is defined by mutually exclusive characters, each with a set of states. Taxa are multivariate classes that reside in particular mapped locations in morphospace. They are defined by combinations of particular character states (see below). The number of characters (and the number of states within a character) included in a particular classification is restricted only by the limits of the computer program used to sort the taxa.

To create a paradigmatic classification—in other words, to define morphospace—the classifier lists all characters that he or she views as analytically important. Note the last part of that sentence. *Only* those characters that are viewed as analytically important are considered. Color, for example, could be of analytical importance in one study but unimportant in another. In the latter case, it would be excluded from consideration when classes are being constructed. For each character used in the classification, the classifier lists the states in which each character might appear. If an unanticipated character state is later found, that state can be added to the list without disrupting it because the order of the states is irrelevant. (Some cladists, however, argue for ordering character states—an issue that we address in the next section.) It is the combination of character states, one state from each character, that both creates a class (taxon) and defines the part of morphospace occupied by that class. Classes can be constructed at various scales. A class can comprise a single character of a discrete object, a particular combination of character states of a discrete object, or multiple kinds of discrete objects (say, the taxa composing a fauna). When constructing a classification with a paradigmatic structure it is important to ensure that all characters are of the same scale. This ensures that, for example, species are not being compared with families or projectile points with all chipped-stone artifacts. In terms of replicators and interactors (Chapter 4), then, classes should be representative of the appropriate interactor of the analysis, whatever the scale at which the interactor is defined.

As an example of paradigmatic classification, we can examine Shaw's classification of conodonts—toothlike phosphatic structures from now-extinct small, eel-like organisms. Shaw specified four characters, two of which included two states and two of which included three states (Table 5.1). Multiplication of the number of states per character ($2 \times 2 \times 3 \times 3$)

TABLE 5.1. Paradigmatic Classification of Conodont Morphology

Character 1: outer platform lobe development
State L: lobed
State U: unlobed
Character 2: outer platform cross-sectional shape
State F: flat
State A: arched
Character 3: blade and ridge (inner platform) plan
State N: nonparallel
State P: parallel
State D: divergent anteriorly
Character 4: inner platform profile
State T: triangular
State R: rounded
State A: alate

Note: Characters and character states from Shaw (1969).

indicates that 36 classes exist within Shaw's classification. For example, the class LFNT is a conodont with a lobed outer platform, flat outer platform cross section, nonparallel blade and ridge, and triangular inner platform profile. Because there are 36 classes, there are 36 positions in that particular analytical morphospace. In paradigmatic classification it is unnecessary for all classes to have empirical members; empty morphospace can be just as important analytically as filled morphospace is (Conway Morris 1998; Gould 1991), especially when the focus is on adaptation.

One important feature of paradigmatic classification with respect to cladistics is that it resolves an objection that has been raised in biology over intraspecific applications of phylogenetic methods: Are the terminal taxa in question related hierarchically (Brower et al. 1996; Davis and Nixon 1992; Goldstein and DeSalle 2000)? In other words, are they nested? If not, then no amount of cladistic analysis is going to tell us anything of interest, and we might as well use phenetics or some other method to create morphological groups. We argue that indeed we *are* dealing with nested hierarchies, irrespective of whether characters or character states are "borrowed" from outside. Cultural phenomena reside in a series of nested hierarchies that comprise traditions at ever more-inclusive scales and that are held together by cultural as well as genetic transmission.

Although it might not be immediately apparent, paradigmatic classification produces units that are directly amenable to hierarchical arrangement, meaning that they are nested. The phylogenetic arrangement of four

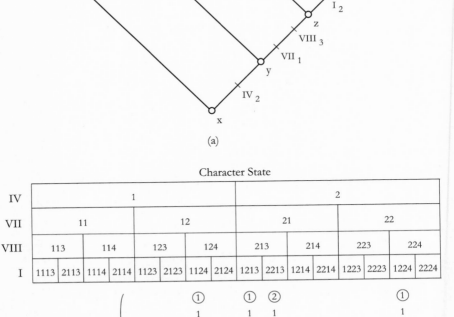

Figure 5.7. Phylogenetic arrangement of four fictional taxa created from eight characters: (a) cladogram of four classes and three ancestors (x, y, and z) showing changes in states (Arabic numerals) of various characters (Roman numerals); (b) nested hierarchical arrangement of character states showing empirically filled morphospace (the classes labeled "Represented Taxa") and empty morphospace; character states common to all classes are not circled (from O'Brien et al. 2002).

hypothetical taxa created from eight characters is shown in Figure 5.7a. The ancestral taxon, x, undergoes one character-state change, in character IV (1 → 2), to produce ancestor y, which is represented by terminal taxon 11222324. Ancestor y undergoes two state changes, in characters VII (2

→ 1) and VIII (4 → 3), to produce ancestor z, represented by terminal taxon 11222313. Ancestor z undergoes one state change in character I (1 → 2) to produce terminal taxon 21222313. This arrangement can be conceived of as an ordination, but it also is a hierarchical arrangement in the sense of a nesting of less-inclusive, lower-level entities within more-inclusive, higher-level entities (Valentine and May 1996).

Considering only those characters that change states—I, IV, VII, and VIII—in order to simplify, and ranking the characters in the order listed in Figure 5.7a, the hierarchy of possible combinations of character states yields the 16 possible classes, or taxa, shown in Figure 5.7b. Note that the order in which the characters are listed does not affect the resulting combinations of character states. Those combinations would be the same irrespective of the ordering of characters, and only the order in which the character states are listed would vary. Only four of the taxa are actually represented by empirical specimens in Figure 5.7a (the terminal taxa). Importantly, the hierarchy potentially has phylogenetic implications. Whether that potential is realized is a separate issue that has nothing to do with the suitability of paradigmatic classification for cladistics.

We agree that in practice the lines between nested hierarchies and reticulating (not hybridizing [Chapter 4]) networks are sometimes blurred, just as we agree that without a boundary around the reticulating networks there can be no nested hierarchy and hence no monophyly (Goldstein and DeSalle 2000). Such boundaries are often difficult to delimit, but they are by no means beyond our power to determine archaeologically, as several studies have shown (e.g., Bellwood 1996; Bettinger and Eerkens 1997, 1999; Harmon et al. 2000, 2003; Kirch 1997; Kirch and Green 2001; Lipo 2001; Lipo et al. 1997; O'Brien et al. 2001, 2002; VanPool et al. 2000). In most cases we can at least identify which side of the boundary we are on (Brower 1999). Archaeology's long-standing recognition of "traditions" lends strong support to that statement.

CHARACTERS AND CHARACTER STATES

How do we choose appropriate characters for cladistic analysis? In our opinion there is no more important question in phylogenetic systematics, but just as important is the realization that there is no textbook answer. We define "appropriateness" in this context in terms of how well a character performs in allowing us to separate taxa phylogenetically, but this definition begs the question of how we know a priori that a particular character will produce a phylogenetic signal. The bottom line is that character choice is a classic case of trial and error, with a good measure of inductive reasoning thrown in. Archaeologists, like biologists, do not go into phylogenetic reconstruction with no prior knowledge of which characters might be useful. They know, or strongly suspect, how certain characters change states over time. For example, anyone familiar with early projectile points from the United States knows that hafting areas usually exhibit heavy grinding. Most later points do not. Similarly, most early points are lanceolate, but certainly in the Southeast and on the Plains this shape gave way to other shapes. Other characters might not be so obvious in terms of state changes, or in terms of which state is ancestral and which states are derived, but even here prior experience offers at least a reasonable means of selecting useful characters. If characters turn out not to be particularly useful, they can be dropped from analysis.

Kinds of Data

One of the numerous methodological issues in cladistics is the suitability of quantitative versus qualitative data and continuous versus discrete data. There is a tendency to favor qualitative and discrete data, but many so-called qualitative characters—for example, a *corner-notched* projectile point—are in reality characters that have a quantitative base filtered through what Peter Stevens (1991:553) referred to as "reified semantic discontinuities of . . . terminology." The distinction between qualitative and quantitative refers more to "mode of expression rather than to intrinsic properties of the data" (Kitching et al. 1998:20). Our take on the matter is that we should not worry too much about whether characters are quantitative or qualitative. The same applies to the use of continuous versus discrete data. Rather, we should pick characters that we suspect will give the strongest phylogenetic signals, irrespective of their precise nature.

Data Coding and Character Transformation

Another issue in cladistics concerns the actual coding of data—the "bête noir of systematics" (Pogue and Mickevich 1990:319)—with some cladists arguing for the use of multistate characters with linked states and others opting for treating the states separately, as in paradigmatic classification. A simple example will show the difference between the two. Figure 5.8 shows four taxa (1–4) that exhibit conflicting character states.

Taxa

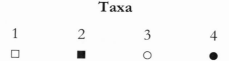

1	2	3	4
□	■	○	●

Figure 5.8. Four taxa (1–4) that exhibit conflicting character states. Taxon 1 is square and white, Taxon 2 is square and black, Taxon 3 is round and white, and Taxon 4 is round and black. For classification purposes we could handle the differences as multistate characters with linked states—square and white; square and black; round and white; and round and black—or as multistate characters with independent states—square and round for the character "shape," and white and black for the character "color." Either way, the classification yields four classes.

Taxon 1 is square and white; Taxon 2 is square and black; Taxon 3 is round and white; and Taxon 4 is round and black. There are several ways of handling the differences, and the way in which we handle them has a bearing on how we code the character states. If we handle them as multistate characters with linked states, then we would code them as four different states: (1) square and white; (2) square and black; (3) round and white; and (4) round and black. Alternatively, if we handle them as multistate characters with independent states, then we have two separate codings, one for shape and the other for color. For the character "shape" we have (1) square and (2) round; for the character "color" we have (1) white and (2) black. Either way, the classification yields four classes. Our opinion is that cladistic analysis should represent independent hypotheses of relationship among taxa. Indeed, one of the strongest tests of hypothesized relationships is congruence—two or more independent character states that map the same topology on a cladogram. Therefore, we recommend that characters and their states be treated as being independent. In reality some character states probably *are* linked, but this is an avenue for analysis, not for a priori assessment.

Notice that in our example above, as well as in our earlier discussion of Shaw's conodont classes, the order in which characters and character states are coded is irrelevant. For purely classificatory purposes it does not matter if a conodont class is defined as an LFNT (lobed outer platform, flat outer platform cross section, nonparallel blade and ridge, and triangular inner platform profile) or as an NTLF—characters 3 and 4 could switch places with characters 1 and 2 in the classification. Nor does it matter if character 1 is the shape of the outer platform or the shape of the blade and ridge. Because paradigmatic classification is nonhierarchical, one character is not more important than another. (Don't confuse the fact that paradigmatic classification itself is nonhierarchical with the fact that it produces units that are amenable to hierarchical arrangement, meaning that they are nested [Figure 5.7].) The characters can be ordered in any possible way, and the system still works the same. The only thing that matters is that we are consistent in applying the classification. Does this hold true for character states? In our opinion the answer is yes *for most cases,* although in rare cases there may be good reasons to order them. This topic deserves a bit of discussion because of the importance that character transformation assumes in cladistics.

Character transformation refers to the change in state that a character goes through, say as a group of organisms evolves from the five-toed state to the four-toed state. A *transformation series* can be binary, meaning that there are only two homologous states present (one ancestral and one derived), or multistate, meaning that there are three or more homologous states (either one ancestral and two or more derived directly from that state or one that is ancestral to another, which in turn is ancestral to a third). Transformation series can be *ordered,* meaning there is a particular sequence of steps that a character takes during its change in state, or *unordered,* meaning there are several pathways that can be taken. Thus, for example, it may be the case that evolutionary "laws" dictate that an organism can lose or gain only one toe at a time. It could move from five toes to four toes, or vice versa, but never from five to three or from two to four. The meristic character "number of toes," then, is said to be ordered. In reality, an ordered transformation series is a *hypothesis* about a particular pathway, because rarely will we know absolutely what is possible in nature. What about the direction of change? A transformation series is *polarized* if the relative apomorphic (derived) and plesiomorphic (ancestral) states are known. Again, polarity is usually a hypothesis. The four possible types of character transformation series are shown in Figure 5.9: (a) ordered, unpolarized; (b) unordered, unpolarized; (c) ordered, polarized; and (d) unordered, polarized.

Despite the prevalence of the term *transformation series,* which has been around since the days of Hennig, it is at best a misleading term, because it brings to mind an anagenetic process by which one character state becomes (is transformed into) another character state. This perspective is more metaphorical than real and results from having inadequate samples of organisms or artifacts that span the block of time from the point at which we first recognize one character state—call it A—and the point at

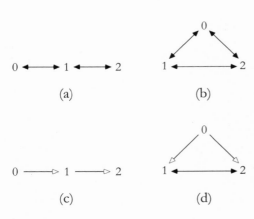

Figure 5.9. Kinds of transformation series: (a) ordered, unpolarized (information about pathway; no information about direction); (b) unordered, unpolarized (no information about either pathway or direction); (c) ordered, polarized (information about both pathway and direction); (d) unordered, polarized (no information about pathway; information about direction). Zero is the ancestral character state; 1 and 2 are derived character states (after Brooks and McLennan 1991).

which we first recognize a succeeding character state—A'. Better resolution would demonstrate that character-state A is not being transformed into state A'. Rather, the relative frequency of character-state A within the population is changing (declining) relative to the relative frequency of state A' (increasing) (Kitching et al. 1998; O'Brien and Lyman 2000). Plotting such changes at the more-inclusive scale of discrete object is the basis of frequency seriation in archaeology (Lyman, Wolverton, and O'Brien 1998; O'Brien and Lyman 1999, 2000).

Should character states be ordered, or should they be left unordered? Change is often ordered, or "channeled." Do not read this as saying that change is "guided"—that *the* direction in which a set of organisms changes is preordained. To the contrary, the precise direction, or course, is not set. All we are saying is that once a course of change is determined by the selective environment, organismal change tends to follow it. Think of a meandering river channel. There is a course that the water follows, even though the channel can wander back and forth across the countryside, first in one direction, then in another, but it is channeled in the sense that it always loses elevation. The channeling of evolutionary change driven by selection constitutes the creative force of natural selection (Gould 1982, 2002). We suspect change effected by drift will often display similar channeling. Given this perspective, we would conclude that through time a set of five-toed organisms might become a set of four-toed or six-toed organisms but probably not three-toed organisms. We might also conclude with even more certainty that the set of five-toed organisms would not evolve into a set of two-toed organisms, then into four-toed organisms, then into six-toed organisms, and finally into three-toed organisms. Nature exhibits

Figure 5.10. Corner- and side-notched points from the Midwest. Specimen on the left is 11.8 cm long.

more order than that. Even given this, biologists typically do not order character states, particularly when evidence of polarity is lacking.

As opposed to organismic pathways of evolutionary change, many of which are highly channeled, it would seem at first glance that cultural developmental pathways are not. A projectile-point maker, for example, could place notches at the sides or corners of a point, could place them along the base, or could leave a point unnotched. Provided the maker knew how to notch a point, it would appear that any of those is as likely as any others. If the manufacture of projectile points were a random process, any of those states would be as likely as any other to appear on a given point, but we know such is not the case. The location of notching, when taken into consideration with other characters, is an excellent means of keeping track of archaeological time. For example, many of the projectile points from the central Mississippi River valley that date roughly 10,000–9000 RCYBP are deeply corner notched, whereas many of the points that date 7000–5000 RCYBP are side notched (Figure 5.10). At least with respect to notching, there was a certain amount of cultural conservancy, which resulted in nonrandom patterning in human behavior—notches moved from corners to sides over time. As we saw in Chapter 4, these kinds of patterns have led archaeologists to talk about "cultural traditions," which are simply aggregative repetitive behaviors at a scale (spatial and/or temporal) that is recognizable.

Sometimes we have insights into select aspects of the patterns, and sometimes we do not. With respect to projectile points, modern skilled flint knappers can provide significant information as to how prehistoric points were manufactured—for example, the sequence of steps that Clovis-point manufacturers took to produce the final piece. Flint knappers also understand the limitations of certain technologies or what performing the steps out of sequence might mean with respect to the intended outcome. Thus it might be possible to use such technological information to order character-state transformations. At the present time, however, we do not think the requisite data are available to warrant the creation of a priori hypotheses with respect to ordering. Also, we believe that in many cases data are unavailable to create similar hypotheses with respect to polarization. Thus we suggest that character states remain unordered and unpolarized for most analyses. Remember that a priori determinations of polarity will affect the outcome of analysis. If we miscalculate whether a character state is apomorphic or plesiomorphic, no computer program in the world is going to save us. If we want to remain faithful to the paradigm of parsimony and to exorcise "hidden evolutionary assumptions from character descriptions (e.g., a priori designation of character polarity)" (Brower 2000:147), then a system that employs unordered multistate characters with equal weights is the least burdened by ad hoc assumptions.

We used such an unordered multistate-character system for the phylogenetic analysis of Paleoindian points from the Southeast. Table 5.2 lists the characters and character states used to create our taxa, and Figure 5.11 shows the locations of the characters. Characters are defined as follows:

I. Location of maximum blade width: the quarter section of a specimen in which the widest point of the blade occurs.

II. Base shape: qualitative assessment of the shape of the basal indentation.

III. Basal indentation ratio: the ratio between the medial length of a specimen and its total length; the smaller the ratio, the deeper the indentation.

IV. Constriction ratio: the ratio between the minimum blade width (proximal to the point of maximum blade width) and the maximum blade width; the smaller the ratio, the higher the amount of constriction.

V. Outer tang angle: the degree of tang expansion from the long axis of a specimen; the lower the angle, the greater the expansion.

VI. Tang-tip shape: the shape of the tip ends of tangs.

VII. Fluting: the removal of one or more large flakes (≥ 1 cm long) from the base of a specimen and parallel to its long axis; subsequent flake removal may obliterate earlier flake scars.

VIII. Length/width ratio: the maximum length of a specimen divided by its maximum width.

Our choice of characters was based on expectations as to which parts of a projectile point would change the most over time as a result of transmission and thus create a strong phylogenetic signal. All other things being equal, characters that show a higher degree of variation are more likely to have detectable phylogenetic signals than characters that do not. Considerable variation exists in the overall size and shape of Paleoindian points from the Southeast, so we selected characters I, IV, and VIII to explore changes in size and shape. All three avoid potential bias (created by some points having been resharpened) that could be introduced by using direct measurements of length and width. Previous research (e.g., Beck 1995; Howard 1995; Hughes 1998) indicates that the hafting element of Paleoindian projectile points—the part that fits into a wooden or bone shaft—is a likely region in which to find other good candidates for use in phylogenetic analysis. Five characters (II, III, V, VI, and VII) were selected to monitor changes in such features as base shape, the shape of tang tips, and the angle formed by a tang relative to the long axis of a specimen.

Stylistic versus Functional Characters

This brings us to an important point that has been raised in archaeology: the difference between stylistic characters and functional

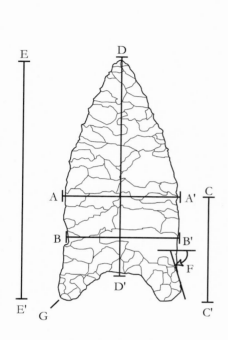

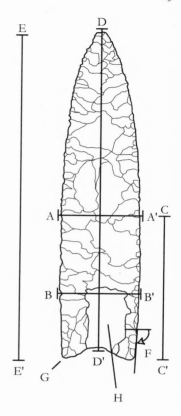

Landmark Characters

A–A' = maximum blade width

B–B' = minimum blade width

C–C' = height of maximum blade width

D–D' = medial length

E–E' = maximum length

F = outer tang angle

G = tang tip

H = flute

Base Shapes

arc-shaped

normal curve

triangular

Folsomoid

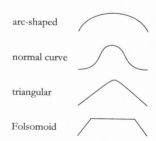

Figure 5.11. Locations of characters used in the analysis of projectile points. See Table 5.2 for character states; states for base shape are shown at the lower right.

TABLE 5.2. System Used to Classify Projectile Points from the Southeast

CHARACTER *Character State*	CHARACTER *Character State*

I. Location of Maximum Blade Width
  1. proximal quarter
  2. secondmost proximal quarter
  3. secondmost distal quarter
  4. distal quarter
	V. Outer Tang Angle
	  1. 93°–115°
	  2. 88°–92°
	  3. 81°–87°
	  4. 66°–80°
	  5. 51°–65°
	  6. ≤ 50°

II. Base Shape
  1. arc-shaped
  2. normal curve
  3. triangular
  4. Folsomoid
	VI. Tang-Tip Shape
	  1. pointed
	  2. round
	  3. blunt

III. Basal-Indentation Ratio[a]
  1. no basal indentation
  2. 0.90–0.99 (shallow)
  3. 0.80–0.89 (deep)
	VII. Fluting
	  1. absent
	  2. present

IV. Constriction Ratio[b]
  1. 1.00
  2. 0.90–0.99
  3. 0.80–0.89
  4. 0.70–0.79
  5. 0.60–0.69
  6. 0.50–0.59
	VIII. Length/Width Ratio
	  1. 1.00–1.99
	  2. 2.00–2.99
	  3. 3.00–3.99
	  4. 4.00–4.99
	  5. 5.00–5.99
	  6. ≥ 6.00

[a] The ratio between the medial length of a specimen and its total length; the smaller the ratio, the deeper the indentation.
[b] The ratio between the minimum blade width (proximal to the point of maximum blade width) and the maximum blade width as a measure of "waistedness"; the smaller the ratio, the higher the amount of constriction.

characters and the suitability of each for particular kinds of analysis. Some archaeologists (e.g., Dunnell 1978; Lyman and O'Brien 1998; O'Brien and Holland 1990; papers in Hurt and Rakita 2001) have argued that, according to Darwinian theory, two kinds of units must be constructed to allow the measurement of two kinds of variation among artifacts. Units that measure stylistic (adaptively neutral) variants allow the detection of transmission (e.g., Lipo and Madsen 2001; Lipo et al. 1997; Neiman 1995), a process that must be monitored to ensure that heritable continuity between sequential forms is being measured. Units that measure functional, or adaptive, variants must also be constructed, as these contribute significantly to the writing and explanation of evolutionary history as it is driven by natural selection (e.g., O'Brien et al. 1994). The distribution of stylistic variants—because they are adaptively neutral and thus do not affect fitness—should, theoretically, often be different from the distribution of functional forms over time and space. Stylistic features measure interaction, transmission, and inheritance, whereas functional features *sometimes* measure transmission as mediated by natural selection and at other times measure adaptational difference alone (Beck 1995; Meltzer 1981; O'Brien and Lyman 2003b).

As opposed to the continuous, unimodal frequency distribution exhibited by stylistic characters—the familiar "battleship-shaped" curves of frequency seriation (Figure 1.4)—functional characters can display one of several distributions. They might display a sharp rise in popularity followed by a steep decline (O'Brien and Holland 1990, 1992) as they are quickly replaced by other functional characters; they might display unimodal frequency distributions similar to those of stylistic characters; or they might display discontinuous, multimodal frequency distributions as a result of convergence or fluctuation in the selective environment. This brings us to an important point—the equation of style with homology and the equation of function with analogy. No other single issue has done more to confuse the style-function dichotomy in the archaeological literature than these seemingly straightforward equations (O'Brien and Leonard 2001; O'Brien and Lyman 2003b). Unless we clear the matter up, and in the process debunk the myth that function necessarily implies analogy, someone familiar with the style-function issue might wonder why we use functional characters in a phylogenetic analysis.

In the case of style and homology, an equation is justified, but in the case of function and analogy, it is not. Functional characters can be either analogous or homologous, which is why we noted above that functional forms sometimes measure transmission as mediated by natural selection and other times measure adaptational change alone. Homologous characters result from common ancestry. If we are sure that the characters with which we are dealing are homologous, then the phenomena exhibiting those characters are by definition related back through a common ancestor. In archaeology the objects are related because of cultural transmission of various kinds. But this tells us nothing about whether the homologous characters are functional or stylistic. O'Brien and Leonard (2001:5) state: "Do not be misled by the use of the term 'function' in defining what an analog is. . . . The key to whether a feature is homologous or analogous is strictly a matter of its history." A better way of putting it would be: "Although analogous characters can always be assumed to be functional, the reverse is not always true. Functional characters can be either homologous *or* analogous." In other words, functional characters—those that by definition affect the fitness of the bearer—can show up in two different lineages as a result of either common ancestry or convergence.

In archaeology we assume that such things as decorations on ceramic vessels are so complex that the probability of duplication by chance is small. If we find, say, two pots that are relatively close in time and space and that contain identical decoration, we conclude that they are from the same tradition or line of cultural heredity (Rouse 1955). They are homologous. We would normally not suspect that two completely independent groups of people arrived at exactly the same way of decorating their vessels, given the myriad possibilities available. There is no reason to suspect that we will never find such an example, but the more parsimonious explanation of such a phenomenon is that the vessels share a common developmental history and are from the same tradition.

Evolutionary archaeologists have emphasized the usefulness of stylistic traits for chronological purposes, making it appear that those traits are the only kind that can be used, but this again masks the real issue: Is a character or set of characters homologous or analogous? If only stylistic characters or sets of characters (styles) can be used, then changes in, say, the hafting elements of projectile points—which we not only assume to be functional but can demonstrate empirically to be functional (e.g., Hughes 1998)—would be useless not only in phylogenetic analysis but as a basis for measuring the passage of time. This decidedly is not the case, as countless studies have shown (e.g., Beck 1995, 1998; Wilhelmsen 2001). The bottom line is to use characters that will potentially emit strong phylogenetic signals. If stylistic characters—decoration on pots, for example—are available, use them. But when stylistic characters are difficult to come by—on projectile points, for example—then use whatever is available.

Southeastern Projectile-Point Taxa

We classified 621 points from the Southeast. We measured actual specimens if available or used published drawings or photographs if the requisite data could be obtained (Box 5.1). For each specimen we listed (1) the state of each character in numerical order I through VIII, (2) the type

Box 5.1. Scanning Projectile Points

We used electronic scans of points in assigning specimens to classes. Measuring a scan was chosen over measuring the actual point for two reasons. First, it is easier and more precise to take measurements from a scan, as the image of the point is static. You can't jostle or budge the point while measuring it and take the reading from the wrong place (see Tompkins 1993). Second, the dimensioning tool of Canvas®, a vector-based drawing program similar to Adobe Illustrator®, draws a horizontal line when the measurement is made, allowing you to double check that the area selected was the widest or narrowest point on the specimen. Each point was scanned at original size at 200 dots per inch (dpi). While not of print quality, 200 dpi is of sufficient resolution to allow measurement at high magnification, and file size is 2.25 times smaller than at print quality.

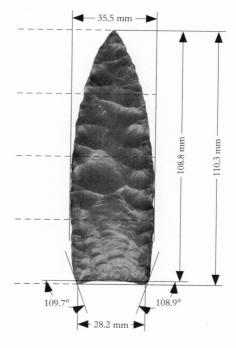

To take a measurement (A–A', B–B', D–D', and E–E' [Figure 5.11]), you set the landmarks to be measured, and the program draws guide rules and calculates the distance between them. Measurements were made at 400 percent magnification. This value was chosen because it allows easy and quick selection of the end points for the dimensioning tool and minimizes the amount of scrolling needed to make length measurements. To calculate the location of maximum blade width, a point was subdivided into quarters by using the Canvas® align/distribute tool to draw five horizontal lines over the point (see figure above)—one at the distal end, another at the proximal end, and three equally spaced interior lines. The five lines now divide the point into four equal quarters, and the one with maximum blade width can be determined visually. Measuring the outer tang angle was done by selecting two lines and having the program calculate the angle of intersection.

Remeasurement of points showed that no value varied more than 0.2 mm from the first measurement, and the majority were exactly the same.

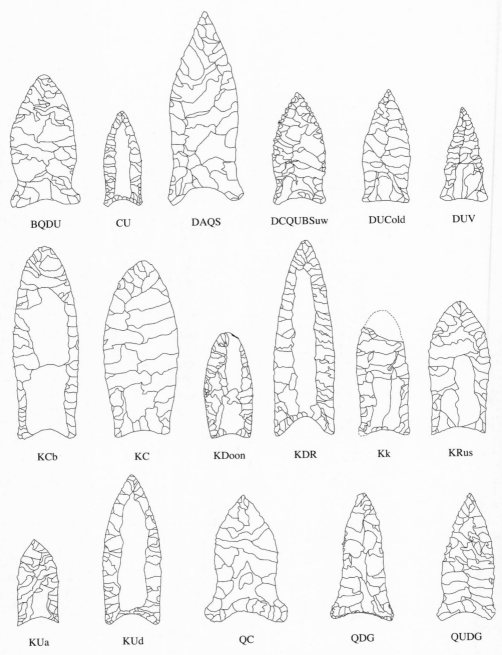

Figure 5.12. Illustrations of specimens in each of 17 projectile-point taxa used in the analysis; taxon abbreviations appear under each example (from O'Brien et al. 2001). See Table 5.3 for taxon definitions.

TABLE 5.3. Taxon Definitions, Abbreviations, and Common Type Names
of 17 Projectile-Point Taxa

Taxon	Abbreviation	Common Type Names[a]
21225212	BQDU	Beaver Lake–Quad–Dalton–Unidentified
21214322	CU	Cumberland–Unidentified
21214312	DAQS	Dalton–Arkabutla–Quad–Simpson
21224312	DCQUBSuw	Dalton–Cumberland–Quad–Unidentified–Beaver Lake–Suwannee
21224212	DUCold	Dalton–Unidentified–Coldwater
21214222	DUV	Dalton–Unidentified–Vandale
21223223	KCb	Clovis–Cumberland
31234322	KC	Clovis–Cumberland
21221122	KDoon	Clovis–Doon
12212223	KDR	Clovis–Dalton–Redstone
21223322	Kk	Clovis
31222122	KRus	Clovis–Russellville
11212122	KUa	Clovis–Unidentified
21212222	KUd	Clovis–Unidentified
21235312	QC	Quad–Cumberland
11214312	QDG	Quad–Dalton–Greenbrier
21215312	QUDG	Quad–Unidentified–Dalton–Greenbrier

[a] Names taken directly from archaeological reports producing the sampled specimens.

name for that specimen given in the literature, and (3) the state from which it was reported. The 621 specimens fell into 491 taxa, 86 of which contained multiple specimens. We used only those taxa that contained a minimum of four specimens, the rationale being that although any taxon is as real analytically as any other taxon, we were interested more in repetitive behavior and less in idiosyncratic behavior. Secondarily, we reasoned that fewer taxa would have been insufficient to reveal nuances of history.

The analyzed subset comprised 17 taxa that together contained 83 projectile points. Taxon definitions are listed in Table 5.3 and illustrated in Figure 5.12; Table 5.4 lists the number of specimens per taxon by state. Recall that the taxa—paradigmatic classes—are defined by the intersections of character states. Taxon 21225212, for example, contains specimens in which the widest part of the blade is in the secondmost proximal quarter (character-state 2 of character I); the base is arc-shaped (character-state 1 of character II); the basal-indentation ratio is shallow (character-state 2 of character III); the constriction ratio is 0.90–0.99 (character-state 2 of character IV); the outer tang angle is 51–65 degrees (character-state 5 of character V); the shape of the tang tip is round (character-state 2 of

TABLE 5.4. Frequencies of 17 Projectile-Point Taxa by State

| | STATE | | | | | | | | | | | |
Abbreviation	Ala.	Ark.	Fla.	Ga.	Ky.	Miss.	Mo.	N.C.	S.C.	Tenn.	Va.	Total
BQDU	—	—	—	—	—	1	—	—	—	3	—	4
CU	2	—	—	—	—	—	—	1	—	1	—	4
DAQS	3	—	—	1	1	1	—	—	—	—	—	6
DCQUBSuw	5	—	1	—	—	—	—	—	1	1	—	8
DUCold	4	—	—	—	—	1	—	—	—	1	—	6
DUV	2	2	—	—	—	—	—	—	—	—	—	4
KCb	1	—	—	—	—	—	—	—	1	4	—	6
KC	—	—	—	—	—	—	2	—	—	2	—	4
KDoon	1	2	—	—	—	—	2	—	—	2	—	7
KDR	1	—	—	—	—	—	2	—	—	1	—	4
Kk	1	—	—	1	—	—	—	1	—	1	—	4
KRus	—	1	—	—	1	—	—	—	—	2	—	4
KUa	1	—	—	—	—	—	—	—	—	—	3	4
KUd	2	—	—	—	—	—	1	—	—	—	2	5
QC	1	—	—	—	3	—	—	—	—	—	—	4
QDG	3	—	—	—	1	—	—	—	—	—	—	4
QUDG	3	—	—	—	—	1	—	—	—	1	—	5
Total	30	5	1	2	6	4	7	2	2	19	5	83

character VI); fluting is absent (character-state 1 of character VII); and the length/width ratio is 2.00–2.99 (character-state 2 of character VIII) (Table 5.2). Because it is easier to use taxon abbreviations than it is to write out taxon definitions (the number strings), we usually refer to taxa by using the abbreviations listed in Table 5.3 and shown under each example in Figure 5.12.

As an important aside, note that the abbreviations are based on commonly used type names, which appear to the right of the abbreviations in Table 5.3. In each case the type names appearing in that column were taken directly from the literature in which the specimens were illustrated. For example, Taxon DAQS contains six specimens (Table 5.4), at least one of which was originally referred to as a Dalton point, at least one as an Arkabutla point, at least one as a Quad point, and at least one as a Simpson point. This plethora of type names for points that are identical in terms of eight characters ought to give us pause the next time we consider using traditional projectile-point types as analytical taxa.

DETERMINING POLARITY
THROUGH OUTGROUP COMPARISON

Once the taxa have been coded in terms of characters and character states, the next step is to determine the polarity of the character states—which state or states of a character are derived and which one is ancestral. One method of doing this involves the use of an outgroup. Briefly reviewing our discussion in Chapter 3, an outgroup is defined as a taxon that is outside the taxa being analyzed (the ingroup taxa). The working assumption is that a character state in the outgroup is ancestral relative to the ingroup taxa. Any taxon technically can serve as an outgroup, but the more closely it is related to the ingroup taxa, the greater the number of character states that might be clarified relative to polarity. To root a cladogram means to select a particular taxon as a basal group from which other taxa are derived.

In situations where considerable prior knowledge of phylogeny exists, it might not be too difficult to select an appropriate outgroup. But what about situations where we know little about the phylogeny of the taxa? Our goal is to find a taxon that lies completely outside the ingroup taxa and yet is close enough to them phylogenetically that it clarifies the polarity of as many character states as possible. In biology it would not make much sense to use a species of sponge to try to order taxa containing trout, deer, and snakes. Based on our knowledge of phylogeny in general, we would assume that so much time has passed since the common ancestor of those four taxa existed that such an exercise would be pointless. In archaeology—where we are dealing with the remains of cultural evolution, which because of the kind of transmission involved has a much faster tempo than biological evolution—we need to be sensitive to the potential strength of the phylogenetic signal. A tradition, however it might be defined, can be a short- or long-lived phenomenon, but even in the latter case, transmission can occur at a high rate, which can cause rapid change in character states. That turnover might be so rapid that phylogenetic signals are of such short duration that they will never be detected.

The most difficult decision we faced in our study of southeastern projectile points was in choosing an appropriate outgroup. Given the age of the taxa with which we were dealing, it was difficult to select an appropriate ancestral taxon from outside those taxa. The earliest generally accepted date for the occupation of North America is about 11,500 RCYBP, and the earliest accepted projectile-point type is Clovis. Again, this temporal placement is based almost solely on evidence from the Plains and Southwest, not from the Southeast. If, for the sake of argument, Clovis is ancestral to the rest of the taxa in the southeastern sequence, then it would make sense to select Clovis as the outgroup. But specimens of what most archaeologists would term Clovis occur in eight separate taxa (Table 5.3). This is not simply a result of our perception of how the points would be termed. As noted above, when we chose a specimen for use in the analysis, we listed the type name of the specimen that appeared in the literature. What were referred to as Clovis points in the original reports are distributed across eight of our taxa, just as specimens of various types are included in a single taxon (DAQS, for example).

One of the eight taxa, Kk (21223322), contains only specimens identified as Clovis points, so maybe it qualifies as an outgroup candidate. But such a choice would be based on little more than supposition. There is, however, an objective means of selecting an outgroup. That method is seriation, an archaeological procedure that produces an ordering of units such that the position of each unit reflects its similarity to other units. Several kinds of seriation (we have mentioned phyletic seriation and frequency seriation) have been used as archaeological chronometers (Lyman and O'Brien 2000a; O'Brien and Lyman 1999, 2000). If seriation is taken to be a method of comparing phenomena so that they can be ordered in such a manner as to reflect the passage of time, then the phenomena to be ordered must be measured identically. This means they must be measured with theoretical units or classes. It also means that the phenomena must meet certain conditions if a seriation is to produce a chronological ordering. First, phenomena to be seriated must be of similar duration. Meeting this requirement ensures that the positions of particular phenomena in an ordering are the result of their age and not of duration. Second, the phenomena to be ordered must come from the same region. This requirement is meant to ensure that what is being measured is variation in time rather than difference in geographic space. It attends the fact that transmission over geographic space can influence the results of a seriation. Meeting the second requirement increases the probability of—but certainly does not ensure—meeting the third requirement, which is that the phenomena to be ordered in a seriation all belong to the same cultural tradition. If the third requirement is met, then heritable continuity is assured, and phylogenetic affinities between the seriated phenomena are guaranteed. Techniques of identifying local areas—those within which transmission was

	I	II	III	IV	V	VI	VII
A	1	(6)	6	(1)	4	3	6
B	1	4	6	4	4	(3)	6
C	1	4	(6)	4	4	2	(6)
D	1	4	5	(4)	4	2	4
E	1	(4)	5	3	(4)	2	4
F	1	3	5	(3)	3	(2)	4
G	1	3	(5)	5	3	1	4
H	1	3	4	5	(3)	1	(4)
I	1	(3)	4	5	2	(1)	3
J	1	2	4	(5)	2	4	3
K	1	2	(4)	2	(2)	4	3
L	1	2	1	2	5	4	3

Taxon (rows A–L); Character (columns I–VII)

Figure 5.13. Occurrence seriation of 12 taxa (A–L) showing the evolution of character states through time (from O'Brien et al. 2002). Each row is a particular character (I–VII); each Arabic numeral in a column denotes a particular character state. Circled character states denote a change from the state immediately below, as if time passed from bottom to top. If time passed from top to bottom, each circle would drop down one row.

relatively unlimited but outside of which it was minimal—are founded on seriation as a method for monitoring cultural transmission (Lipo 2001; Lipo et al. 1997).

The kind of seriation we used in the outgroup determination is *occurrence seriation,* which orders phenomena on the basis of presence/absence of characters or character states (Dempsey and Baumhoff 1963; Rowe 1959). The phenomena to be seriated can be sets of things or individual things. Table 5.5 shows how this works for a fictional case. Ten taxa are examined in terms of the presence or absence of six characters (top), and those data are used to produce the only logical solution as to the order of the taxa (bottom). Note that this technique measures time continuously because of the overlap in character presence across adjacent taxa. The result is strong supporting evidence that we are dealing with heritable continuity. A similar kind of analysis is illustrated in Figure 5.13, but instead of a character analysis we have switched to a character-state analysis and recorded individual states of each character as opposed to recording simply the presence/absence of a character. Each row is a unique taxon (A–L). In this fictitious example, we can track changes in individual characters (a column signified by a Roman numeral) through shifts in

TABLE 5.5. An Example of an Occurrence Seriation Using Six Characters to Order 10 Taxa

	CHARACTER					
	A	B	C	D	E	F
Unordered Taxa						
1	+	+		+		
2	+	+		+	+	
3		+				
4	+	+	+			
5	+			+	+	
6		+	+			
7	+	+	+	+		
8	+				+	
9	+					+
10	+				+	+
Ordered Taxa						
3		+				
6		+	+			
4	+	+	+			
7	+	+	+	+		
1	+	+		+		
2	+	+		+	+	
5	+			+	+	
8	+				+	
10	+				+	+
9	+					+

character states (signified by Arabic numerals within a column). Circled character states signify a change in state from the preceding taxon (presuming that time passes from bottom to top). For example, there are two changes in character state—one in character III (1 —> 4) and another in character V (5 —> 2)—from Taxon L at the bottom to the next taxon above (K). Importantly, all 12 taxa share either five or six character states with their immediate neighbor(s). Given the sequence as we constructed it, heritable continuity is evident because of considerable overlap in character states across adjacent classes. Importantly also, the direction in which time passes—from top to bottom or from bottom to top—is not inherent or evident in the ordering. That must be ascertained with independent temporal data such as stratigraphy.

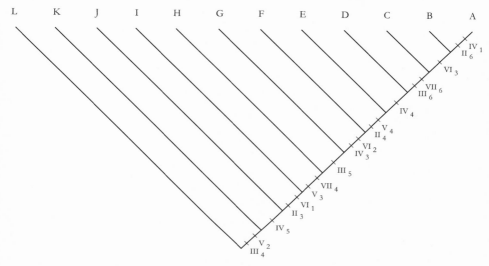

Figure 5.14. Cladogram of 12 taxa (A–L) from the occurrence seriation shown in Figure 5.13, showing changes in states (Arabic numerals) of various characters (Roman numerals). Because there is no homoplasy, the consistency index is 1.0.

In practice, with a small number of taxa and relatively few characters, occurrence seriation will usually produce only a single optimum ordering, which will be similar or identical to the ordering of taxa produced by cladistic methods. Additionally, the length of the phylogenetic tree will be equal to the least number of steps needed to produce the seriation. Figure 5.13 shows the best (meaning the least number of steps used) seriation of taxa A–L. Eighteen steps, or character-state changes (each change is circled), are required. This fictitious example is also a "perfect" solution, meaning there are no character-state reversals. The tree shown in Figure 5.14, with a length of 18, is the optimal solution to ordering taxa A–L using apomorphies. Because there is no homoplasy, the consistency index (CI) is 1.0. This example is a useful heuristic device, but it is only that. It typically is the case that many more taxa and more characters are involved, as are character-state reversals and other forms of homoplasy, all of which together greatly increase the number of optimal orderings (as with our 17-taxon orderings of projectile points from the southeastern United States). Occurrence seriation monitors change in character states, but it cannot account for all instances of complex homoplasy. Also, evolution is primarily a cladogenetic (branching) process as opposed to an anagenetic (linear) one; thus only in a textbook example could we expect a one-to-one correspondence between the number of steps in an occurrence seriation, which recognizes only anagenesis, and the length of a tree, which depicts cladogenesis. Similarly, only in a perfect world could we expect to generate a tree that has a CI of 1.0.

To produce the orderings of our projectile points we used an algorithm that searched the taxa continuously for the ordering or orderings that could be produced using the fewest number of steps. A straightforward approach to finding all optimal solutions is to generate all possible permutations of the set $\{1, 2 \ldots n\}$ and pick the ones that have the least number of steps. Even for a small number of vectors (here 17 taxa), this approach proved time consuming. It took about four days on a 700 MHz Pentium PC to generate 14 solutions that had the apparent optimal value of 28 steps (O'Brien et al. 2001). We subsequently improved the basic search method using a branch-and-bound approach that detects at an early stage that some permutations are not going to have less cost—fewer character-state reversals—than the best solution obtained to that point (Chapter 3). Therefore, some pruning takes place, and fewer than $n!$ permutations are generated and tested for optimality. With this approach we generated 172 optimal solutions of 28 steps for the 17-taxon problem in less than 1 CPU second (see O'Brien et al. 2002 for details on the algorithm). Here Taxon KDR is the single most represented unit at one end of an ordering, appearing 65 out of 172 times (38 percent) (Figure 5.15). As with any seriation, either end of an ordering could be early or late. We viewed KDR as anchoring the early end of the ordering based on the consistent occurrence of various taxa at the opposite end of orderings that had KDR at one end. Those taxa contain specimens of traditional types that from all available evidence occurred relatively late in the Southeast (ca. 10,500–10,000 RCYBP). Thus we selected KDR as our outgroup.

Having located what appeared to be an appropriate outgroup, we then used it to produce a phylogenetic tree of the 17 taxa. We examine that tree in detail in Chapter 6 and then turn attention to what happens to the number of trees produced when we raise or lower the number of taxa.

STARTING POINTS

Ronald Mason's (1962) article is still one of the best overviews of the Paleoindian period in the southeastern United States. Although recent work has contributed significantly to our knowledge of that period in the

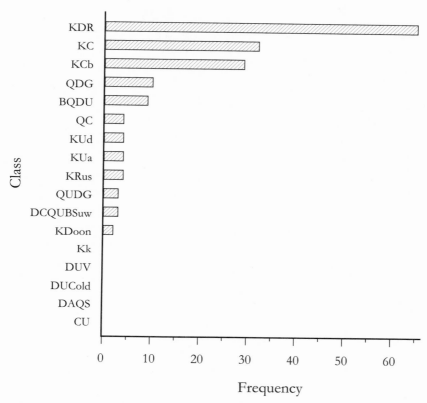

Figure 5.15. Histogram showing the frequency of occurrence of each of the 17 projectile-point taxa at one end of 172 occurrence seriations.

Southeast, it is remarkable how fresh Mason's perspective still is. Also of considerable interest is the work by David Anderson (1990, 1991) and his colleagues (e.g., Anderson and Faught 1998, 2000) in mapping the distribution of various types of Paleoindian points across the United States. For Paleoindian-period lithic technology, see Bruce Bradley's (1997) analysis of Dalton points from the Sloan site in northeastern Arkansas and his treatment of Clovis-point technology based on specimens in the Fenn Cache from southwestern Wyoming or northeastern Utah that he and George Frison examined (Frison and Bradley 1999). Bradley and Dennis Stanford recently speculated that Clovis points could have been derived from European Solutrean points as a result of people from southwestern Europe exploring along the glacial-maximum North Atlantic sea ice front about 18,000 years ago. They base this speculation on the large number of perceived technomorphological characters shared by Solutrean and Clovis points. Not many archaeologists are convinced by the argument— Lawrence Straus (2000) wrote an interesting rebuttal—but one potential means of addressing the problem is through cladistics.

For more in-depth discussion of paradigmatic classification and the difference between intensionally and extensionally defined units, see our book *Applying Evolutionary Archaeology: A Systematic Approach* (O'Brien and Lyman 2000). You should also look at Robert Dunnell's (1971) early formulation of paradigmatic classification in *Systematics in Prehistory*. Ian Kitching et al.'s (1998) *Cladistics: The Theory and Practice of Parsimony Analysis* and Daniel Brooks and Deborah McLennan's (1991) *Phylogeny, Ecology, and Behavior: A Research Program in Comparative Biology* contain excellent treatments of the pros and cons of various approaches to character coding, as does a short paper by Steven Poe and John Wiens (2000). For extended treatment of occurrence seriation, including its assumptions, see our book *Seriation, Stratigraphy, and Index Fossils: The Backbone of Archaeological Dating* (O'Brien and Lyman 1999).

SIX

Trees and Clades

MICHAEL J. O'BRIEN, DANIEL S. GLOVER,
R. LEE LYMAN, AND JOHN DARWENT

EVERY STEP we take in cladistics moves us closer to the final analytical goal, which is the production of a phylogenetic tree. Perhaps we should term this the penultimate step, because we still have to analyze the tree in terms of what it tells us about the evolution of taxa—when they evolved relative to each other, changes in character states that taxa went through, and maybe even geographic differences in the distribution of taxa and clades (Chapter 7). Rarely will we obtain a tree with a consistency index (CI) of 1.00 (which means there is a complete absence of homoplasy); and more often than not we will obtain multiple trees of the same length and CI. At this point we have two options: Either analyze each of the multiple trees in turn or sample the trees. Regardless of which option we choose, we can also create consensus trees of various kinds (Chapter 3). Quite often, phylogenetic analysis is an iterative process, which means that the initial trees we produce are starting points for a further round of analysis. We might want to add or subtract a taxon to see how that affects the phylogeny, and we might even want to go back and collapse some taxa to determine what effect that has on the ordering.

We examine several of these topics by focusing first on the phylogenetic tree produced from the 17 taxa discussed in Chapter 5 and then on the effects of removing or adding taxa. We eventually expand the sample to include 36 taxa and show how to build consensus trees. One of those consensus trees becomes the focus of the remainder of the chapter, in which we discuss the geographic patterning of taxa and clades. What these clades might mean for the evolution of weapon-delivery systems in the southeastern United States is taken up in Chapter 7, where we turn our attention to individual character-state changes.

THE 17-TAXON TREE

The phylogenetic tree—and, interestingly, there was only one most parsimonious tree—generated for the 17 projectile-point taxa is shown in Figure 6.1. We used David Swofford's (1998) PAUP* (version 4) program to generate the tree. Recall from Chapter 3 that PAUP* has an upper limit of 12 taxa for its exhaustive-search routine, so we set the program to construct the tree by the branch-and-bound method. This method quickly establishes a tree and then systematically removes from further consideration partial trees whose length exceeds the length of the initial tree, where "length" is measured as the number of changes in character states or what in Chapter 5 we termed "steps" with respect to the occurrence seriation. When the program encounters a complete tree that is shorter than the initial one, it resets the upper bound and begins the process anew. The algorithm guarantees to find the shortest tree or trees.

The shortest tree we found, shown in Figure 6.1, has a length of 22, a retention index (RI) of 0.70, and a CI of 0.59. The RI and CI values are high enough to offer encouragement that the tree is fairly representative of the true phylogeny, but there are still some problematic features. Notice that the tree contains several *polytomies* (points at which the program cannot make a simple dichotomous split). For example, there is a polytomy in the form of a trichotomous branching that produces KC, CU, and the ancestor of the clade comprising BQDU + DUCold + DCQUBSuw + DAQS + QC + QUDG + QDG. Phylogenetic analysis often assumes that diversification occurs only by a series of bifurcations, but this assumption is unnecessary and may obscure reality (Hoelzer and Melnick 1994). In fact, cultural transmission may result more often in polytomies than in simple bifurcation. Alternatively, in reality there may be a bifurcation, but the phylogenetic signal is too weak for the program to resolve the pattern. Thus it treats it as a polytomy.

Character-state changes—there are 22 of them, hence the tree length of 22—are represented by the small boxes in Figure 6.1. Each box has two numbers associated with it: The Roman numeral refers to the character (Table 5.2 and Figure 5.11), and the subscript Arabic number indicates the evolved state of that character (moving from left to right across the tree). Open boxes indicate nonhomoplasious changes. For example, KDR produced a descendant in which character II changed states from 2 to 1. In fact, all descendants of KDR exhibit character-state 1. Once that character state appeared, it never disappeared and reappeared. Similarly,

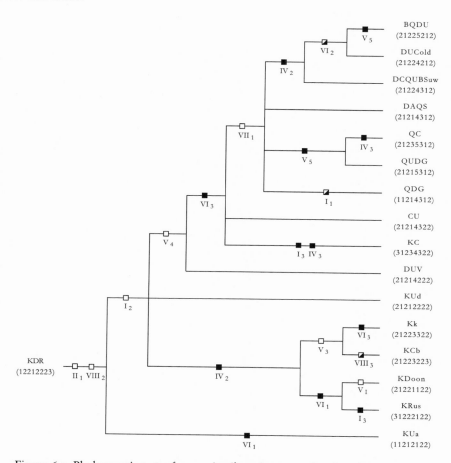

Figure 6.1. Phylogenetic tree of 17 projectile-point taxa, showing character-state changes. The tree has a length of 22 and a consistency index of 0.59. Boxes denote changes in character state, Roman numerals denote characters, and subscript Arabic numbers denote character states. For example, the boxes at the far left indicate that Class KDR underwent changes in characters II (to state 1) and VIII (to state 2) to produce the ancestor of the other 16 taxa. Open boxes indicate nonhomoplasious changes; shaded boxes indicate parallel or convergent changes (homoplasy); and half-shaded boxes indicate characters that reverted to an ancestral state (homoplasy). Note that in this and all succeeding figures, we place the outgroup out to the left to emphasize that it is the outgroup. A more common practice is to place it on the right, at one end of the ingroup taxa. In form, it would appear as KDR does in the phenogram shown in Figure 6.2.

KDR's direct descendant changed states in character VIII from 3 to 2. Later taxa might exhibit a different state of character VIII, but state 2 arose only once. Shaded boxes indicate parallelism or convergence (homoplasy)—that is, a change to a particular character state occurs more than once within the entire set. For example, character IV changes to state 3 in both the line leading to QC and the line leading to KC. Finally, half-shaded boxes indicate characters that reverted to an ancestral state. For example, character VI began in KDR, the outgroup, as state 2; it later changed to state 3 and then changed back to state 2 in the line that produced BQDU + DUCold.

The first characters in the outgroup to change were (1) character II (base shape), which changed from state 2 (normal curve) to state 1 (arc-shaped), and (2) character VIII (length/width ratio), which changed from state 3 (3.00–3.99) to state 2 (2.00–2.99). This produced (1) an ancestor (11212222) that in turn produced KUa after an additional change in character VI from state 2 to state 1 and (2) an ancestor of all other ingroup taxa. The latter ancestor underwent a change in character I (location of maximum blade width) from state 1 (proximal quarter) to state 2 (secondmost proximal quarter). That ancestor is isomorphic with KUd, which means they are identical in terms of character states (21212222). This makes it appear as if KUd is the ancestor, but in cladistics all taxa that are part of the analysis are shown as terminal taxa. As we pointed out in Chapter 3, this solves the problem of having to guess whether a taxon is indeed ancestral to other taxa.

In terms of character stability, the most stable characters—excluding character III, which was found only in character-state 2 and hence could have been deleted from analysis—are characters II and VII, each of which underwent a single change, followed by character VIII, which changed twice (once affecting only a single taxon [KCb]). The most unstable characters are V and VI, each of which changed five times, followed closely by characters I and IV, each of which changed four times. There are six instances of parallelism—in character states I_3, IV_2, IV_3, V_5, VI_1, and VI_3—and three instances of characters (I, VI, and VIII) reverting to an ancestral state. Parallelism might be expected if there are mechanical or technological constraints either on how particular projectile points are made or in terms of performance characteristics (Schiffer and Skibo 1987). We return to this topic in Chapter 7. Instances of character-state reversals are rare in the organic world (if they occur at all); what appear to be reversals there are in our view usually artifacts of classification, especially with respect to

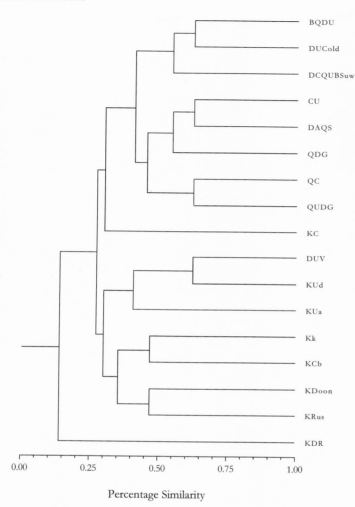

Figure 6.2.
Phenogram of 17
projectile-point taxa
obtained by means of
a clustering algorithm
(Hintze 1999).

Percentage Similarity

measurement scale (Chapter 3). With human-manufactured tools, there is nothing to prevent the recurrence of earlier states, given how cultural transmission works, although in some cases apparent reversals could be attributable to the scale of the classification system.

The 17-Taxon Tree versus a Phenogram

To underscore the difference between a phylogenetic tree and a phenogram, we produced Figure 6.2, using the same data shown in Figure 6.1. We used an unweighted pair-group algorithm (Hintze 1999) to construct the phenogram. Insofar as the phenogram reflects descent with modification, it suggests a different evolutionary history than the tree. For example, at the similarity level of roughly 0.30 in the phenogram, there are two clusters. One cluster includes the same nine taxa as in the large clade shown at the top of Figure 6.1: BQDU, DUCold, DCQUBSuw, CU, DAQS, QDG, QC, QUDG, and KC. The phenogram links these particular taxa differently than the tree does. For example, the phenogram places CU, DAQS, and QDG in a cluster, whereas the tree links these three taxa only through the clade that also contains the other six taxa. The second cluster in the phenogram links DUV and KUd with KUa, Kk, KCb, KDoon, and KRus; although this cluster is similar to the Kk + KCb + KDoon + KRus clade, in the phylogenetic tree DUV is more closely related to the aforementioned clade of nine taxa and KUa is set apart as a distinct taxon after the first instance of branching.

General similarities between the tree and the phenogram were not unexpected. The point here is not that phenetics is incapable of producing phylogenetic relationships but rather that it is not designed solely to do so. Any phylogenetic information that a phenogram projects is strictly a methodological by-product as opposed to a targeted product. Thus, as Mark Ridley (1996) points out, when the issue is phylogeny, we have considerable reason to distrust distance statistics, which are based solely on phenetic dissimilarity.

MULTIPLE TREES

We noted at the beginning of the chapter that we were surprised that PAUP* produced only a single tree for the southeastern taxa. With 17 taxa, eight characters, and numerous character states, we thought prior to analysis that a large number of trees would be produced. Recall that one criterion we used in choosing the taxa was that a taxon had to have at least four specimens in it. Our rationale was twofold. First, we were interested more in repetitive behavior and less in idiosyncratic behavior. The larger the number of specimens, the less likely it is that we are dealing with the latter. Second, we reasoned that fewer taxa would have been insufficient to reveal nuances of phylogenetic history. The first part of our rationale is reasonable, but there is nothing magical about having four specimens in a paradigmatic class as opposed to, say, three. Any class is as real analytically as any other class, regardless of the number of empirical units—here projectile points—it contains. Still, if our phylogeny were full of single-specimen taxa, it is unclear how useful it would be at this stage of analysis.

In this section we extend the analysis beyond the 17 taxa to see how well the original phylogenetic ordering holds up when we subtract and add taxa. By doing this we not only can gain a more in-depth look at southeastern projectile-point taxa in terms of phylogenetic relationships but can also discuss how to handle multiple trees of equal length. We covered multiple trees in Chapter 3, but here we use real data and output instead of talking about multiple trees in general terms. The point to the following discussion—one that we have underscored throughout the book—is that rooted trees are nothing more than phylogenetic hypotheses. They are not the final answer to phylogenetic history, nor can they be. A tree is only as good as the analytical taxa used to produce it, and the taxa are only as good as the characters used to define them. The use of more or fewer taxa, as with the use of more or fewer characters and character states, will usually provide different phylogenetic orderings. It is up to the analyst to interpret the results. Just as there is nothing magical about having four specimens in a class as opposed to any other number, there is no cookbook formula for how many taxa to use or how many characters to include in creating the taxa. The only limitations are those imposed by the computer program used, the power of available computing equipment, and our insights.

Using Fewer Taxa

Decreasing the number of taxa used in a phylogenetic analysis will produce one of three results: It will yield fewer trees, more trees, or the same number of trees. Similarly, tree length will increase, decrease, or remain the same. Inspection of a cladogram will allow some judgments to be made about the possible effect that removal of a taxon might have on the results, but these are confined to the more obvious situations. Figure 6.3 reproduces the 17-taxon cladogram shown in Figure 6.1, but here we have listed on the right side: (1) the number of trees that would result if we removed a particular taxon from analysis and reran the data, (2) the length of the best (shortest) tree(s) that would be produced, and (3) the CI of the best tree(s). Looking at the tree in Figure 6.1, and knowing that only one best tree was produced, we might expect that only a single tree would be produced if we removed many of the taxa individually. We would be correct with respect to several taxa (BQDU, DAQS, QC, QDG,

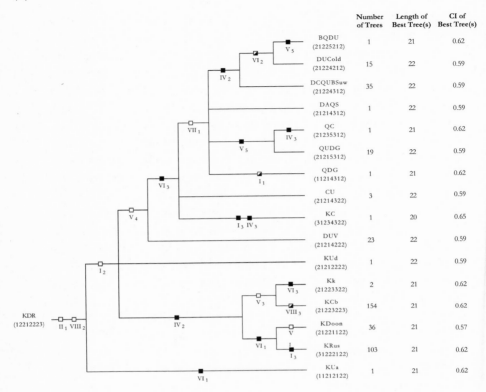

Figure 6.3. Phylogenetic tree of 17 projectile-point taxa, showing the effects of taxon removal. Boxes denote changes in character state, Roman numerals denote characters, and subscript Arabic numbers denote character states. Open boxes indicate nonhomoplasious changes; shaded boxes indicate parallel or convergent changes (homoplasy); and half-shaded boxes indicate characters that reverted to an ancestral state (homoplasy). The columns to the right show the number of trees that would result if the corresponding taxon were removed from the sample; the length of the best (shortest) tree that would be produced; and the consistency index (CI) of that tree.

KC, KUd, and KUa), but we would be wrong about the other taxa. Removing CU results in three trees being produced; removing DUCold results in 15 trees; removing DUV results in 23 trees; and removing DC-QUBSuw results in 35 trees. One might expect from looking at Figure 6.3 that with respect to the Kk + KCb clade the removal of either taxon would have more or less the same consequence on the number of trees, but it does not. Only two trees are produced when Kk is removed, but a surprising 154 trees are produced when KCb is removed. Removal of either

KDoon or KRus creates a large number of trees, but we might have thought beforehand that the effect would be much less and probably not three times greater for one than for the other. As with the other taxa whose removal increases the number of phylogenetic trees, each one of those taxa possesses something that PAUP* needs to create a single tree such as the one shown in Figure 6.1. When one of those taxa is removed, the program cannot find the resolution that it can when that taxon is present.

We need to insert an important caveat here: Do not equate number of trees produced with the "correctness" of a phylogenetic tree. In other words, simply because we have multiple trees does not imply that our results are any worse than they would be had only a single tree been produced. A single tree might make our analysis neater in terms of appearance than if we had 154 trees, but the presence of a single tree should not give us greater confidence in our results. For "correctness," we still rely on indices such as the retention index (RI) and the consistency index (CI). As an example, let's take the two trees that are produced when Kk is removed. Those trees are shown in Figure 6.4. They are exact images of each other except for KCb and KUa, which swap positions between trees. Both trees duplicate the topology of the original 17-taxon tree (Figure 6.1). That KUa and KCb could swap places without lengthening the tree is interesting, because they do not closely resemble one another morphologically, containing different states for five characters. The two trees that are produced after removing Kk have a tree length of 21, one less than the tree generated using all 17 taxa. The CI increases by 0.03 from the CI of the 17-taxon tree, from 0.59 to 0.62. The RI increases by 0.01, from 0.70 to 0.71. Another caveat: The higher CI and RI obtained for the 16-taxon trees do not mean that the trees are superior to the original 17-taxon tree; they are entirely different trees because they were built using different taxa.

Suppose we wanted to show only a single tree for our 16 taxa. We could either pick one of the two trees or compute a consensus tree. Recall from Chapter 3 that there are several kinds of consensus trees; for discussion here we calculated only a semistrict consensus tree and a majority-rule consensus tree. Semistrict consensus trees are more relaxed than strict consensus trees and combine those clades that are not contradicted by one of the trees. Majority-rule consensus trees retain the groupings that occur in a user-determined percentage between 50 percent and 100 percent of the trees in the sample. When there are only two trees in the sample,

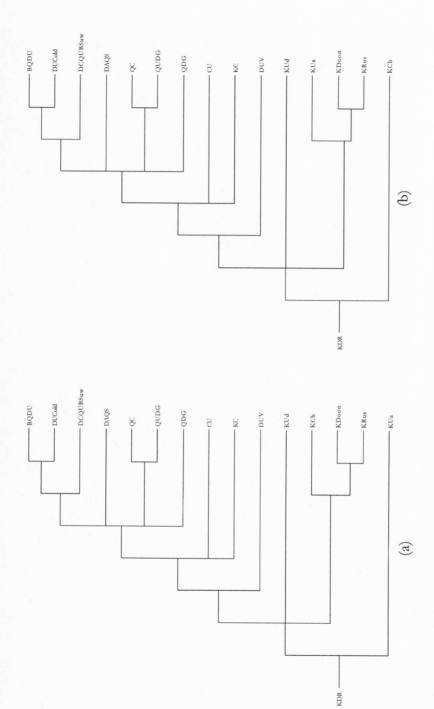

Figure 6.4. The two trees produced when Kk is removed from the 17-taxon sample. They are duplicates of each other except for KCb and KUa, which swap positions between trees.

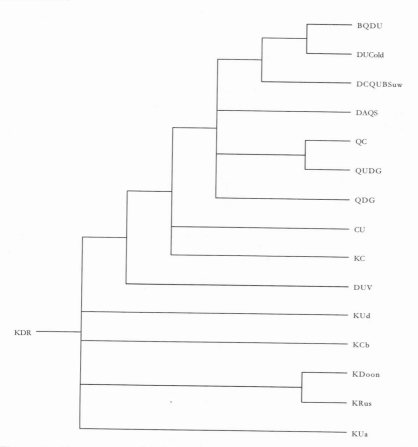

Figure 6.5. Consensus tree for the two trees shown in Figure 6.4. Because there are only two trees, the consensus tree is both a semistrict consensus tree and a majority-rule tree. The only difference between the consensus tree and either of the two nonconsensus trees (Figure 6.4) is the placement of KUa and KCb. Because PAUP* cannot resolve their placement relative to the KDoon + KRus clade, it creates a five-taxon polytomy just above the basal node.

identical consensus trees are produced regardless of kind. In other words, the consensus tree shown in Figure 6.5 is both the semistrict consensus tree and the majority-rule tree. As might be expected, the only difference between the consensus tree and either of the two nonconsensus trees (Figure 6.4) is the placement of KUa and KCb. Because it cannot resolve their placement relative to the KDoon + KRus clade, it creates a five-taxon polytomy at the basal node.

We can move beyond this simple example, where the two consensus

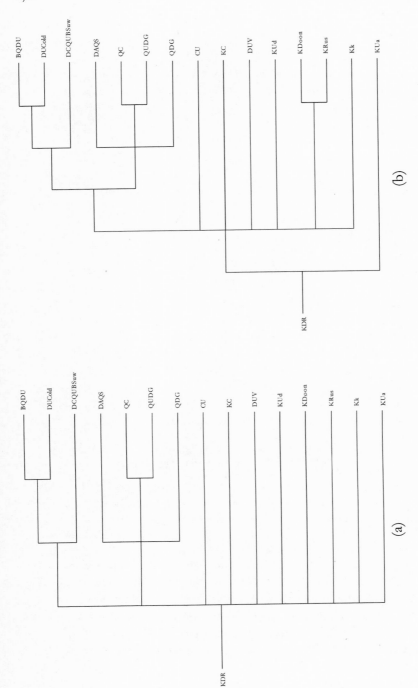

Figure 6.6. Consensus trees created when KCb is removed from the 17-taxon sample: (a) semistrict consensus tree; (b) 50-percent majority-rule consensus tree.

trees are identical, and examine what happens when many more trees are generated. For this exercise, we add Kk back to the 17-taxon sample and this time remove KCb, which we know from inspection of Figure 6.3 will result in the generation of 154 trees. The trees have a CI of 0.62. Figure 6.6a shows the semistrict consensus tree, and Figure 6.6b shows the 50-percent majority-rule consensus tree for the new 16-taxon sample. The semistrict consensus tree preserves some of the clades shown in the 17-taxon tree (Figure 6.1)—for example, the BQDU + DUCold + DCQUB-Suw clade and the QC + QUDG clade—but rearranges others—for example, there now is a four-taxon clade comprising DAQS + QC + QUDG + QDG, where in the 17-taxon tree there was not. Because of the amount of homoplasy present, PAUP* created a 10-taxon polytomy at the basal node. The majority-rule tree (Figure 6.6b) looks similar to the semistrict tree in that it creates both the BQDU + DUCold + DCQUBSuw clade and the DAQS + QC + QUDG + QDG clade, but unlike the semistrict tree it unites all seven taxa into an exclusive clade, which duplicates the seven-taxon clade in Figure 6.1 (but see below). Also, the majority-rule tree preserves the KDoon and KRus clade from the 17-taxon tree.

The important lesson here is that it is often impossible to determine beforehand exactly what effect the removal of a particular taxon will have on the phylogeny. We might have thought beforehand that the removal of KCb would have no impact on the top half of the tree, but it obviously does. Although the seven-taxon clade BQDU + DUCold + DCQUBSuw + DAQS + QC + QUDG + QDG is reproduced from the 17-taxon tree, the internal arrangement of the clade is different. DAQS and QDG are now in a clade with QC and QUDG, whereas before they were not.

Based on what we have seen so far, many of the clades evident in the 17-taxon cladogram are preserved in consensus trees that result from the removal of a single taxon. Although we have shown only two removals here (Kk and KCb), analysis has demonstrated that the clades hold up well when other single taxa are removed. What happens when multiple taxa are removed? Figure 6.7 shows the single tree produced when five taxa—Kk, KCb, KDoon, KRus, and KUa—are excluded. Because there are only 12 taxa remaining, we can perform either a branch-and-bound or an exhaustive search—12 taxa being the upper limit that PAUP* can handle using the latter method. Both methods evaluate the same number of unrooted trees—654,729,075—and produce single rooted trees with a length of 14. The two trees are identical because exhaustive searches and branch-and-bound searches both guarantee finding the shortest tree(s).

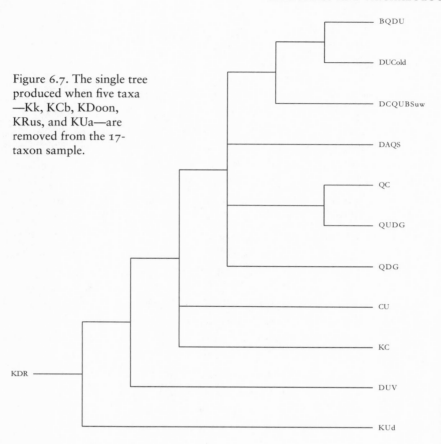

Figure 6.7. The single tree produced when five taxa —Kk, KCb, KDoon, KRus, and KUa—are removed from the 17-taxon sample.

Notice that removing the five taxa did not disturb the clades in the upper two-thirds of the 17-taxon tree (Figure 6.1). This might have been pre-dicted beforehand, given the positions of the five deleted taxa in the 17-taxon tree, but as we saw in the 16-taxon majority-rule consensus tree with KCb removed (Figure 6.6b), we can never be sure until the new tree is generated. There, the removal of KCb, which occurs in the lower third of the 17-taxon tree (Figure 6.1), resulted in the rearrangement of some of the taxa in the upper, seven-taxon clade. The important point is that under certain circumstances whole clades can be pruned without affecting the rest of the tree. In Figure 6.7, the four-taxon clade Kk + KCb + KDoon + KRus has been removed, together with the closely related taxon KUa, and the phylogenetic positions of the remaining 12 taxa have remained unchanged.

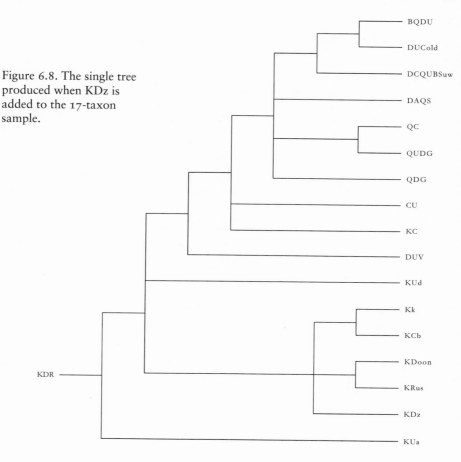

Figure 6.8. The single tree produced when KDz is added to the 17-taxon sample.

Using More Taxa

Had we started out with more than 17 taxa, we obviously would have generated trees with different topologies than shown in Figure 6.1, but how many trees per added taxon might there have been? Figure 6.8 shows the single tree produced when an eighteenth taxon, KDz, is added. That taxon, defined as 21222222 (see Table 5.2), contains three specimens identified in the literature as being Clovis or Dalton points. We chose KDz because we thought it might broaden either the Kk + KCb clade or the KDoon + KRus clade. In the new tree KDz fits in the same clade with Kk, KCb, KDoon, and KRus, but it is not part of either two-taxon clade. The addition of KDz does not increase the tree length because it did not go through any additional character-state changes. The CI

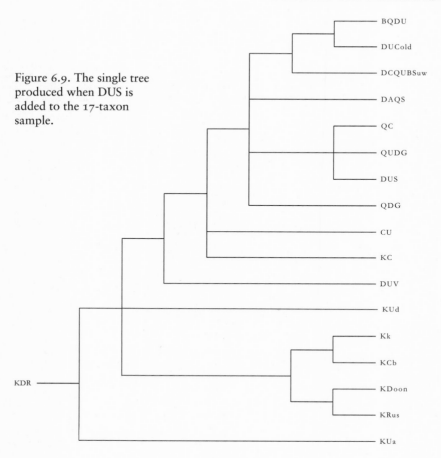

Figure 6.9. The single tree
produced when DUS is
added to the 17-taxon
sample.

of the 18-taxon tree is 0.59—the same as for the 17-taxon tree—and the
RI is 0.73—0.03 higher than for the 17-taxon tree.

Another 18-taxon tree is shown in Figure 6.9. Here DUS instead of
KDz is added to the 17-taxon tree. DUS, defined as 21215313 (see Table
5.2), contains three specimens identified in the literature as a Dalton
point, a Simpson point, and an unidentified point. Not surprisingly, DUS
fits in the upper half of the cladogram, being placed in the same clade with
QC and QUDG. The length of the 18-taxon tree (only one tree was produced) is 23—one more than the length of the 17-taxon tree; the CI is
0.57—slightly less than for the 17-taxon and 17-taxon + KDz trees; and
the RI is 0.70—the same as that for the 17-taxon tree and 0.03 less than
that for the 17-taxon + KDz tree.

Given their individual placement in the trees, and the fact that single

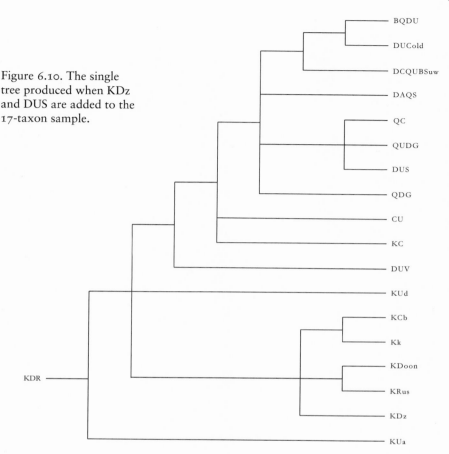

Figure 6.10. The single tree produced when KDz and DUS are added to the 17-taxon sample.

trees were produced, it is not surprising that adding both KDz and DUS simultaneously produces only a single tree (Figure 6.10) and that the two taxa hold their positions in their respective clades. The 19-taxon tree has a length of 23, a CI of 0.57, and an RI of 0.72.

Do not be misled by the fact that to this point our examples make it appear that the addition of a single taxon produces only a single tree. It might, but just as we saw when we deleted certain single taxa, there is every likelihood that numerous trees will result. Figure 6.11 shows the semistrict and the 50-percent majority-rule consensus trees based on the 17 trees that result from the addition of taxon R—defined as 11211322 (Table 5.2) and containing only what were listed in the literature as Redstone points—to the 17-taxon sample. Those 17 trees have a CI of 0.54 and an RI of 0.66. The semistrict consensus tree (Figure 6.11a) more or

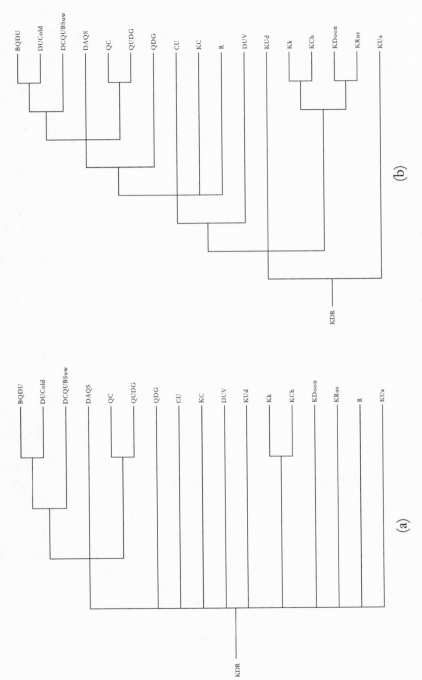

Figure 6.11. Consensus trees created when R is added to the 17-taxon sample: (a) semistrict consensus tree; (b) 50-percent majority-rule consensus tree.

less preserves the clades in the upper half of the 17-taxon tree (Figure 6.1), but with the exception of the Kk + KCb clade it obliterates the clades in the lower half of that tree. The large polytomy at the basal node now includes 11 taxa. The 50-percent majority-rule consensus tree (Figure 6.11b), however, is nearly identical to the 17-taxon tree. Taxon R slides into the same clade with KC, CU, and the other taxa in the upper half of the tree, with no change to the bottom half. This makes sense in light of the fact that Redstone points are considered to be morphologically (and, by extension, temporally) close to Clovis points (Cambron and Hulse 1964; Perino 1985).

We could keep adding taxa ad infinitum, but in most situations we will at some point be overwhelmed by the number of trees produced—the result of homoplasy that PAUP* cannot resolve except through the creation of multiple trees. At some point PAUP*, too, will be overwhelmed, and we will need to switch from the branch-and-bound method of building trees to a heuristic method such as branch swapping. As we pointed out in Chapter 3, with 10 taxa the number of possible unrooted trees is roughly 2×10^6. With 17 taxa—the number of projectile-point taxa in our original analysis—the number of unrooted trees increases to roughly 6×10^{15}. This is a tremendously large number, but PAUP* was able to produce the tree (Figure 6.1) in a few seconds. Even with 19 taxa, the branch-and-bound method found a shortest tree in about the same amount of time. But at around 20 taxa, things begin to slow considerably. At that point we need to implement a heuristic search method.

As our final example of adding taxa, we extend our analysis to include all projectile-point taxa with three or more examples. The original 17-taxon data set contained 83 specimens; the addition of the new specimens (Figure 6.12) raises the projectile-point sample to 141 specimens in 36 taxa (Table 6.1). Because the large number of taxa precluded use of the branch-and-bound method, we used PAUP*'s branch-swapping heuristic search. We then set PAUP* to root the trees at KDR—the same outgroup used in the 17-taxon tree—and to select 100, 10,000, and 100,000 trees at random. All saved trees had an equal length (41), CI (0.37), and RI (0.67). We also set PAUP* to compute 50-percent majority-rule consensus trees for each set of saved trees (Plates 1–3).

Four features of the consensus trees are worth noting. First, the large clade shown in blue, comprising 13 taxa, is identical across the consensus trees. Second, the clade shown in red is also unchanged across the trees. Thus we believe that those clades are very close approximations of the

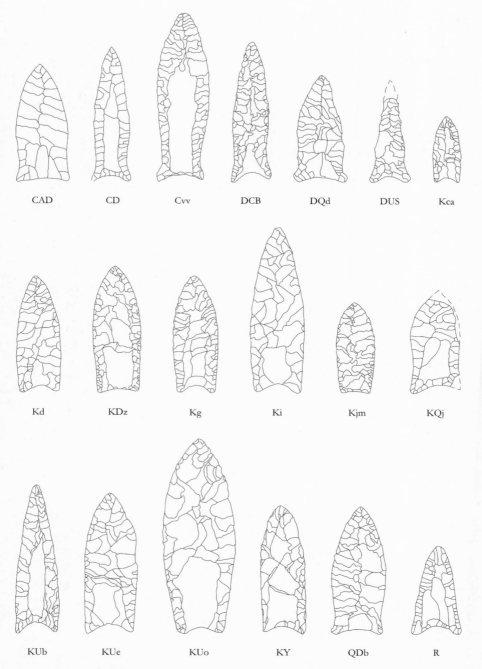

CAD   CD   Cvv   DCB   DQd   DUS   Kca

Kd   KDz   Kg   Ki   Kjm   KQj

KUb   KUe   KUo   KY   QDb   R

Figure 6.12. Illustrations of specimens in each of 19 additional projectile-point taxa used in the analysis; class abbreviations appear under each example. See Table 6.1 for taxa definitions.

TABLE 6.1. Taxon Definitions, Abbreviations, and Common Type Names of 36 Projectile-Point Taxa

Taxon	Abbreviation	Common Type Names[a]
21225212	BQDU	Beaver Lake–Quad–Dalton–Unidentified
21214322	CU	Cumberland–Unidentified
21214312	DAQS	Dalton–Arkabutla–Quad–Simpson
21224312	DCQUBSuw	Dalton–Cumberland–Quad–Unidentified–Beaver Lake–Suwannee
21224212	DUCold	Dalton–Unidentified–Coldwater
21214222	DUV	Dalton–Unidentified–Vandale
21223223	KCb	Clovis–Cumberland
31234322	KC	Clovis–Cumberland
21221122	KDoon	Clovis–Doon
12212223	KDR	Clovis–Dalton–Redstone
21223322	Kk	Clovis
31222122	KRus	Clovis–Russellville
11212122	KUa	Clovis–Unidentified
21212222	KUd	Clovis–Unidentified
21235312	QC	Quad–Cumberland
11214312	QDG	Quad–Dalton–Greenbrier
21215312	QUDG	Quad–Unidentified–Dalton–Greenbrier
. . . .		
21224322	CAD	Cumberland–Arkabutla–Dalton
21224323	CD	Cumberland–Dalton
31235323	Cvv	Cumberland
21214213	DCB	Dalton–Cumberland–Beaver Lake
21216312	DQd	Dalton–Quad
21215313	DUS	Dalton–Unidentified–Simpson
21211222	Kca	Clovis
21211322	Kd	Clovis
21222222	KDz	Clovis–Dalton
21221222	Kg	Clovis
21221323	Ki	Clovis
31231222	Kjm	Clovis
31224322	KQj	Clovis–Quad
11212223	KUb	Clovis–Unidentified
21212122	KUe	Clovis–Unidentified
21241322	KUo	Clovis–Unidentified
11211223	KY	Clovis–Yazoo
21225312	QDb	Quad–Dalton
11211322	R	Redstone

[a] Names taken directly from archaeological reports producing the sampled specimens.

true phylogenies of the taxa within them (Plate 4). Because of the larger number of taxa involved, these clades perhaps are better indicators of relationships than the clades in the 17-taxon tree (Figure 6.1). Addition of the new taxa moves the older taxa around relative to each other. For example, BQDU now is only distantly related to the other terminal taxa, whereas before (Figure 6.1) it formed a clade with DUCold. Together, the older and newer taxa create numerous subclades within the larger ones, and many of the branchings are dichotomous. How the two large clades relate to each other is difficult to ascertain. The 100,000-tree consensus tree (Plate 3) shows them as being much more closely related than either of the other trees does. Third, each consensus tree contains three other clades comprising two or three terminal taxa that are consistent across at least two trees. The (purple) KUa + KUe clade occurs across all three trees, whereas the (green) KDoon + KRus + KDz clade in two of the trees deletes KDz in the third. Similarly, the (yellow) R + Kd + KUo clade in two of the trees is a KDz + Kg + R clade in the third. Fourth, four taxa—Kca, KUd, KY, and KUb—remain isolated in all three trees and also hold consistent topological positions.

There is no hard and fast rule concerning the number of trees that should be included in a sample. We picked 100, 10,000, and 100,000 trees simply to use as examples. As a rule of thumb, we would suggest undertaking a series of runs with increasingly larger samples of trees, as we did here. Any clades/relationships that consistently show up would then be worth taking a closer look at. Although the three majority-rule consensus trees shown in Plates 1–3 are consistent in several major respects—especially the positions of the blue and red clades—the 100,000-tree consensus tree (Plate 3) differs more from the other two trees than either does from the other. In fact, the only major difference between the 100-tree and the 10,000-tree topologies is in terms of how the large clade made up of (1) the red clade, (2) the KDoon + KRus + KDz clade, and (3) Kg is related to other taxa. The 10,000-tree topology (Plate 2) shows that large clade as part of a four-prong polytomy, one prong of which leads to the blue clade. The 100-tree topology (Plate 1) excludes the blue clade.

TREES AND GEOGRAPHY

Now that we have trees, what can we do with them? We pointed out at the beginning of the chapter that phylogenetic ordering is a legitimate end in itself, but there are other issues that perhaps can be addressed with the information. One of those is the changes in character states that taxa went through and what those changes might mean in terms of the overall design changes in taxa as they evolve. For our purposes, those changes are relative to the evolution of Paleoindian weaponry in the southeastern United States. We take up this topic in Chapter 7. Phylogenetic trees can also be used to examine the geographic distribution of taxa and clades. Several research questions might be involved: Are there geographic differences in the distribution of clades and the taxa within them? Can we determine the location of evolutionary "hotspots"—localities in which taxa and clades arose? Do some areas appear to have more such hot spots than chance would allow? Can we learn anything about how transmission effected evolutionary change? That is, what if anything does the geographic distribution of taxa in relation to the phylogenetic pattern say about how a region's population interacted regarding the particular taxa being studied? Does the distribution tell us anything about social boundaries and community and regional organization (e.g., Lipo and Madsen 2001; Lipo et al. 1997)? One term (among many) for this kind of analysis is *phylogeography*. There are multiple approaches to phylogeography (see Brown and Lomolino 1998 for a summary), one of which is to construct area cladograms to depict the geographic distributions of taxa within clades. There are several ways to draw area cladograms, depending on the amount of phylogenetic and/or biogeographical information available. As James Brown and Mark Lomolino (1998) point out, some diagrams provide visual representations of the relationships among the areas containing related taxa, whereas others provide enough information to hypothesize explicit sequences of historical interchange and isolation events.

Several examples of area cladograms are shown in Figure 6.13, drawn from the work of Vicky Funk and Warren Wagner (1995) on plant and animal colonization of the Hawaiian Islands. Figure 6.13a shows a simple area cladogram predicted for colonization of the five largest islands based on a simple rule of lineage progression. But why that pattern as opposed to another? Because we know from geological and geophysical data that of the major islands that make up the Hawaiian Archipelago, Kauai, the northwesternmost island, is the oldest, followed by Oahu, Molokai, Maui, and finally Hawaii, the southeasternmost island. That pattern is the one shown in Figure 6.13a. If groups of organisms followed simple rules of progression, then we would expect to see the least differentiated taxa on the oldest island (Kauai) and the most derived taxa on the youngest is-

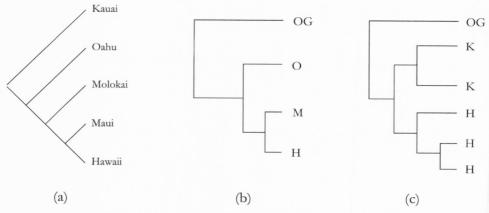

Figure 6.13. Area cladograms for the five largest islands in the Hawaiian Archipelago (after Funk and Wagner 1995): (a) area cladogram predicted on a simple progression rule, where taxa colonize each island in turn as it is formed by the emergence of a volcano from beneath the ocean surface; (b) actual area cladogram for a group of *Drosophila* flies; and (c) actual area cladogram for the endemic plant genus *Hibiscadelphus* (OG = outgroup, K = Kauai, O = Oahu, M = Maui, and H = Hawaii).

land (Hawaii). But groups of organisms rarely follow simple rules, especially when it comes to colonization. Or they might follow the basic blueprint but add their own twists. Figure 6.13b illustrates an area cladogram for a group of fruit flies (*Drosophila* spp.). True to the prediction, the flies inhabited Oahu before they inhabited Maui and Hawaii, but they never inhabited Kauai, and they skipped over Molokai on their way to Maui and Hawaii. The plant genus *Hibiscadelphus* exhibits a somewhat similar pattern (Figure 6.13c), where the ancestral taxa occur on Kauai and the more derived taxa on Hawaii, but none occur on the three middle islands. Further, there were multiple speciation events within the two islands.

Our sample of projectile points from the Southeast is amenable to analysis through area cladograms, although at present the sample is not robust enough to talk about historical interchange and isolation events in all but the broadest of terms. For one thing, we need more specimens of each of the 36 taxa so that we can place greater faith in the geographic distribution of the taxa. Nonetheless, we can scan the data available to determine, even in preliminary fashion, if there are patterns in the geographic distribution of taxa. For this exercise we use the 100,000-tree consensus tree. We picked it based strictly on the fact that it contains one or two orders of magnitude more trees than either of the other two 36-

Figure 6.14. Area cladogram of 36 projectile-point taxa, with state abbreviations replacing taxon names.

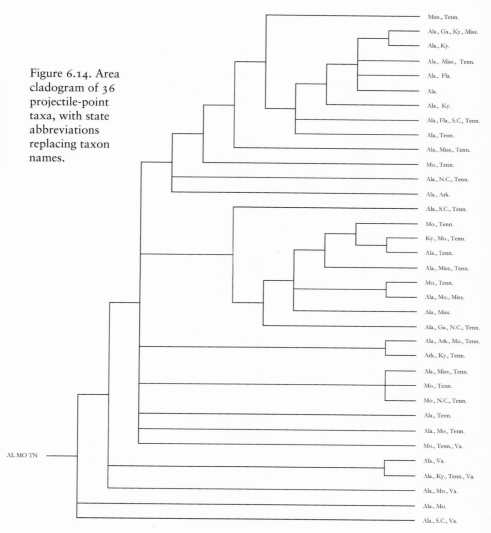

Miss., Tenn.
Ala., Ga., Ky., Miss.
Ala., Ky.
Ala., Miss., Tenn.
Ala., Fla.
Ala.
Ala., Ky.
Ala., Fla., S.C., Tenn.
Ala., Tenn.
Ala., Miss., Tenn.
Mo., Tenn.
Ala., N.C., Tenn.
Ala., Ark.
Ala., S.C., Tenn.
Mo., Tenn.
Ky., Mo., Tenn.
Ala., Tenn.
Ala., Miss., Tenn.
Mo., Tenn.
Ala., Mo., Miss.
Ala., Miss.
Ala., Ga., N.C., Tenn.
Ala., Ark., Mo., Tenn.
Ark., Ky., Tenn.
Ala., Miss., Tenn.
Mo., Tenn.
Mo., N.C., Tenn.
Ala., Tenn.
Ala., Mo., Tenn.
Mo., Tenn., Va.
Ala., Va.
Ala., Ky., Tenn., Va.
Ala., Mo., Va.
Ala., Mo.
Ala., S.C., Va.

AL MO TN

taxon consensus trees does. It should therefore, at least potentially, be a more conservative approximation of the phylogeny.

Figure 6.14 shows the tree with geographic states replacing the taxa. The information is easier to read, however, if we plot the taxa spatially, using branching information from the tree to organize the taxa sequentially in terms of their appearance. But there are caveats in so doing. Phylogenetic trees can provide varying degrees of chronological information—all of it in a relative sense (what came before what)—but we often have to make assumptions as to the precise order of splitting, especially where polytomies are involved. The outgroup in Plate 3, KDR, produced an ancestor to all other ingroup taxa. That ancestor is isomorphic with KUb (Plate 5), meaning that they carry identical character states, but remember that in cladistics ingroup taxa get placed at branch tips, not at nodes. That ancestral taxon also produced an ancestor of all other taxa—an ancestor isomorphic with KUd (Plate 5). That ancestor produced the ancestor of the two-taxon purple clade (KUa + KUe) as well as an ancestor, isomorphic with Kca (Plate 5), of all remaining taxa. But after that, things are not as clear cut. The ancestor that is isomorphic with Kca produced a large polytomy, which includes the ancestors of the blue and red clades and the ancestors of the smaller green and yellow clades.

Within the two larger clades the chronological ordering of taxa is fairly straightforward—chronology here being equated with the order of splitting events—but interclade chronology is not as straightforward. In fact, in and of itself our tree is of no help in resolving chronological differences between the red and blue clades—the topological position of the red and blue clades is moot when it comes to chronology. But all is not lost, with help coming from what at first might appear to be an unlikely source: historical types that routinely are used in the Southeast to partition projectile-point variation. As we hope we have made clear, historical types are in no sense analytically useless entities. They are not well suited for phylogenetic work because of the manner in which they were created, but many of them are excellent *marker types,* akin to *index fossils* in paleontology (O'Brien and Lyman 1999). That is how we are using them here.

Archaeological work in the Southeast (e.g., Anderson et al. 1996; Anderson and Faught 2000) suggests that points placed in types such as Dalton, Quad, Beaver Lake, and Greenbrier postdate Clovis points. Further, several investigators (e.g., Anderson and Faught 2000) have suggested that Cumberland points postdate Clovis and predate Dalton, Quad, Beaver Lake, and Greenbrier. The phylogenetic tree (Plate 3) suggests that this general ordering is more than simply received wisdom. Notice that the ingroup taxa not connected with the large, seven-taxon polytomy—KUb, KY, KUd, and the ancestor of the two-taxon purple clade (KUe + KUa)—all contain specimens that traditionally are placed in the Clovis type (symbolized in the class name with the capital letter "K"). They appear earlier on the tree than any other taxa, consistent with the proposition that Clovis is the earliest point type in the Southeast. Overall morphological aspects of Clovis points carry over into taxa such as Kca, KUo,

Kd, those in the yellow and green clades, and many of the red-clade taxa. Six of the nine taxa in the red clade contain specimens identified in the literature as being Clovis points. Five of the nine taxa (those with a "C" in the class name) contain specimens identified as Cumberland points. One of the two earliest taxa in the clade, KCb, contains both. The overlap between Clovis and Cumberland points in the red clade is not too surprising if Cumberland points were evolving out of Clovis points, which is exactly what we think happened. A little more surprising is the occurrence of Cumberland points in several blue-clade taxa, given the derived nature of many of the taxa in the red and blue clades. Without exception, however, specimens in the blue clade that were referenced in the literature as being "Cumberland" are unfluted, whereas all those in the red clade are morphologically fluted (Bradley 1997).

There are several ways of looking at the chronological relationship between the red and blue clades. First, we could propose that there were two parallel and more or less contemporaneous traditions in the Southeast, perhaps regional traditions, each of which, in typological terms, grew out of a Clovis base. One tradition continued to produce Clovis points, which soon evolved into Cumberland points, whereas the other tradition produced Dalton, Simpson, Suwannee, Quad, Arkabutla, and Beaver Lake points. Second, we could propose that there were two traditions but that, broadly speaking, taxa in the red clade are earlier than many of the blue-clade taxa. This in no way should be taken to mean that *all* taxa in the red clade appeared before those in the blue clade or that they died out before blue-clade taxa appeared. Rather, it means that on average one set of taxa appeared before the other. How long any individual taxon might have lasted is unknown.

At this point it is difficult to judge between the two proposals. What is clear is the separation of the red and blue clades and the derived nature of their immediate roots. The ancestors of both clades went through character-state changes subsequent to their common ancestry (Chapter 7). In the case of the red-clade ancestor (defined as 21223222), both characters IV (constriction ratio) and V (outer tang angle) changed. In the case of the blue-clade ancestor (isomorphic with DUV), only character V changed. Of more significance is what happened to character VII, fluting. In the blue clade, DUV contains fluted specimens, as does CU, a sister taxon to DUV. Those two taxa share that feature with all taxa in the red clade. But *all* other taxa in the blue clade are unfluted. This signifies to us that in typological terms there was an evolution of two traditions in the Southeast

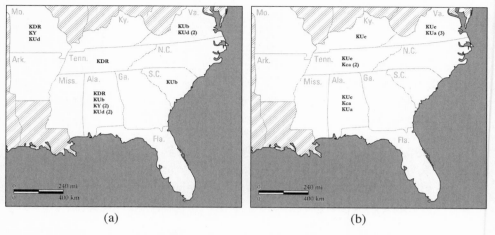

Figure 6.15. Locations (by state) of specimens in (a) KDR, KY, KUb, and KUd and (b) Kca, KUa, and KUe.

arising out of Clovis—fluted Cumberlands in one clade and unfluted Daltons, Quads, and related types in the other. In terms of timing, the split could have occurred around 10,950 RCYBP. We base that date solely on the generally accepted ending date of Clovis in the Southwest (Haynes 1991; Taylor et al. 1996). There is, however, no reason to believe that that same date applies to the Southeast, although we would guess that it is not off by more than 50–100 years on either side.

Given the proposed sequence outlined above, we can examine the geographic distribution of clades and individual taxa. Figure 6.15a shows the distribution of specimens in outgroup KDR, together with those in the first two taxa to split off—KY and KUb—and in KUd, which is isomorphic with the ancestor of all remaining taxa. Figure 6.15b shows the distribution of specimens in what might be the next taxa to split off—Kca (which is isomorphic with its ancestor), KUa, and KUe, the latter two of which are related to KUd through an unnamed ancestor. The two figures show fairly similar distributions of the seven early taxa, one major exception being the presence of three taxa in Missouri in Figure 6.15a and the absence of taxa in Missouri in Figure 6.15b. One significant feature of the combined distributions is that Virginia contains four taxa, the last time that specimens of any taxon appear in that state.

Figure 6.16a shows the distribution of specimens in taxa in the green clade (KDoon + KRus), and Figure 6.16b shows the distribution of specimens in taxa in the yellow clade (KDz + Kg + R). Missouri contains at

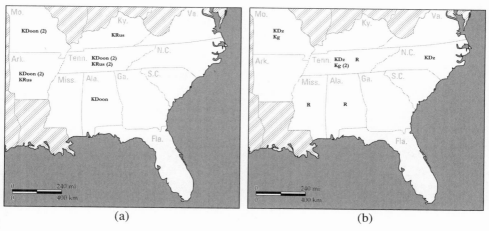

Figure 6.16. Locations (by state) of specimens in (a) KDoon and KRus and (b) KDz, Kg, and R.

least one taxon in both, and Arkansas contains two in Figure 6.16a. There appear to be several differences between Figures 6.15 and 6.16 that may not be driven by sample size. Whereas Alabama is an evolutionary "hot spot" in Figures 6.15a and 6.15b, which show the distribution of the earliest taxa, it contains but a single taxon in Figures 6.16a and 6.16b. The evolution of KDoon and KRus was primarily to the west and north of Alabama, and the evolution of KDz and Kg was in a band from Missouri to North Carolina. Notice the clustering of specimens in Taxon R, which consists solely of specimens in the Redstone type. Taxon R is one of the most highly derived taxa in the entire 36-taxon sample (Chapter 7).

Several taxa in the red clade also exhibit patterns that may not be tied to sample size. Figure 6.17a shows the distribution of specimens in KCb and Kk—perhaps the two earliest taxa in the red clade. The distribution is toward the eastern half of the Southeast. Figure 6.17b shows the distribution of specimens in the subclade Cvv + KC + Kjm + KQj—four of the later, more derived taxa in the red clade. What the distributions tell us about social transmission during the Paleoindian period is open to question, but we could propose that the center of projectile-point experimentation moved west through time. This does not mean that areas to the east (Georgia and the Carolinas) were vacated. It simply means that the evolutionary center had shifted to the west.

Figures 6.18 and 6.19 show the distributions of specimens in taxa in the blue clade, beginning with CU and DUV (Figure 6.18a), continuing

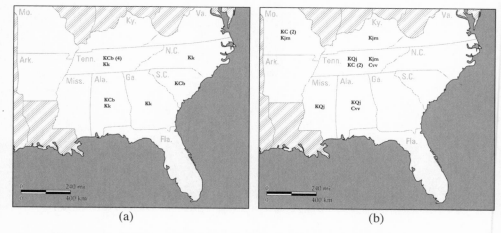

Figure 6.17. Locations (by state) of specimens in (a) KCb and Kk and (b) Cvv, KC, Kjm, and KQj.

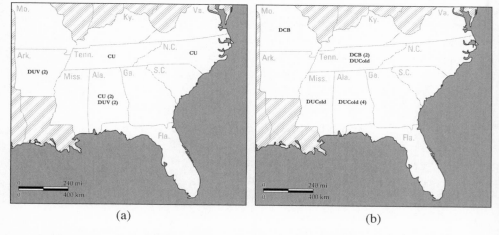

Figure 6.18. Locations (by state) of specimens in (a) CU and DUV and (b) DCB and DUCold.

with DCB and DUCold (Figure 6.18b), then BQDU, DCQUBSuw, and QDb (Figure 6.19a), and ending with the six-taxon clade QC + DQd + DUS + QUDG + QDG + DAQS (Figure 6.19b). The highest concentration of points is in Alabama, but this is more a function of our sampling scheme than anything else. More important is the distribution of individual taxa, not the frequency of occurrence of a specific taxon or which

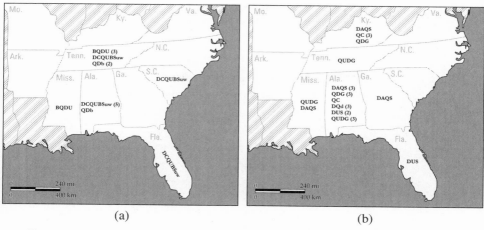

Figure 6.19. Locations (by state) of specimens in (a) BQDU, DCQUBSuw, and QDb and (b) the QC + DQd + DUS + QUDG + QDG + DAQS clade.

state contains the most taxa. Several taxa exhibit distributions that may be independent of sample size—for example, DCB and DUCold (Figure 6.18b), which occur in the western half of the region. Likewise, the presumably slightly later BQDU is found in only two states, Tennessee and Mississippi (Figure 6.19a).

DISCUSSION

Phylogenetic trees derive their topology not only from the taxa used, which in turn are defined by the characters and character states selected, but from the kind of algorithm employed. In other words, it is a long way from character selection to tree construction, with the entire process resting largely on human decision making. How many characters to use? Which characters to use? How to break up continuous characters into states? How many taxa to use? Which search method to use? Which kind of consensus tree to use? No wonder that Niles Eldredge and Michael Novacek (1985:68) made the remark quoted in Chapter 3: "[C]ladistics is no panacea. It is hard to do a good piece of systematics research using cladistics—indeed, harder than ever before. The system is logically much more rigorous, requiring every available item of evidence." We could not agree more with that statement. It is difficult to do good systematics research using cladistics. The mechanics are not difficult. They might be foreign, but they can be mastered. It is the decision making that goes into good cladistics that is the killer.

In this chapter we have explored several issues connected with the decision-making process, including what happens to tree topology when we add and subtract taxa and what happens to topology when we construct consensus trees in the face of conflicting information. One thing that should be obvious is that it is difficult if not impossible to guess beforehand what the effect on a tree of adding or subtracting taxa will be. The only approach that works is trial and error. Does the resulting tree yield more information than the previous one? Is the resolution better than it was previously? If so, then build on the new tree. If not, discard it and try another one.

One measure (among many) of tree support is the recurrence of a topology across a set of trees. That recurrence could be based on the addition or subtraction of taxa, or it could be based on a sample of trees built using the same taxa. We have demonstrated that it was possible to maintain fairly consistent phylogenetic ordering of the original 17 projectile-point taxa by subtracting or adding a few taxa and that this also applied to 100-tree, 10,000-tree, and 100,000-tree consensus trees built using 36 taxa. When the same clades appear across a sample of trees, and they assume the same position on the trees, it is good evidence that we have a reasonable phylogenetic ordering. In the case of the projectile-point taxa, it appears that two large clades can be viewed as separate trajectories that grew out of a Clovis base, one containing fluted points and the other unfluted points.

The phylogenetic ordering can be viewed as an end in itself, or we might apply it to other problems, such as the geographic distribution of clades and the taxa within them. Although the sample of projectile-point taxa is small, there are a few geographic patterns that suggest centers of development for some of the taxa. We can also examine the topological position of individual character states that compose the taxa. Changes in character state create taxonomic differences in the first places—changes that, in the present case study, are related to evolving weaponry in the southeastern United States. To understand something about that evolution requires that we track character-state changes across the tree we have created. We take up that topic in Chapter 7.

STARTING POINTS

For the proposed dating of Paleoindian projectile points from the Southeast, see David Anderson et al. (1996). For one of the best introductions to phylogeography in its many guises, see James Brown and Mark Lomolino's (1998) *Biogeography.* The book covers many more topics than simply phylogeography, but their Chapter 11 is unbeatable in terms of being a jargon-free discussion of some of the ways in which phylogeographical analysis has been used. Another good discussion can be found in Chapter 7 of Daniel Brooks and Deborah McLennan's (1991) *Phylogeny, Ecology, and Behavior: A Research Program in Comparative Biology,* although it assumes much more knowledge of cladistics than Brown and Lomolino's discussion does. For an informative and lively discussion of the growth of phylogeography out of the American Museum of Natural History–style vicariance biogeography (sister groups replacing each other spatially), which itself replaced the earlier idiosyncratic panbiogeography of Leon Croizat, see Chapter 5 of David Hull's (1988b) *Science as a Process: An Evolutionary Account of the Social and Conceptual Development of Science.* Gareth Nelson and Norman Platnick's (1981) *Systematics and Biogeography: Cladistics and Vicariance* is a state-of-the-art treatment of biogeography and phylogeny as it was practiced in the late 1970s. It remains a classic reference.

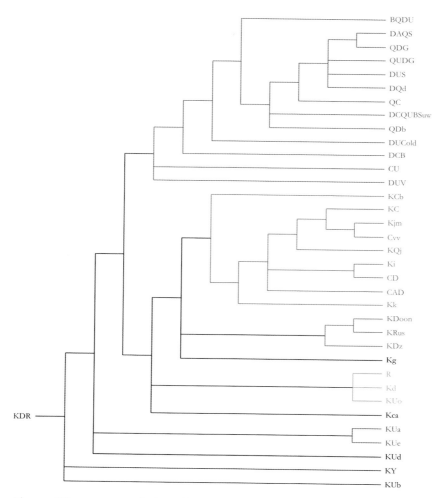

Plate 1. Fifty-percent majority-rule consensus tree of 36 taxa based on 100 trees selected at random from a much larger number of equal-length trees generated by PAUP*'s branch-swapping heuristic search.

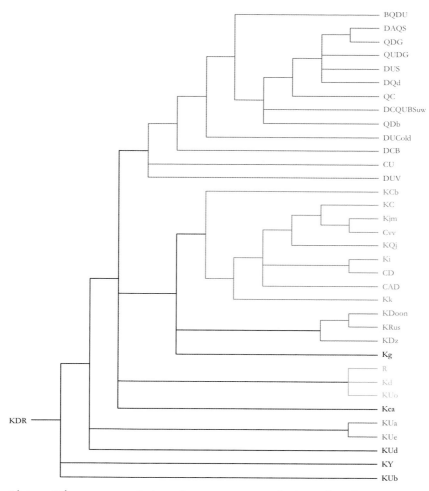

Plate 2. Fifty-percent majority-rule consensus tree of 36 taxa based on 10,000 trees selected at random from a much larger number of equal-length trees generated by PAUP*'s branch-swapping heuristic search.

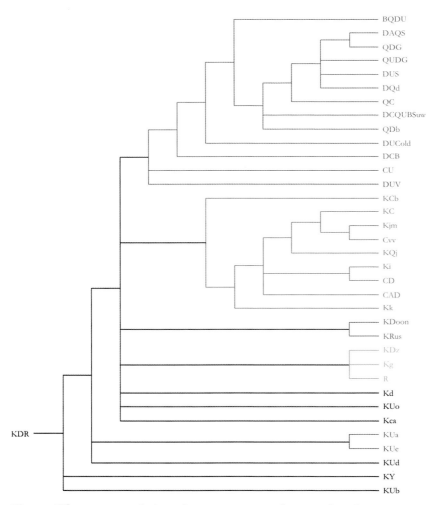

Plate 3. Fifty-percent majority-rule consensus tree of 36 taxa based on 100,000 trees selected at random from a much larger number of equal-length trees generated by PAUP*'s branch-swapping heuristic search.

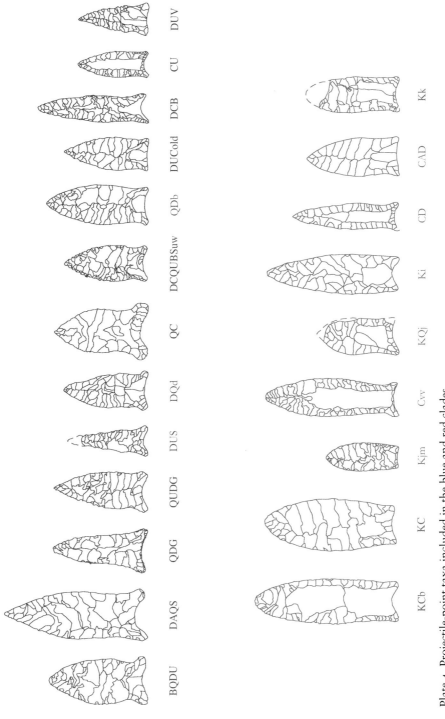

Plate 4. Projectile-point taxa included in the blue and red clades.

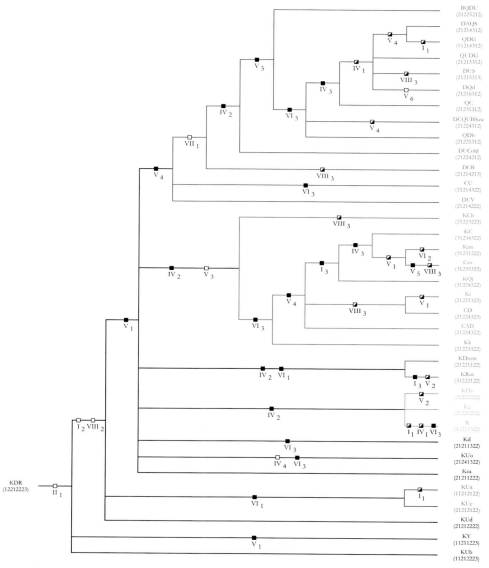

Plate 5. Fifty-percent majority-rule consensus tree of 36 taxa based on 100,000 trees (same tree as shown in Plate 3), with various clades highlighted. Boxes denote changes in character state, Roman numerals denote characters, and subscript numbers denote character states. Open boxes indicate nonhomoplasious changes; shaded boxes indicate parallel or convergent changes (homoplasy); and half-shaded boxes indicate characters that reverted to an ancestral state (homoplasy).

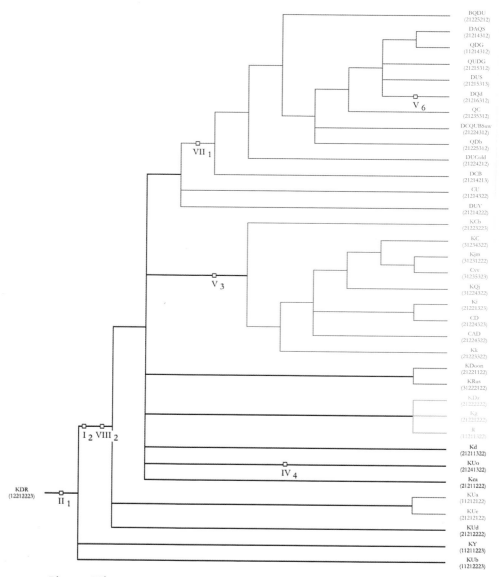

Plate 6. Fifty-percent majority-rule consensus tree of 36 taxa based on 100,000 trees (same tree as shown in Plate 3), with various clades highlighted. Nonhomoplasious changes in character state are denoted by boxes, Roman numerals denote characters, and subscript numbers denote character states.

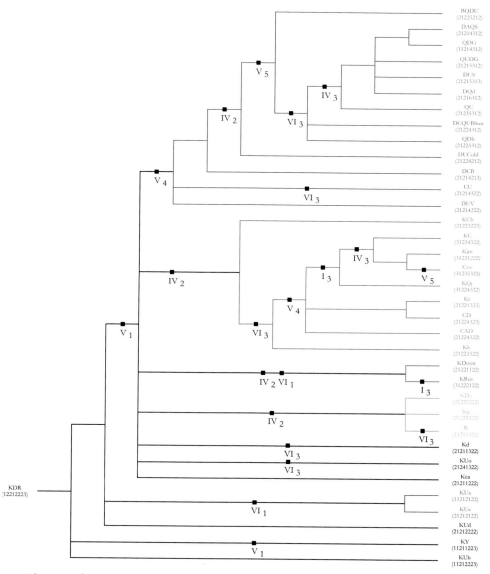

Plate 7. Fifty-percent majority-rule consensus tree of 36 taxa based on 100,000 trees (same tree as shown in Plate 3), with various clades highlighted. Boxes denote parallel or convergent changes in character state (homoplasy), Roman numerals denote characters, and subscript numbers denote character states.

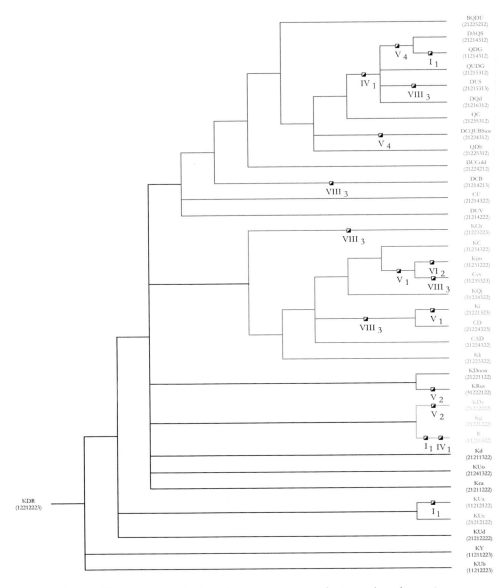

Plate 8. Fifty-percent majority-rule consensus tree of 36 taxa based on 100,000 trees (same tree as shown in Plate 3), with various clades highlighted. Boxes denote character-state reversals (homoplasy), Roman numerals denote characters, and subscript numbers denote character states.

SEVEN

Character-State Tracking

Michael J. O'Brien, Daniel S. Glover, and R. Lee Lyman

GENERATING information about the geographic distribution of clades and taxa can be an important component of phylogenetic analysis, but so, too, is tracking changes in character states that create the taxa. Taxa are the actual units of evolution, but it is the character-state changes that are the accounting units of the evolutionary process. If one goal of our phylogenetic analysis of projectile points is to understand the evolutionary development of weaponry in the southeastern United States, then tracking character-state changes takes on added significance. We view character-state changes in cultural phenomena no differently than we do similar changes in organisms—that is, as the products of evolutionary processes such as selection and drift. Both are tied intricately to transmission. We know that cultural transmission provides a mechanism for character-state change that far outstrips anything in the purely biological realm. Phylogenetic trees do not in and of themselves allow us to assess rates of change (tempo), but they do allow us to assess the direction and perhaps the magnitude of change (pattern). If we map the distribution of character states and character-state changes across a phylogenetic tree, what kinds of patterns do we see? With respect to southeastern projectile points, do the patterns tell us anything about evolving weapon-delivery systems? As noted in Chapter 5, to address this issue fully will require considerable experimentation by lithic technologists possessing not only the ability to reverse engineer projectile points but also a deep understanding of such things as mechanical constraints and performance characteristics. In the meantime, we can at least make note of changes that occurred at different points along the phylogenetic tree.

Although we in no way view our paradigmatic classes as some loose equivalent of biological species or other organismic taxa, there should be little doubt that, like species, classes have distributions not only in time but in space. With species—more specifically, populations that together make up a species—genetic transmission between individual organisms is the glue that holds the species together (Figure 4.3). With projectile-point taxa, cultural transmission is the glue. Adhesives, however, have their spatial and temporal limits. Those limits define what we refer to as the *problem of scale* (O'Brien and Lyman 2000). At one scale, units look homogeneous, but within what appears to be a relatively homogeneous unit, such as a species, change is occurring continually. We know that change is more apt to occur at the edges of a species's distribution than at its core because of the chances of transmission with individuals outside the unit. We also know that reproduction between organisms, even at the core of a distribution, produces less than 100 percent fidelity—meaning that two organisms do not produce clones. Nonfidelity in terms of offspring is one source of the fuel that drives natural selection, and it also produces drift, which further spurs speciation. But what about fidelity at the edges? To us, one of the interesting issues in phylogenetic analysis is how character states change at the edges of their distributions. Is the pattern of change different than it is at the core? This applies equally to organismic and cultural taxa.

In the discussion that follows we examine a few of the temporal and spatial trends in character-state changes in southeastern United States projectile points, using the phylogenetic tree shown in Plate 3. This is the 100,000-tree majority-rule consensus tree constructed using 36 taxa. Our discussion of character-state change is divided into four parts: phylogenetic changes and how they compare to changes on the 17-taxon tree; nonhomoplasious changes; homoplasious changes; and character-state changes in terms of projectile-point design.

OVERVIEW OF CHANGES

Plate 5 shows the aggregate character-state changes for the 36 taxa. There are 46 changes; hence the tree has a length of 46. As in Figure 6.1, two numbers are shown for each change: a Roman numeral referring to the character (Table 5.2) and a subscript number indicating the evolved state of that character (moving from left to right across the tree). Character-state changes are of three kinds, also as in Figure 6.1. Open boxes indicate nonhomoplasious changes; shaded boxes indicate parallelism or convergence (homoplasy)—that is, a change to a particular character state occurs more than once within the entire set; and half-shaded boxes indicate characters that at some point in the tree revert to an ancestral state (homoplasy).

As with the 17-taxon sample (Figure 6.1), the first three characters to change were II (base shape), I (location of maximum blade width), and VIII (length/width ratio), although the timing of the changes differed slightly. For the 17-taxon sample the outgroup, KDR, produced an offspring that changed in terms of both characters II and VIII; for the 36-taxon sample only character II changed. For both samples the changes were identical in terms of derived character states. The next significant change in both samples—"significant" defined as affecting a large clade—was in character V (outer tang angle). In the 17-taxon sample character V changed from state 2 (88°–92°) to state 4 (66°–80°), whereas in the 36-taxon sample character V changed to state 1 (93°–115°). After that, the two trees differ markedly in topology, although there are still some similarities. For example, a change in character VII (fluting) from state 2 (fluting present) to state 1 (fluting absent) defines a 7-taxon clade on the 17-taxon tree and an 11-taxon clade on the 36-taxon tree.

There are several similarities between the two trees in terms of character stability. For both trees, character III (basal-indentation ratio) exists in a single state (2 [shallow]) and hence could have been excluded. It is a parsimony-uninformative character. In both trees characters II (base shape) and VII (fluting) change only once. Character II is interesting because its only change occurs at the basal node. The outgroup, KDR, has a normal-curve base (state 2), whereas all the other taxa have arc-shaped bases (state 1). Character instability in the 17-taxon tree is paralleled in the 36-taxon tree, but the percentage of change contributed by the character changes differs. The differences, however, are about what one would expect if the changes were making more or less equal contributions to the two trees. Table 7.1 compares character-state changes between the two trees. Notice that character I, with its four changes, contributes 18 percent (4/22) of the total change in the 17-taxon tree, whereas it contributes only 13 percent (6/46) of the total change in the 36-taxon tree. Likewise, character VIII contributes 9 percent (2/22) of the total change in the 17-taxon tree and 13 percent (6/46) of the total change in the 36-taxon tree—another insignificant difference. Even characters IV, V, and VI do not differ markedly between the two trees.

TABLE 7.1. Number of Character-State Changes on the 17-Taxon and
36–Taxon Trees

Character	17-Taxon Tree	36-Taxon Tree
I	4	6
II	1	1
III	0	0
IV	4	9
V	5	13
VI	5	10
VII	1	1
VIII	2	6
Total	22	46

What do these data tell us? They perhaps indicate that our sample of 36 taxa fairly well represents the dynamics of projectile-point change in the southeastern United States. Increasing the number of taxa would yield different topological arrangements, but the overall nature of the change, particularly in terms of the contribution of various characters, probably would not differ significantly from what is represented in Table 7.1. We can't be sure what the data are telling us, however, because we used two different samples of taxa, although the larger one encompasses the smaller one. This means that we have to exercise caution when we assess intertree similarities in such things as overall character stability. We are on far safer ground treating the similarities on a character-by-character basis than we are in making generalizations about the entire character assemblage.

NONHOMOPLASIOUS CHANGES

Plate 6 shows the character-state changes that occur only once in the 36-taxon consensus tree. With the exception of character VI (and ignoring character III, which remains constant across taxa), each character is represented at least once; character V is represented twice. With the exception of V_6 (outer tang angle $\leq 50°$), which occurs only in Taxon DQd, the changes occur early in the tree. The change from II_2 to II_1 (from a normal-curve base to an arc-shaped basal concavity) defines all taxa except the outgroup. The change from I_1 to I_2 (a shift in the location of maximum blade width from the proximal quarter to the secondmost proximal quarter), which occurs just above the basal node, defines a large number of taxa, including all but one taxon (QDG) in the blue clade, five taxa in the red clade, and eight other taxa. The change from VIII₃ to VIII₂ (a change in length/width ratio from 3.00–3.99 to 2.00–2.99), which also occurs just above the basal node, similarly defines a large number of taxa. The change from VII₂ (fluted) to VII₁ (unfluted) defines 11 of the 13 taxa in the blue clade. All other taxa are defined by the ancestral state. Character state V₃ appears fairly early in the tree, but character V is so unstable (see below) that V₃ shows up in only two of the nine taxa in the red clade.

HOMOPLASIOUS CHANGES

As one might expect, the amount of homoplasy increases between the 17-taxon tree and the 36-taxon consensus tree. Whereas the former has six instances of parallelism and three reversals, the latter has eight cases of parallelism and 17 reversals. In terms of parallelism, the same four characters (I, IV, V, and VI) are affected in both trees. The highest incidence of parallelism in the 36-taxon tree occurs in character VI, where VI₃ (blunt tang tip) arose six times (Plate 7). The only other case of multi-parallelism is in character IV, where IV₂ (constriction ratio of 0.90–0.99) arose four times. Character state VI₃ defines 19 of the 36 taxa, and character state IV₂ defines 14 taxa.

What do we make of the high incidence of parallelism or convergence in some of the characters? In biology parallelism is viewed as a result of common developmental history among taxa (Chapter 3). That is, related organisms, perhaps because of anatomical constraints, independently evolve the same character state. It is similar to convergence, in which organisms, because of environmental constraints, independently evolve the same character state. Here we cannot distinguish between parallelism and convergence, so we treat them together. Regardless, both are forms of homoplasy, and they yield the same result: suppression of the phylogenetic signal given off by apomorphic characters. Homoplasy is a fact of life, irrespective of whether the taxa under examination are organismic or cultural. And, with respect to cultural phenomena, perhaps some homoplasious characters are "real." Given that there are mechanical constraints in making such things as projectile points—as well as various desired performance characteristics—there is no a priori reason to suppose that a certain character state could not have arisen in separate projectile-point lineages that had a common ancestor at some distant point in the past but had long been separated when the character state arose in each of them. With respect to character VI (tang-tip shape), independent experimentation might have led to the conclusion that for certain mechanical/performance reasons blunt tang tips (state 3) were preferable to round tang tips (state 2). There is no a priori reason to suspect that this change occurred only once in the Southeast. Plate 5 suggests that unless the phylogenetic ordering is completely wrong—and we know that this is not true—then indeed the change from round to blunt tang tips *did* occur more than once.

With respect to the second kind of homoplasy, character-state reversal, single reversals affecting characters I, VI, and VIII occur on the 17-taxon tree. Those same characters are affected on the 36-taxon tree, but so, too, are characters IV and V. In fact, the largest number of reversals (six) occurs in character V. These consist of two reversals each of character states 1, 2, and 4 (Plate 8). What do we make of the high incidence of reversal in some of the characters? As pointed out in Chapter 3, we tend to view this kind of homoplasy more as a classification problem (O'Brien et al. 2001, 2002), meaning that rarely if ever will precisely the same character state reemerge after it disappears, especially if it involves complex structures. This is true with respect to organisms, but with respect to cultural phenomena, perhaps some characters will occasionally revert to previous states. Again, the production of projectile points is a highly constrained process, meaning there are only so many ways of manufacturing a useful tool. (Stone-tool manufacture, being a subtractive process, is much more constrained than pottery manufacture, which is an additive process. You can always add clay to a vessel if you remove too much during manufacture. You cannot add flakes back on to a half-finished projectile point.) Humans can pick and choose among a wide range of options when manufacturing projectile points, but the choice of options is in large part predetermined. Social learning creates a deep pool of stored variants, any of which conceivably can be selected at any time for a given purpose. Thus it is not surprising to see reversals crop up here and there in a cultural phylogeny.

Are some of the reversals we see in Plate 8 a sign that the variation is neutral? In other words, (1) Are there several different methods of doing something, all of which are acceptable from the standpoints of engineering and function? and (2) Do manufacturers randomly select from among those variants? Those are difficult questions to answer. Notice that all five reversals in character VIII are to state 3. In fact, character VIII occurs in only two states—the ancestral condition, state 3 (length/width ratio of 3.00–3.99), and derived state 2 (length/width ratio of 2.00–2.99). Thus a reversal in character VIII can be of only one form: ancestral $\rightarrow$ derived

TABLE 7.2. Character States Represented in the 36 Taxa

Character	States					
I	1[a]	1	1			
II	1	1	3	4	—[b]	6
III	1	1	3	4		
IV	1	1	1	1	5	6
V	1	1	1	1	1	1
VI	1	1	1			
VII	1	1				
VIII	1	1	1	4	5	6

[a] States underlined are represented in the 36 taxa. States not underlined are represented in other taxa from the Southeast not included in the 36-taxon sample. The complete array of character states defines southeastern projectile-point morphospace.
[b] Character-state II_5 does not exist in the larger sample.

—→ ancestral. Therefore we would have to concede that based on the phylogenetic tree it is impossible to determine whether reversals in character VIII are directly related to function or are a result of drift.

What about other character-state reversals, especially the six reversals in character V? Character V is interesting because the reversals are limited to three of six possible states (Table 5.2). All the various states of the eight characters help define southeastern projectile-point morphospace, but not all states are represented in the 36 taxa. Thus it is illogical to talk about how significant reversals might be if we do not know the boundaries of the sampled morphospace. Table 7.2 shows the character states (in bold) represented in the 36 taxa. Note that all six states of character V are represented, which makes it additionally significant that the reversals confine themselves to only three of the six states. We explore that significance below, where we summarize some of the step-by-step changes in individual character states.

CHARACTER-STATE CHANGES AND PROJECTILE-POINT DESIGN

As pointed out in Chapter 5, our choice of characters was based on expectations as to which parts of a projectile point would change the most over time as a result of transmission and thus create a strong phylogenetic signal. Obvious choices are characters that define the hafting element, which previous observation and research indicate changed significantly during the Paleoindian period. Accordingly, we selected five characters—II (base shape), III (degree of indentation), V (the angle formed by a tang relative to the long axis of a specimen), VI (tang-tip shape), and VII (presence or absence of fluting)—to monitor changes in the proximal end of projectile points. Hafting itself is technological in nature, which translates into morphology, but we know that some if not all morphological characters are related directly to performance in carrying out specific functions. Form and function are independent, but they are also correlated. This means that changes in form can lead to or result from changes in intended function. It is up to the analyst to determine, through experimental means, how and why certain engineering designs were superior to others and the effects these changes might have had on the bearers of the traits—in this case humans who depended on hunting as one means of making a living.

We believe that some of the engineering changes that the blades of Paleoindian points went through—such as the addition of bevels to what typically are referred to as Dalton points (Figure 5.4)—were tied to the appearance of the atlatl, or throwing stick, as an addition to the hunting arsenal (O'Brien and Wood 1998). Equally important, but for different functional reasons, was the reengineering of the proximal ends of projectile points to coincide with improvements made in fastening the points to bone or wooden foreshafts or main shafts (see Hughes 1998 and Lyman, O'Brien, and Hayes 1998 for discussions and references on Paleoindian-period hafting). In an interesting and highly readable discussion of projectile-point hafting, Robert Musil (1988) tackled some of the important issues related to engineering design. Whether or not all his conclusions are correct is immaterial. What is significant is that he laid out in clear language the kind of study needed to explain projectile-point lineages.

Musil titled his paper "Functional Efficiency and Technological Change: A Hafting Tradition Model for Prehistoric North America," which clearly ties technological change—the ways in which points were hafted—to functional efficiency—how well the products of technology performed their intended tasks. Musil's emphasis on functional efficiency as the independent variable in the hafting equation differs significantly from approaches that have emphasized such things as ethnicity (different groups made different kinds of points), chronology (different points were made at different times), and economy (different points were used for different game). His explanation for the observed temporal sequence of projectile-point form in the Plains and Southwest—from what he termed the fluted/lanceolate tradition to the stemmed tradition and finally to the notched tradition—is that

> each new hafting tradition and change in hafting technology rendered each successive design a more effective killing implement, allowed for more efficient reuse of broken projectile points and better prevented damage to the wooden shaft. These changes in point form usually involved the haft element, the feature of projectile points on which most type designations are based. In this view, then, the variety of forms represented among projectile points is not seen as derivative of the migration of peoples or as the result of different adaptations to a specific environment or hunting economy, but as technological change in one element of material culture—the projectile point. In this view, successive changes in projectile point form were made and adopted because they were functionally more efficient than designs of the preceding tradition. (Musil 1988:373)

Projectile points, Musil (1988:373) noted, are only one component of a complete weapon, the others being the shaft (which itself might be a compound piece, especially if it is a spear or dart), the method of binding, and the hafting technique. He distinguished among four dimensions of the design of a projectile point that allow it both to function as a piercing implement and to conserve the wooden shaft and the projectile point. These are a sharp point, which permits the projectile to pierce an animal's hide; sharp blade edges to open a sizable wound; a haft-element design that absorbs the force of the impact without splitting the shaft; and an overall haft design that minimizes damage to the projectile point and allows it to be reworked in case of breakage (see also Howard 1995). Musil identified three major hafting traditions for the Plains and Southwest, one of which he divided into two subtraditions. The fluted/lanceolate tradition includes points assigned to the Clovis, Folsom, Goshen, Midland, and Plainview types. The stemmed-point tradition consists of a parallel-sided subtradition of lanceolate points with shoulders and a stem added (including Alberta, Scottsbluff/Eden, Hardin barbed, and Windust types) and a contracting-sided subtradition of lanceolate points with thicker cross sections and stems (including Agate Basin, Hell Gap, and Haskett types). The third tradition, containing notched points, occurred after the period of interest here.

Musil found the fluted/lanceolate tradition, which contains the oldest points, to be the least efficient of the three major hafting traditions

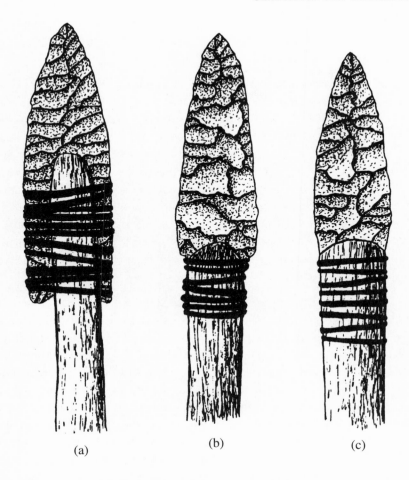

Figure 7.1. Proposed techniques for hafting a projectile point to a shaft or fore-shaft: (a) split-shaft hafting of a parallel-edge lanceolate point; (b) split-shaft hafting of a stemmed point; and (c) socketed hafting of a contracting-sided point (after Musil 1988).

because a considerable amount of lithic material is discarded when a point breaks, less opportunity exists for remanufacture, and there is greater possibility of shaft damage. Based on the width of their bases, Clovis, Folsom, and related lanceolate points, including Dalton points, apparently were hafted in split-end shafts (Figure 7.1a). On impact, most of the force travels through the projectile point—which, in the case of specimens that normally would be placed in those point types, already have thin bases—down into the wooden shaft. George Frison and Larry Todd (1986:123–128) noted, as did Musil (1988:376), that this arrangement invites damage to the shaft by further splitting it (see also Howard 1995). Also, based on the number of lanceolate-point bases that have been found with transverse breaks at the haft area, the method of hafting these specimens would have done little to extend the use-life of the points.

Within the stemmed tradition, points belonging to the parallel-sided subtradition appear to have been more suited to a split shaft (Figure 7.1b), whereas points belonging to the contracting-sided tradition, because of their thick cross sections and rounded stem, probably were placed in socketed foreshafts (Figure 7.1c). Musil (1988:379) noted that "resting of the shoulders [of the parallel-sided points] on the bindings may have reduced the impact at the base/shaft juncture, thus reducing shaft damage more than in nonshouldered lanceolate points while also removing the bindings from the blade edges." If the purpose of the blade is to create a large wound, then the more blade that is exposed, the deeper the dart/spear point will penetrate (Howard 1995). The advantages of a socketed contracting-sided design over a fluted/lanceolate design are twofold: "the contracting of the stem removes the bindings from the blade edges, thus increasing the penetrating ability of the point; and . . . the long, thick contracting stem is in contact with the wooden shaft over the entire stem length and the blunt thick base absorbs more of the force of the thrust" (Musil 1988:379).

In terms of historical relationships, some stratigraphic associations in the Plains (such as at the Hell Gap site in Wyoming), coupled with radiocarbon dates, suggest that Agate Basin contracting-sided points are older than Hell Gap contracting-sided points (10,500–10,000 RCYBP for Agate Basin and 10,000–9500 RCYBP for Hell Gap [Agenbroad 1978; Frison 1991]), and some associations suggest that they were contemporary forms but that Hell Gap outlasted Agate Basin. It appears that both types of points are older than parallel-sided Alberta, Scottsbluff, and Eden points, which span portions of the period 9500–8500 RCYBP (Frison 1991), although Musil (1988:382) suggested the possibility that parallel-sided points may have overlapped temporally with contracting-sided points on the Plains (Agenbroad 1978).

Regardless of whether there was a sequence that led from fluted/lanceolate points to contracting-sided points and then to parallel-sided points—or from the earlier fluted/lanceolate points to two parallel traditions of point manufacture—they eventually were supplanted by notched points, which, as Musil (1988:382) noted, contained features that "rendered all of the earlier hafting techniques obsolete." Although this perhaps is a bit of an overstatement, the fact that notching persisted from ca. 9500 RCYBP until historical times forces us to admit that it was "the most efficient hafting technique to have developed in prehistoric North America" (Musil 1988:382).

Two of Musil's traditions—fluted/lanceolate and stemmed—occurred in the southeastern United States, although the timing of the traditions is not as secure as it is for the Plains and Southwest. Phylogenetic ordering can help us sort out the appearance of various traditions and subtraditions, as can radiometric dates, but phylogenetic methods such as cladistics give us something that radiometric dating cannot: an evolutionary history of changes to projectile points. It could be argued that a rigorous radiometric-dating program will allow us to pinpoint the dates of occurrence of slight changes, and this is true. But the only kind of evolutionary sequence it will permit us to construct is an anagenetic one, whereas we cannot help but believe that the vast majority of evolution—both biological and cultural—is cladogenetic, albeit with some reticulation present. No amount of radiometric dating will help us construct a cladogenetic evolutionary pattern. It will help us identify the timing of events, but not their relations to one another.

PHYLOGENETIC TRENDS IN PROJECTILE-POINT DESIGN

In broad terms, Musil's fluted/lanceolate tradition consists of all taxa not included in the blue clade (Plate 5) plus CU and DUV. All 25 taxa (including KDR, the outgroup) contain specimens that are fluted (character state VII₂) and lanceolate. In typological terms those taxa contain specimens that fall into commonly named types such as Clovis, Redstone, Cumberland, Doon, Russellville, and Yazoo. The other 11 taxa are unfluted and contain a variety of stem forms, primarily expanding stems. In typological terms those taxa contain specimens that fall into commonly named types such as Quad, Beaver Lake, Dalton, Coldwater, Suwannee, and Simpson. The separation between the two groups of taxa is not absolute in terms of Musil's traditions, but it is evident that the phylogenetic signal is strong enough to create fairly robust groupings based on the characters used.

Five ancestral taxa stand between the outgroup and the ancestor that produced the 11-taxon stemmed clade. In summary terms, a change in base shape (character II) from a normal curve (II$_2$) to an arc-shaped curve (II$_1$) separates the outgroup (KDR) from all other taxa. Once that character changed, it remained constant throughout both traditions. KDR produced an ancestor (isomorphic with KUb) of three taxa that cannot be distinguished as to their relative age: KUb, KY, and the ancestor of all other taxa (Plate 5). KY went through one character-state change, and the ancestor to all other taxa went through two. Those two derived character states affected the location of maximum blade width (proximal quarter → secondmost proximal quarter) and the length/width ratio (3.00–3.99 → 2.00–2.99). This produced an ancestor (isomorphic with KUd) that was wider toward the middle and slightly stouter than its own ancestor. That derived state of the maximum blade width would subsequently show up in 25 of the possible 33 taxa (excluding KDR [the outgroup] and KUb and KY, both of which had already split off). The nearest competitor of character state I$_2$ in terms of frequency is I$_3$ (maximum blade width in the secondmost distal quarter), which occurs in only five taxa, four of them (KC + Kjm + Cvv + KQj) in the same small clade. Three taxa—KUa, R, and QDG—reverted to the ancestral state. Based on this pattern, it is safe to conclude that, like characters II and III, character I was highly conservative in nature. For the most part, once point manufacturers lowered the maximum point of the blade from the proximal quarter to the secondmost proximal quarter, they stuck with it. Thus it became an analogue of what in biology is referred to as a *Bauplan,* or basic organizational plan (Chapter 3).

The next multitaxa change was a change in character V (outer tang angle) from the ancestral state V$_2$ (88°–92°) to derived state V$_1$ (93°–115°). The resulting ancestor (isomorphic with Kca) produced all remaining taxa, including the direct ancestors of the red and blue clades. As noted previously, character V is very unstable, contributing 14 of the 46 character-state changes to the phylogenetic tree. It is so unstable that the two immediate ancestral taxa of the blue and red clades themselves changed states, the blue-clade ancestor to V$_4$ (66°–80°) and the red-clade ancestor to V$_3$ (81°–87°). Both large clades contain four more changes each to character V. As we suggested earlier, it appears at this point that from a technofunctional standpoint the outer tang angle was free to vary all over the map, but this is true only to a point. The scale of the map is important. At the scale of all 35 ingroup taxa, the state of character V appears to be rather hit or miss. But at the scale of individual clades, the options are pared down considerably. In the blue clade, seven of the 13 taxa exhibit V_4, five exhibit V_5, and one exhibits V_6. No other character states are represented. Seventeen of the remaining 22 ingroup taxa, however, exhibit V_1, V_2, or V_3. Thus, although there is freedom for character V to vary, the choices have been pared considerably, depending on the scale of analysis. As it turns out, V_4 to V_6 define the blue clade, whereas V_1 to V_3, with a few exceptions, define all other taxa. This is not surprising, given that V_1 to V_3 include outer tang angles of 81°–115° and thus help define a lanceolate form, whereas V_4 to V_6 include outer tang angles of ≤ 50°–80°, thus creating small "feet," which are characteristic of the stemmed points. The fact that the states for character V are not random across the phylogenetic tree strongly suggests that outer tang angle is a functional character.

Fluting (character VII) is another character that shows consistent patterning across the tree. Fluting (VII_2) is the ancestral state and occurs in 24 of the ingroup taxa. Once fluting disappears, it never reappears in the other 11 ingroup taxa. Thus there is clear separation between the clade containing the upper 11 taxa shown in Plate 5 (almost all of the blue clade) and all other taxa. That 11-taxon clade is supported by V_4 to V_6.

DISCUSSION

Like their biological counterparts, archaeological taxa are complex, which is brought home forcefully by our projectile-point classes. Even with as few as eight characters, each with only a handful of states, the taxa are slow to give up their phylogenetic relationships. One reason for this undoubtedly lies in the nature of cultural phenomena and the kind of transmission process that creates them. If nothing else, we should by now have a deep appreciation for the difficulties involved in creating cultural phylogenies, with the numerous instances of parallelism, convergence, and trait reversal that act to damp the underlying phylogenetic signal. And yet, with all the noise that a tree such as the one in Plate 5 exhibits, there is still enough of a signal that a reasonable tree can be produced. We say "reasonable" because the general topology of the tree is supported by external lines of evidence (Chapter 6).

The strength of the phylogenetic signal rests in the character states and their pattern of change. Looking at Plate 6, which shows the distribution of nonhomoplasious character-state changes, we might wonder how only six "clean" derived character states could ever be enough to create a reasonably accurate tree. If these changes were all that went into the analysis, such doubt would be well placed, but they are not the only changes.

PAUP* and other similar programs use all changes, including instances of homoplasy, to create a tree. Some instances of homoplasy are worse than others. If an instance of homoplasy is the result of parallelism or convergence, it still counts as a derived character state. There will be multiple instances of that state, but we can increase our overall number of derived states by one. The correct way to look at this is to say that at least there is change, without which no computer program can create a phylogeny. If we had to dichotomize kinds of homoplasy in terms of the degree to which they disrupt our phylogenetic efforts, we could say that parallelism and convergence are "better" kinds of homoplasy and that character-state reversals are "worse." True, reversals are instances of change, but they tend to confuse phylogenetic ordering much more than the other kinds of homoplasy do. The degree of confusion is tied directly to their location on the tree. Luckily, in the case examined here, reversals tend to occur out toward the branch tips, where they do not significantly disrupt the clades. Notice, for example, that 13 of the 17 reversals in the 36-taxon tree (Plate 8) occur in terminal taxa as opposed to ancestral taxa.

In technological terms, the character-state distribution for the southeastern projectile-point taxa creates an image parallel in several key respects to what Musil (1988) painted for the Plains and Southeast: two separate traditions built around how points were hafted to foreshafts. The earlier tradition consisted of a basic fluted/lanceolate *Bauplan*. Through time, and probably with regional variation, that basic form was tinkered with (moving it in one direction, then another) before it spun off a new *Bauplan*, the backbone of the stemmed/unfluted tradition.

With a much larger sample of specimens, it might be profitable to examine the geographic distribution of individual character states and possible linkages of states from different characters. We explored these avenues using the available sample, with unspectacular results. We could find no significant geographic clustering of character states, although we think that a larger sample would show that some clustering occurs. Not only sample size but also the number of character-state reversals and the geographic scale at which we are operating work against the detection of patterning. On the one hand, the scale should make it possible to detect some regional patterns, but on the other hand, the sample requirements are so severe that it might be impossible to meet them. Broad-scale analysis does not have such steep data requirements. For example, Julie Morrow and Toby Morrow (1999), adopting a continental scale, were able to show conclusively that mean lateral-indentation-index values—a measure of

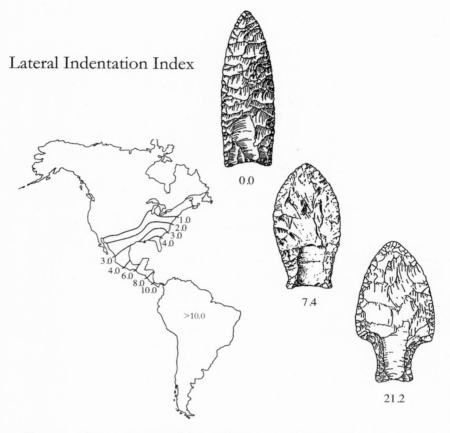

Lateral Indentation Index

Figure 7.2. Geographic variation in mean lateral-indentation-index values, used as a measure of "fishtailness" of projectile points (after Morrow and Morrow 1999). The three forms illustrate various index values.

"fishtailness"—increased monotonically from North America into South America for early fluted points (Figure 7.2). Radiocarbon dates on a whole support the notion that South American fluted points are slightly later than Clovis points in western North America. Morrow and Morrow (1999:227) conclude that instead of invoking adaptive convergence as the cause of the pattern, "we choose to interpret the changes . . . to be the result of stylistic drift . . . a process inherent in the ongoing translation of cultural practices from one generation to another under specific geographic and historical circumstances." They are using the term "drift" in the way that historical linguists do, not in the way that biologists do (equaling neutrality).

It is difficult to argue with either the findings or the explanation for the change in lateral-indentation-index values. Importantly, a mere 449 points were used in the analysis. Compare that number, which spans two continents, to our 141 specimens from one small part of one continent. Morrow and Morrow (1999) were able to see significant geographical patterns in their data in terms of character-state change, but we were not. This tells us that in order to see such patterning, we are going to need a very large sample. Even in that case, though, the area might be small enough that the tempo and mode of cultural transmission during the Paleoindian period swamp any geographical patterning except at the level of taxa.

STARTING POINTS

We highly recommend Robert Musil's (1988) discussion of hafting traditions for Paleoindian projectile points on the Plains because he links them directly to functional efficiency and technological change—two important considerations in any evolutionary study. We also recommend what could be considered a companion piece, by Alan Bryan (1988), on the stemmed and fluted traditions in the Great Basin. George Frison and Larry Todd's (1986) *The Colby Mammoth Site: Taphonomy and Archaeology of a Clovis Kill in Northern Wyoming* presents useful information on the manufacture and use of Clovis points. On the dating of different Paleoindian traditions on the Plains, see Frison et al. (1996), R. E. Taylor et al. (1996), and Stuart Fiedel (1999). For more information on fishtail points from South America, see Gustavo Politis (1991).

PART III

For the Future

EIGHT

Concluding Remarks

G IVEN that the Linnaean taxonomic system enjoys such a dominant position in biology and is so pervasive in the popular and scientific literature, it is little wonder that a call for its abandonment as a source of phylogenetic information from some quarters (e.g., Cantino 2000; Cantino et al. 1999; de Queiroz and Gauthier 1994; Ereshefsky 2001) has evoked such a vocal reaction (e.g., Brummitt 1997; Dominguez and Wheeler 1997). The general sentiment among supporters of the taxonomy seems to be "if it ain't broke, don't fix it" (Benton 2000:647). Understandably, many biologists and paleobiologists are committed to keeping Linnaeus's system around. It offers an immediate remedy to a host of thorny problems, not the least of which is that it provides a framework for placing look-alike organisms together and separating them from organisms that differ in looks. For years after Linnaeus first proposed the system, naturalists were content for the most part simply to pigeonhole the various flora and fauna they encountered, secure in knowing that the system at least gave them a means to communicate objectively with other naturalists. When someone provided a sufficiently specific description of a particular kind of plant or animal, it was unlikely that this kind would be confused with any other kind. Organizing various kinds under more-encompassing kinds was a separate and potentially more difficult issue, but here, too, degree of specificity could save the day. All you needed to do was to extract more-general characteristics from the specific kinds to create a higher-order kind, and so on. Linnaeus started out with five levels of hierarchical units, but naturalists saw that they could easily expand that number as needed to account for the burgeoning number of kinds that were being identified.

No one seriously questions the utility of Linnaeus's system as a convenient means of quickly conveying information about taxa in terms of their morphological similarities and differences. Even the most ardent supporter of PhyloCode—the proposed replacement for the Linnaean taxonomic system—undoubtedly on occasion refers to a taxon by its binomial designation. At issue are not morphological similarities and differences but what they tell us about phylogenetic relationships. That issue began taking shape immediately upon publication of Darwin's *On the Origin of Species* in 1859. Darwin's contribution to biological taxonomy was that he provided not only a causal mechanism for why there were kinds in the first place—a mechanism that did not rely on divine providence—but also an explanation for why various kinds were often so similar to one another. They were similar because they were related phylogenetically.

Darwin's thesis in its basic form was not antithetical to the prevailing biological view of the mid-nineteenth century. Naturalists assumed that relatedness provided the glue that bound kinds together hierarchically, but the means of creating differences among the kinds was missing. Natural selection provided that means. With the appearance of *On the Origin of Species,* naturalists now had a system that provided not only a hierarchical organization of taxa but also a means of reading the phylogenetic history of those taxa. This dual-purpose system was carried essentially wholesale into the Modern Synthesis of the 1940s, with its emphasis on species recognition, and became formalized in the paradigm that was the major product of the synthesis, evolutionary taxonomy. The architects of the synthesis—Ernst Mayr in particular—showed how critical classification was to the success of evolutionary biology. Classification began with identifying species; without proper regard for such things as isolating mechanisms, which keep separate populations of a species from merging, "real" species could not be recognized. The process of hierarchical classification was difficult enough (polyphyletic taxa, for example, had to be identified and discarded) without having to worry about whether the basic building blocks—species—had been identified correctly. Mayr and other taxonomists were clear: Mistakes made at the crucial step of species recognition rendered all subsequent discussions, including those regarding phylogenetic relationships, suspect.

Evolutionary taxonomists might have questioned specific phylogenetic schemes, but there was no question that if taxa were arranged correctly the Linnaean taxonomic system produced a phylogenetic ordering. In fact, Mayr (1942) thought that the only taxa that should ever be admitted to the taxonomy were those based solely on phylogenetic relationship. This meant that the taxonomist should strive for monophyly and avoid paraphyly and polyphyly. This might have been Mayr's goal in 1942, but he and other evolutionary taxonomists soon came to the conclusion that monophyly was next to impossible to achieve up and down the Linnaean taxonomy. Thus they began to relax their standard of monophyly, believing that no one should become a slave to it, especially if it meant discarding taxonomic groupings that had historical prominence. Trained taxonomists could always deal with a little nonmonophyletic noise if behavioral, developmental, and morphological similarities between taxa strongly supported their concatenation.

There was no denying the pull that morphological similarity had on the classification of taxa. It seemed patently obvious that morphological similarity and phylogeny were so intertwined that with careful analysis one could almost serve as a proxy for the other. This is not to say that mistakes could not be made, but that is where "careful analysis" came in. To an untrained naturalist, a North American wolf looks so similar to a Tasmanian wolf that they must surely belong in closely related groups. But a trained naturalist knows that the former is a placental mammal and the latter a marsupial mammal. The trained naturalist understands the difference between homologous and analogous characters and how convergence can trip us up, as in the case of the two kinds of wolves. Once analogous characters are discarded, the remainder of the characters can be used to place specimens in their natural kinds, to relate those kinds to other kinds at greater and lesser degrees of specificity, and then to read their phylogenetic history. German entomologist Willi Hennig, however, had other ideas.

To Hennig, it made no sense to treat the Linnaean biological taxonomy as a phylogenetic chronicle because of the undifferentiated nature of the homologous characters used to create it. He distinguished between ancestral characters (those inherited from distant ancestors) and derived characters (those inherited from an immediate ancestor) and focused solely on the latter as his phylogenetic measurement units. This meant that recency of common ancestry became a criterion of ranking individual taxa—an approach that represented a break with classical evolutionary taxonomy and its focus on ancestral characters in order to ascertain phylogenetic affinity. To Hennig, ancestral characters might be useful in assessing general affinity among taxa, but they are of little use in assessing specific relationships among taxa. Hennig further distanced himself from then-current evolutionary taxonomy by claiming, as Mayr himself had done early in the Modern Synthesis, that phylogeny should be the *only* criterion used in taxonomic classification. In other words, whereas evolutionary taxonomy kept an eye on both evolutionary pattern *and* process, Hennig's method—what later became known as cladistics—excluded process from consideration.

In our opinion, the differences between the way evolutionary taxonomy views taxonomic relationships and the way cladistics views them are ontologically irreconcilable. There may be some holdouts in biology who optimistically believe that the two *can* be reconciled (see Wiley 1981 for an early attempt); but the majority of taxonomists and cladists agree they cannot (e.g., de Queiroz and Gauthier 1992, 1994; Ereshefsky 2001; Mayr 1995). Evolutionary taxonomy is built on the recognition of species. The only kind of classification to which cladistics can contribute is one based on the creation of monophyletic groups, not on the recognition of specific, real taxa. Mayr (1997) refers derisively to this systematic as "cladification." Cladistics creates taxa not on the basis of similarity but on the basis of proximity of descent as defined by the possession of shared derived characters (synapomorphies). In cladistic analysis there are no known ancestors to any descendant taxa, nor will we ever be able to identify one. That is why a rooted cladogram—a phylogenetic tree—is an abstraction of reality and not "real" history. This, however, is its strength, not a weakness. Conversely, evolutionary taxonomy cannot exist without "real" as opposed to hypothetical ancestors. Given the vast number of species that must have existed from the beginning of time and the relatively few that have left fossil records, it is not very likely that actual ancestors have even been found (Hull 1979). Yet evolutionary taxonomists continue to insist that ancestor recognition is integral to the creation of groups—an insistence derived from the perspective that the groups themselves are real.

If we are interested in producing phylogenetic orderings, cladistics is clearly superior to evolutionary taxonomy because relatedness is the only thing that it tracks. Although it renders pattern visible, cladistics in and of itself says nothing about process (Brower 2000). A phylogenetic tree is simply a statement of relationship among taxa. In its most basic form, a tree states that two taxa resemble each other more than either does a third taxon. It does not tell us why two taxa came to resemble each other or why those two taxa and not some other taxon came to resemble each other. That is why cladistics is a nontautological procedure. We can even go a step further and explain the pattern using evolutionary theory (descent with modification), but nothing forces us to do so. Again, there is no tautology built in. Instead, we have a nice, linear operation that goes pattern recognition —→ historical relationship —→ theory-based explanation.

If we are interested in pattern and process simultaneously, then evolutionary taxonomy is an option. But in such cases we have to acknowledge that paraphyly will be present to some unknown degree. As a result, evolutionary taxonomy cannot *on average* produce as correct a phylogenetic result as cladistics can. Evolutionary taxonomists try to work around this conundrum by moving back and forth between the two methods, first constructing evolutionary taxonomies and then testing derived groupings for monophyly (Mayr 1969; Mayr and Ashlock 1991). Only in those cases where exactly the same characters, and only those characters, are used to define taxa will there be a correspondence between taxa defined cladistically and those defined by evolutionary taxonomy. It should go without saying that all those characters would be putative synapomorphies. We have no way of knowing the percentage of taxa in the Linnaean system that have been defined strictly or largely on the basis of synapomorphies, although we suspect it is quite high (see Eldredge and Cracraft 1980; Wiley 1981). The key question is, how would we know that only synapomorphies were used, given that such characters are for the most part indistinguishable from the total set of homologous characters used in evolutionary taxonomy? The answer is that we would not know. In fact, there is no way of ever knowing that only shared derived characters are being used until we subject taxa to a cladistical analysis.

CLADISTICS IN ARCHAEOLOGY

Americanist archaeology has also seen its share of evolutionary taxonomic schema, although the debates that so characterize the development of evolutionary biology have been largely absent. Early attempts to apply biological taxonomy to cultural phenomena—that by Harold Colton and Lyndon Hargrave (1937) being a prime example—were met with disdain. To critics such as J. O. Brew (1946), there are no such things as phylogenetic relationships among artifacts. Brew was correct that genes do not produce artifacts, but he apparently never considered that tool forms are modeled on preexisting tool forms. Tools certainly do not breed, but tool makers do breed, and they do transmit information to other tool makers, irrespective of whether those other tool makers are lineal descendants. Transmission creates what archaeologists have long referred to as tool traditions. Given this perspective, things found in the archaeological record are appropriate for phylogenetic analysis.

There are no "natural" taxa in archaeology, except as they are nested on a phylogenetic tree. Therefore, we create them. We have advocated using paradigmatic classification to do this, although we can envision other methods that would work. The critical issue is that the taxa are both unique in terms of their defining character states and comparable in terms of rank. If either of these criteria is unmet, then the taxa, regardless of how they are constructed, are not useful for phylogenetic purposes. Anyone using archaeological taxa faces many of the same problems a biologist does. By definition, our archaeological taxa—classes—cannot be polyphyletic (or paraphyletic) because they consist only of themselves. In a strict sense, a biological species is not polyphyletic either. It is only at higher ranks that taxa can be polyphyletic, just as they can be paraphyletic. Paradigmatic classes as used here are all of equal rank, although they can be turned into a nested set of less-inclusive, lower-level entities within more-inclusive, higher-level entities (Figure 5.7). It is this "nestability" that makes paradigmatic classes appropriate units for cladistics. Ideally, paradigmatic classification guarantees monophyly at greater levels of inclusivity; but so, too, does the Linnaean taxonomy. This means simply that there is one true phylogeny, and in theory either paradigmatic classification or the Linnaean taxonomic system is capable of representing it. It is the less-than-ideal situations that cause problems, irrespective of whether the taxa are species or classes.

Paradigmatic classes are superior to normative archaeological constructs such as traditional projectile-point types, which are jumbles of polyphyletic and paraphyletic taxa. Note the number of times that the names "Clovis" and "Cumberland" in Table 6.1 appear alongside other type names for specimens in the same class—specimens that are identical in terms of eight morphological characters. A traditionalist might argue that we left out the most important "Clovis" or "Cumberland" character—that one essential trait that allows an expert to identify a specimen as a Clovis or Cumberland—but we would counter by saying that classification should not depend on one's "expert" ability. Moreover, we have seen plenty of instances where experts are sharply divided over the placement of a projectile point in one type or another. If Mayr and other evolutionary taxonomists are correct that phylogenetic ordering in biology depends on our ability to eradicate mistakes in basic taxonomic identity, then the same applies in archaeology.

Lest we be misinterpreted, we point out, as we have elsewhere (e.g., O'Brien and Lyman 2000, 2002a), that traditional archaeological units are not worthless constructs, despite the fact that they are extensionally derived. Type names and the like serve useful purposes, primarily as shorthand devices to facilitate communication. If you report that you found a Clovis point, that term immediately imparts useful information. We know that the specimen is lanceolate, has a concave base and a ground hafting element, and does not have notches. You would not, in normal speech, say, "I found a specimen of class 21211222." No one, including us, would know what you were talking about. Types convey information, and that in and of itself makes them useful, but only at a particular level. Rarely if ever will that level be at or near what a historical science demands.

Archaeology is just that: a historical science. Its sole claim to unique status within the human sciences is its access to portions of past phenotypes—something that ethnographers, sociologists, psychologists, historians, and others who study humans do not have. Only archaeologists have access to the entire time span of culture, however it is defined. Historical questions are the most obvious ones archaeologists can ask, although this is hardly a strong warrant for asking them (Eldredge 1989). We believe, however, that archaeologists should ask historical questions not only because they have access to data that provide a direct test of historical hypotheses but also because answers to historical questions are critical to gaining a complete understanding of cultural manifestations occupying particular positions in time and space. Thus we take as archaeology's most important goals the writing and explaining of the history of human phenotypes (Lyman and O'Brien 1998; O'Brien and Lyman 2000; O'Brien et al. 1998). From an evolutionary perspective, to "*explain* means to identify a mechanism that causes evolution and to demonstrate the consequences of its operation" (Bell 1997:1). From a Darwinian perspective, two of the more important mechanisms are selection and transmission, and the causes precede the consequence of the working of the mechanisms. Selection and transmission are historical mechanisms; they operate every moment, at some times more strongly or more rapidly than at others, creating the varying tempo of evolutionary change over time.

To understand the operation of historical processes means not only that we have the units upon which the processes act in correct historical sequence but that we have them in a sequence that is correct from the standpoint of heredity. With only the first we might be able to demonstrate that change has taken place, but we are left with the unanswered question: "Change in what?" Many of our efforts in the past few years (e.g., Lyman and O'Brien 2000b, 2001a; O'Brien and Lyman 1999, 2000; O'Brien et al. 2001, 2002) have been directed toward developing methods to demonstrate that we indeed are examining heritable continuity and not simply historical continuity. We view cladistics as the most important of the various methods. Cladistics is not a method that depends on genetic continuity as a basis for reconstructing phylogeny. Rather, it depends solely on heritable continuity, irrespective of the mode of transmission. Proper use of cladistics in archaeology recognizes biological (genetic) and cultural transmission, both of which play a role in the evolution of such things as tool traditions. Artifacts are not replicators; rather, they are what gets replicated (Lyman and O'Brien 1998). Ideas in the minds of individual people are the replicators that are transmitted; social learning is both the transmission mechanism and the source of variation that results from transmission errors and recombination. If there is phenotypic change, and if over time enough variation is generated, cladistics might indeed be able to detect the phylogenetic signal. If so, we should be able to create phylogenetic orderings that have testable implications.

Cladistics might be the most important of the various methods available for documenting and examining heritable continuity, but it is also the most intellectually demanding. We wish it were as simple as the command that the King gave to the White Rabbit during the trial to determine who stole the Queen's tarts. Before reading a piece of evidence, the White Rabbit asks, "Where shall I begin, please your Majesty?" "Begin at the beginning," the King says gravely, "and go on till you come to the end: then stop." Unfortunately, there is no end in cladistics. You cannot simply stop, unless you get a perfect tree—one that contains no instances of homoplasy. If that ever happens, consider yourself to be living in Wonderland.[1] More likely, you will get a suboptimal solution filled with instances of convergence, parallelism, and character-state reversals. At this point it might seem that phenetics, or even evolutionary taxonomy, is a whole lot simpler, but don't despair. See where the tree or trees you produced might lead. Use the trees to produce historical narratives about intertaxa relationships and notice what kind of patterning there is. See if that allows

---

1. With apologies to John Avise (2000), whose review of Quentin Wheeler and Rudolf Meier's (2000) *Species Concepts and Phylogenetic Theory* is titled "Cladists in Wonderland."

you to pick up on clues about how to improve the trees, which will then provide more narratives, which might provide more clues, and so on. Cladistics is an iterative process, and it demands patience and persistence. But in our view what it can tell us about evolutionary history is well worth the effort.

Glossary

adaptation: Any attribute (*character* or *character state*) of an organism that allows it to survive and reproduce in a given environment better than if it lacked the attribute. As the term is used here, the attribute must have been shaped by *selection* for the function it presently serves.

affinity: The particular relation of analytical interest between formally similar specimens within a *group* or between groups of formally dissimilar specimens.

aggregative hierarchy: A set of nested *units* (*taxa*), with each higher level encompassing greater inclusiveness than the ones below. Compare with *positional structure*.

allele: Alternate state of a gene and the *genotypic* equivalent of a *character state*. For example, if there were a single gene for hair color, one allele would code for red, whereas another allele would code for brown.

anagenesis: Linear evolution of a *character*, a combination of characters, or a *taxon* within a *lineage* without diversification, or branching, of the lineage. Compare with *cladogenesis* and *reticulate evolution*.

analogue: An identical *character/character state* shared by a set of *taxa* that is not present in their common ancestor. Analogues can arise through *convergence, parallelism,* or *reversal*. Compare with *homologue;* see also *homoplasy*.

analogy: See *analogue*.

ancestral character state: The original condition of a *character* before it changes. Also referred to as a "primitive character state" and as a "plesiomorphy." Compare with *derived character state;* see also *symplesiomorphy*.

apomorphy: See *derived character state*.

archetype: A model phenomenon constructed from the sum of morphological *characters* shared by a *group* of phenomena.

autapomorphy: A *character state* that one *taxon* exhibits that a *sister taxon* does not. The taxon exhibiting the character state developed it after the two taxa diverged.

auxiliary principle: Principle formulated by Willi Hennig that says that *homology* should always be assumed in the absence of contrary evidence. See also *parsimony*.

Bauplan: A basic structural design with a long history. For example, we can speak of a bilaterally symmetrical *Bauplan,* a vertebrate *Bauplan,* a mammalian *Bauplan,* or a quadrupedal *Bauplan.*

branch: A line on a *cladogram* that connects two *nodes* or a node and a *terminal taxon.*

branch-and-bound: An exact method of *cladogram* construction, meaning that the method guarantees to find the shortest cladogram(s). It works by checking only those cladograms that are likely to be shorter than the shortest cladogram already found. As soon as it finds a cladogram of shorter length, that cladogram becomes the one against which to compare new cladograms. Once the method finds a partial solution that looks promising, it continues building in that direction until it finds a shorter cladogram or decides it is moving toward a longer cladogram and abandons that search vector. Compare with *branch swapping.*

branch swapping: A heuristic method of *cladogram* construction, meaning that although the program searches for the shortest cladogram(s), there is no guarantee that it will find one. In local swapping, adjacent branches of a tree are systematically swapped until a shorter length is found. The routine continues swapping branches until no shorter trees are found (or until the operator terminates the search). In global swapping, the program slices the trees into subtrees and then rearranges the various subtrees into new trees and calculates their length. Compare with *branch-and-bound.*

character: A set of mutually exclusive alternative attributes, or *character states.* For example, character 1 might be base shape, which contains an infinitely expandable set of mutually exclusive character states; character 2 might be notch angle, again with an infinitely expandable set of character states; and so on.

character argumentation: See *outgroup comparison.*

character state: One of the expressions of a *character,* such as hair color, and the phenotypic equivalent of an *allele.* Red, brown, and blond are alternate states of the character "hair color."

character-state polarity: The temporal order of appearance of one character state relative to another. See also *ancestral character state, derived character state, symplesiomorphy,* and *synapomorphy.*

clade: A complete set of *taxa* descended from a common ancestor, plus that ancestor. Also known as a "monophyletic group." Compare with *paraphyletic group* and *polyphyletic group.*

cladistics: A system of phylogenetic analysis that classifies things on the basis of the sequence by which they diverged from a common ancestor. Time is irrelevant except in a relative sense, and only derived *characters/character states,* termed "apomorphies," are used to classify things.

cladogenesis: The branching and diversification of *lineages* during *evolution.* It involves the multiplication of *taxa* within a lineage. Compare with *anagenesis* and *reticulate evolution.*

cladogram: A branching diagram specifying hierarchical relationships among *taxa* based solely on derived *characters/character states,* termed "apomorphies." Cladograms are often confused with *phylogenetic trees,* but the latter carry connotations of ancestry and descent, whereas the former do not. When rooted, cladograms become phylogenetic trees. Compare with *phenogram.*

class: An *ideational unit* that has been defined intensionally in terms of its *character states;* the definition specifies the necessary and sufficient conditions—*significata*—that must be displayed by a specimen in order for it to be considered a member of the class. Unlike a *group,* which has a location in space and time, a class has a distribution in space and time.

classification: The creation of new *units* and the modification and revision of old units by stipulating the necessary and sufficient conditions—*significata*—that something must exhibit to qualify for membership within a particular unit.

consensus tree: A *phylogenetic tree* that combines information from several alternative trees according to a predetermined algorithm. There are numerous kinds of consensus trees, including strict, semistrict, and majority-rule.

consistency index (CI): A measure of the amount of *homoplasy* in a *cladogram.* The index ranges from zero (complete homoplasy) to 1.0 (no homoplasy) and is calculated by dividing the number of *characters* in a data matrix by the number of characters on the resulting cladogram.

contingency: An event that is in part predicated on what comes before it. Thus we say that whatever happens at a particular point in time is contingent on everything that led up to that point; those previous points conditioned the outcome at the future point.

convergence: A case of an identical *character state* arising in two unrelated *taxa* as a result of similar adaptive paths. Convergence is one kind of *homoplasy*. See also *analogue, parallelism,* and *reversal.*

deme: A local population of a *species.*

denotata: The empirical members of a *class.*

derived character state: The secondary (or later) condition of a *character.* If, for example, the character "number of toes" started out at five and later changed to four, "four-toed" would be the derived character state. Also referred to as "apomorphy." Compare with *ancestral character state;* see also *synapomorphy.*

differentia: See *significata.*

diffusion: The movement of a culture trait from one culture to another by whatever means. See also *transmission.*

Dollo's Law: Principle stating that rarely if ever will precisely the same *character state* reemerge after it disappears, especially if it involves complex structures. Also known as the Law of Phylogenetic Irreversibility.

drift: Random changes in the relative frequency of *character states* in a population resulting from the vagaries of *transmission.* In biology it is typically defined as intergenerational sampling error of the available *alleles.* Compare with *selection* and *sorting.*

empirical unit: An analytical *unit* that has a physical existence, as opposed to an *ideational unit.*

epistemology: The branch of philosophy that examines the origin and nature of knowledge. Compare with *ontology.*

essentialism: A metaphysic that presumes the existence of discoverable, discrete kinds of things. Membership within a kind is based on a shared essence among all things placed in that kind. Compare with *materialism.*

evolution: In a broad sense, the generation of entities that vary in terms of *character states* relative to their ancestors and of changes in their proportional representation over time.

evolutionary taxonomy: *Classification* of organisms according to their phylogenetic relationships and their subsequent evolutionary divergence.

extensional definition: A definition that establishes the necessary and sufficient conditions for membership in a *unit.* The conditions are derived by enumerating selected *character states* of the members placed in a previously constructed set as opposed to being imposed on specimens to derive a set. Compare with *intensional definition.*

frequency seriation: A technique for ordering collections of presumably historical *types* such that each type has a continuous distribution and a unimodal frequency distribution. The ordering is based on relative frequencies of types and is inferred to be chronological.

function: Usually a term synonymous with "use." In evolutionary archaeology the term has a restricted meaning and refers to the *adaptational* aspects of an object or organism. Compare with *style.*

genotype: The set of genes that an organism possesses.

grade: See *paraphyletic group.*

group: A phenomenological *unit* comprising empirical things. Groups can be derived from *intensional* classification or from *extensional* clustering approaches. As opposed to a *class,* which has a distribution in space and time, a group has a location in space and time.

heredity: The result of *transmission* of information, whether in the form of genes or ideas, from one organism to another.

heritable continuity: A geneticlike connection between things, produced by *transmission,* that results in an unbroken sequential ordering of those things along a temporal continuum. *Sequences* are based on *overlapping.* Compare with *historical continuity;* see also *frequency seriation* and *occurrence seriation.*

historical continuity: A sequential ordering of things based on their similarity and assumed to reflect the passage of time. *Heritable continuity* may be the implicit basis for the ordering, in which case *overlapping* is the principle of ordering, or it may be an inference derived from observed overlapping. Failure to explicitly distinguish between heritable continuity and historical continuity results in this awkward situation in archaeology. Compare with *sequence.*

homologue: A similar *character/character state* shared by a set of *taxa* that is present in their common ancestor. Compare with *analogue.*

homology: See *homologue.*

homoplasy: *Character states* that are not *homologous;* or more precisely, character states that, based on the evidence at hand, cannot be shown to be homologous. Homoplasy can result from any of three situations: parallel development of identical character states in unrelated *taxa* (*parallelism*); *convergence* upon the same state by unrelated taxa; and character-state *reversal.* See also *analogue* and *Dollo's Law.*

hybrid: An individual created by mating between unlike forms.

ideational unit: A conceptual *unit* that does not have an empirical existence, as opposed to an *empirical unit*. Ideational units can be either theoretical units—the kind most important in evolutionary archaeology—or descriptional units.

index fossil: See *marker type*.

ingroup taxa: The groups being examined in a phylogenetic analysis.

intensional definition: A definition that establishes the necessary and sufficient conditions for membership in a *unit*. The conditions are imposed on empirical specimens in order to sort them into sets as opposed to being extracted from previously constructed sets. Compare with *extensional definition*.

interactor: An entity that directly interacts as a unified whole with its environment in such a manner that it is differentially replicated over time as a result of its adaptedness (an example would be a mammal's skin, endoskeleton, circulatory system, and so on). Compare with *replicator*. See also *function* and *style*.

lineage: A temporal line of direct descent from a particular ancestor or ancestral group owing its existence to the *heredity* between ancestors and descendants produced by *transmission*. Compare with *tradition*.

Linnaean taxonomic system: A hierarchical arrangement of nested sets of *taxa* such that less-inclusive, lower-rank taxa are included in more-inclusive, higher-rank taxa. By the late nineteenth century Linnaean taxonomy was widely viewed as evidence of evolutionary descent with modification. Also known as "Linnaean biological taxonomy."

marker type: An *ideational unit* used to denote a particular time period—the briefer the better—within a particular area. It allows the temporal correlation of geographically separate units; its function is the same as that of an "index fossil."

materialism: A metaphysic that holds that phenomena cannot exist as discrete kinds because they are constantly in the process of becoming something else. Compare with *essentialism*.

meme: A particle of information that is held in an individual's memory and that is capable of being copied to another individual's memory.

mode: Patterns and processes of *evolution*. *Anagenesis* is an evolutionary mode, as are *cladogenesis* and *reticulate evolution*. Compare with *tempo*.

Modern Synthesis: Term coined by Julian Huxley (1942) to highlight the reconciliation of Darwin's notion of natural *selection* with the empirical evidence of genetics that occurred in the late 1930s and early 1940s. The product of that union often is referred to as neo-Darwinism.

monophyletic group: See *clade*.

morphological classification: See *typological classification*.

morphospace: Multidimensional space encompassing the range of morphological variation of a specific set of *taxa*.

multistate transformation series: The changes that a *character* with more than one state goes through. If there are only two changes—from an *ancestral character state* to one *derived character state*—it is called a binary transformation series. See also *character-state polarity*, *ordered transformation series*, and *unordered transformation series*.

node: A point on a *cladogram* where three or more *branches* intersect.

numerical taxonomy: See *phenetics*.

occurrence seriation: A technique for ordering collections of presumably historical *types* such that each type has a continuous distribution. The ordering is based on the presence or absence of the types in the collections and is inferred to be chronological.

ontogenetic: Pertaining to the growth and development, or life history, of a thing.

ontology: The branch of philosophy that deals with existence. Compare with *epistemology*.

operational taxonomic unit: The lowest-level taxonomic *unit* employed in a given *phenetic* study.

ordered transformation series: A series of transformations in which *character states* are ordered based on some principle. If a *character* changes from one state to an adjacent state (in either direction), it counts as one step. If it changes to a nonadjacent state, the number of skipped states is added to that one step to arrive at a total number of steps. Compare with *unordered transformation series*.

orthogenesis: Long-discredited proposition that a vaguely defined nonphysical force propels *evolution* in a predetermined direction until a perfect structure is formed.

outgroup: A *taxon* that diverged from a set of taxa prior to the point at which those taxa diverged from each other.

outgroup comparison: The use of an *outgroup* (or outgroups) to identify *ancestral* and *derived character states* within a set of *ingroup taxa* (the logic being that the ancestral state will be found in the outgroup but not in the other, more closely related ingroup taxa).

overlapping: The occurrence of a kind of phenomenon in multiple contiguous time periods. Multiple instances of overlapping serve to connect sets of material from different periods, such as in *seriation.* Overlapping often serves as part of the basis for inferring *heritable continuity* between sets of material ordered chronologically.

paradigmatic classification: A nonhierarchical *classification* procedure in which *classes* are created by the intersection of *character states.* Compare with *taxonomic classification.*

parallelism: A case of an identical *character state* arising in two distantly related *taxa* as a result of common developmental histories that channel a *character* in a certain direction. Parallelism is one kind of *homoplasy.* See also *convergence* and *reversal.*

paraphyletic group: A *taxon* that includes some but not all descendants of a common ancestor. Gorillas, chimpanzees, and orangutans form a paraphyletic group because humans are excluded. Compare with *clade* and *polyphyletic group.*

parsimony: The scientific principle of choosing from among competing hypotheses the one that explains the data most simply. Applying this to *cladistics,* it is more parsimonious to make as few ad hoc phylogenetic hypotheses as possible. See also *auxiliary principle.*

pattern cladism: A school of thought in cladistics that holds that the only thing that matters is *synapomorphy* patterns, meaning that the process that created the pattern is irrelevant. Compare with *process cladism.*

performance standards: A set of measurable criteria used to gauge how poorly or how well something functions.

persistence: The generic process resulting in what came to be known in archaeology as a *tradition.* See also *stasis.*

phenetics: A kind of *classification* system based solely on *phenotypic* similarity of the *taxa* in question. As opposed to *cladistics* and *evolutionary taxonomy,* phenetics makes no distinction among different kinds of phenotypic *characters.*

phenogram: A branching diagram showing relations among *taxa* that is based on *phenotypic* similarities among the taxa, regardless of whether the similarities are *homologous* or *analogous.* Compare with *cladogram* and *phylogram.*

phenon: A sample of *phenotypically* similar specimens.

phenotype: Properties of an organism created by the *genotype* interacting with the environment.

phyletic seriation: Ordering of objects based on similarity in appearance and inferred to be chronological. For example, ceramic vessels could be ordered based on suspected change in form or decoration.

phylogenetic systematics: See *cladistics*.

phylogenetic tree: An arrangement of *taxa* based on *synapomorphies* and showing patterns of descent. Compare with *cladogram*.

phylogeny: A reconstruction of historical patterns and relationships among a set of *taxa*.

phylogeography: The examination of geographic distributions of *clades* and the *taxa* in them.

phylogram: A branching diagram that shows both the branching points and the degrees of subsequent divergence of *taxa*. This is a result of the fact that two classificatory criteria—formal (*phenotypic*) similarity and shared ancestry—are included in the classification. Compare with *cladogram* and *phenogram*.

plesiomorphy: See *ancestral character state*.

polarity: See *character-state polarity*.

polarized transformation series: A series of *character states* where the relative apomorphic (*derived*) and plesiomorphic (*ancestral*) states are known.

polyphyletic group: A set of *taxa* comprising members derived from more than one ancestral taxon. Compare with *clade* and *paraphyletic group*.

polythetic: Comprising multiple *characters*.

polytomy: Three or more *taxa* that cannot be differentiated in terms of a dichotomous split.

positional structure: An arrangement of *units* based strictly on priority of appearance. Compare with *aggregative hierarchy*.

primitive character state: See *ancestral character state*.

process cladism: A school of thought in *cladistics* that holds that a *phylogenetic* pattern can be explained through the invocation of a process—Darwinian evolution (descent with modification). Compare with *pattern cladism*.

replicative success: Term coined by Robert Leonard and Tom Jones (1987) to denote the differential persistence of the traits of organisms from one generation to the next. It implies neither a mode of trait *transmission* nor that a selective advantage is attained by an organism as a result of trait transmission and retention.

replicator: An entity that passes on its structure directly in replication—for example, genes. Compare with *interactor*.

retention index (RI): A measure of the fit of *characters* to a *cladogram* (the ratio of apparent *synapomorphy* to actual synapomorphy). It is calculated by subtracting the number of characters on a cladogram from the maximum number of steps in the data matrix. That value is then divided by the maximum number of steps in the matrix minus the number of characters in the matrix.

reticulate evolution: A mode of evolution characterized by the branching and merging of lineages. Compare with *anagenesis* and *cladogenesis*.

reversal: A kind of *homoplasy* resulting from a change in a *character* back to its former *state*. See also *convergence* and *parallelism*.

scale: A particular degree of inclusiveness or rank. For example, one scale of analysis might be at the level of a *character* of a discrete object (e.g., the temper in a pot), a second scale at the level of a discrete object (e.g., the pot itself), and a third at the level of a set of discrete objects (e.g., an assemblage of pots).

selection: Process by which certain forms in a population that are better adapted to a particular environment increase in proportion to less well-adapted forms. Compare with *drift*; see also *sorting*.

sequence: A temporal ordering of things. It may be based on chronological data independent of the things or based on an assumption of *historical continuity* between the things. An inference of *heritable continuity* might be derived from a sequence, but not all sequences measure heritable continuity.

seriation: The arrangement of a set of things in order on the basis of some logical principle other than superposition. The order is inferred to be chronological and is based on intrinsic properties of the *units* being ordered rather than on extrinsic properties such as the geographic or geological positions of the things. The seriation method has several techniques housed within it, including *frequency seriation, occurrence seriation,* and *phyletic seriation*.

shared ancestral character: See *symplesiomorphy*.

shared derived character: See *synapomorphy*.

significata: The necessary and sufficient conditions that must be displayed by a specimen in order for it to be considered a member of a *class*. Also referred to as "differentia."

sister taxa: Two or more *taxa* sharing an immediate common ancestor. This means that they are more closely related to each other than any of them is to any other taxon.

somatic: Bodily, such as somatic *characters* (e.g., hair color) and *character states* (e.g., red hair).

sorting: A general description of differential representation of traits in succeeding generations. Used by itself it contains no statement about cause. *Selection* and *drift* are two sorting mechanisms.

species: A basic *taxonomic* category in which organisms are placed. A biological species is a *group* of populations, the members of which actually or potentially interbreed with one another under natural conditions. A paleobiological species is a group of fossil organisms, each member of which more resembles the other members of that group *phenotypically* than it does a member of another group. It is assumed that phenotypically similar fossil organisms classified as members of the same species actually or could have interbred.

stasis: A state of static balance or equilibrium. See also *tempo*.

stem group: A term used in linguistics to refer to an actual as opposed to a hypothetical ancestral language.

stemmatics: The study of the history of related sets of manuscripts.

stratigraphic debt: A method used in *stratocladistics* to determine how much of the record of a particular suite of fossils might be missing—a calculation viewed as being similar to *tree length*. The debt is calculated by counting the number of strata that a *taxon* passes through but that contain no evidence of that taxon.

stratocladistics: A method involving the use of temporal data, such as from superposition, to assist in constructing a *cladogram*.

style: Usually a catchall term used to denote a particular look or design of a thing, including such dimensions as form and decoration. In evolutionary archaeology the term has a restricted meaning and is used to refer to the nonfunctional (nonadaptational) aspects of an object or organism, similar to the way in which biologists use the term "neutrality." For example, we could say that style A confers no fitness value on its possessor different than that conferred by style B. Compare with *function*.

symplesiomorphy: *Ancestral character* or *character state* that two or more *taxa* share in common with their immediate ancestor and the preceding ancestor(s). Also known as "shared ancestral character." Compare with *synapomorphy*.

synapomorphy: *Derived character* or *character state* that two or more *taxa* share in common with their immediate ancestor but not with the preceding ancestor. Also known as "shared derived character." *Cladistics* depends solely on the identification and use of synapomorphies. Compare with *symplesiomorphy*.

systematics: Procedures for creating *units* derived logically for a specific analytical purpose. The units are used to characterize and measure similarities and differences between phenomena and to sort them into sets such that like goes with like. Typically, things that are alike are thought to have a particular affinity. As used in this book, one critically important kind of affinity is evolutionary, or geneticlike, affinity.

taxon: A named taxonomic *unit* of unspecified rank (e.g., family, genus, *species*) to which individual organisms or sets of organisms are assigned.

taxonomic classification: A hierarchical classification made up of lower-level *classes* nested within higher-level classes, which themselves are nested in even higher-order classes, and so on. Compare with *paradigmatic classification*.

taxonomy: Theories of *classification,* their bases, principles, procedures, and rules. Compare with *systematics*.

tempo: The rate of evolutionary change. The rate can be zero, in which case the rate represents *stasis;* it can be gradual; or it can be relatively rapid. Compare with *mode*.

terminal taxon: A *taxon* placed at the end of a terminal branch on a *cladogram*.

three-taxon statement: A declaration that two *units* (*taxa*) are more like each other than either is to any third unit.

topology: The basic arrangement of *taxa* on a *cladogram*. Note that cladograms can look different in terms of branch placement but still have the same topology. This is because any *clade* can be swiveled at any of its *nodes* without changing the topology.

tradition: A temporal continuum represented by persistent configurations of related forms. See also *heredity, lineage,* and *persistence*.

transmission: The movement of information, whether genes or cultural ideas, from one organism to another. Thus it is not necessarily intergenerational. This process produces inheritance and drives *heritable continuity*. See also *diffusion* and *heredity*.

tree length: The sum of the fit of all *character states* to a *cladogram*. Minimum length is the number of character-state changes necessary to account for the data.

type: Synonymous with kind or category of unspecified derivation. Compare with *class*.

typological classification: A kind of *classification* based on morphological *characters* chosen haphazardly, without explicit effort to measure a particular kind of affinity other than *phenetic* similarity.

unit: A conceptual entity that serves as a standard of measurement.

unordered transformation series: A series of transformations in which *character states* are left unordered. This means that a *character* can change from one state to any other state and is counted as only one step. Compare with *ordered transformation series*.

References

Adams, E. N., III
  1972   Consensus Techniques and the Comparison of Taxonomic Trees. *Systematic Zoology* 21:390–397.
Agenbroad, L. D.
  1978   *The Hudson-Meng Site: An Alberta Bison Kill in the Nebraska High Plains.* University Press of America, Washington, D.C.
Alroy, J.
  2002   Stratigraphy in Phylogeny Reconstruction—Reply to Smith (2000). *Journal of Paleontology* 76:587–589.
Anderson, D. G.
  1990   The Paleoindian Colonization of Eastern North America: A View from the Southeastern United States. In *Early Paleoindian Economies of Eastern North America,* edited by K. B. Tankersley and B. L. Isaac, pp. 163–216. JAI Press, Greenwich, Conn.
  1991   Examining Prehistoric Settlement Distribution in Eastern North America. *Archaeology of Eastern North America* 19:1–22.
Anderson D. G., and M. K. Faught
  1998   The Distribution of Fluted Paleoindian Projectile Points: Update 1998. *Archaeology of Eastern North America* 26:163–187.
  2000   Palaeoindian Artefact Distributions: Evidence and Implications. *Antiquity* 74:507–513.
Anderson, D. G., and J. C. Gillam
  2000   Paleoindian Colonization of the Americas: Implications from an Examination of Physiography, Demography, and Artifact Distribution. *American Antiquity* 65:43–66.
Anderson, D. G., L. D. O'Steen, and K. E. Sassaman
  1996   Chronological Considerations. In *The Paleoindian and Early Archaic Southeast,* edited by D. G. Anderson and K. E. Sassaman, pp. 3–15. University of Alabama Press, Tuscaloosa.
Anderson, E.
  1949   *Introgressive Hybridization.* Wiley, New York.
Angier, N.
  1997   Ernst Mayr at 93. *Natural History* 106(4):8–11.

Arnold, M. L.
   1997   *Natural Hybridization and Evolution.* Oxford University Press, New
           York.
Aunger, R.
   2002   *The Electric Meme: A New Theory of How We Think.* Free Press,
           New York.
Avise, J. C.
   2000   Cladists in Wonderland. *Evolution* 54:1828–1832.
Bader, R. S.
   1958   Similarity and Recency of Common Ancestry. *Systematic Zoology*
           7:184–187.
Bamforth, D. B.
   2002   Evidence and Metaphor in Evolutionary Archaeology. *American An-
           tiquity* 67:435–452.
Beatty, J.
   1982   Classes and Cladists. *Systematic Zoology* 31:25–34.
   1995   The Evolutionary Contingency Thesis. In *Concepts, Theories, and
           Rationality in the Biological Sciences,* edited by G. Wolters and J. G.
           Lennox, pp. 45–106. University of Pittsburgh Press, Pittsburgh.
Beck, C.
   1995   Functional Analysis and the Differential Persistence of Great Basin
           Dart Forms. *Journal of California and Great Basin Anthropology*
           17:222–243.
   1998   Projectile Point Types as Valid Chronological Units. In *Unit Issues in
           Archaeology: Measuring Time, Space, and Material,* edited by A. F.
           Ramenofsky and A. Steffen, pp. 21–40. University of Utah Press, Salt
           Lake City.
Bell, G.
   1997   *The Basics of Selection.* Chapman and Hall, New York.
Bell, R. E., and R. S. Hall
   1953   Selected Projectile Point Types of the United States. *Oklahoma An-
           thropological Society, Bulletin* 1:1–16.
Bellwood, P.
   1996   Phylogeny vs Reticulation in Prehistory. *Antiquity* 70:881–890.
Benton, M. J.
   1994   Palaeontological Data, and Identifying Mass Extinctions. *Trends in
           Ecology and Evolution* 9:181–185.
   2000   Stems, Nodes, Crown Clades, and Rank-Free Lists: Is Linnaeus Dead?
           Biological Reviews 75:633–648.
Benton, M. J., and R. Hitchin
   1996   Testing the Quality of the Fossil Record by Groups and by Major
           Habitats. *Historical Biology* 12:111–157.
Bettinger, R. L., R. Boyd, and P. J. Richerson
   1996   Style, Function, and Cultural Evolutionary Processes. In *Darwinian
           Archaeologies,* edited by H. D. G. Maschner, pp. 133–164. Plenum
           Press, New York.
Bettinger, R. L., and J. Eerkens
   1997   Evolutionary Implications of Metrical Variation in Great Basin Pro-

jectile Points. In *Rediscovering Darwin: Evolutionary Theory in Archeological Explanation,* edited by C. M. Barton and G. A. Clark, pp. 177–191. Archeological Papers, no. 7. American Anthropological Association, Washington, D.C.

1999   Point Typologies, Cultural Transmission, and the Spread of Bow-and-Arrow Technology in the Prehistoric Great Basin. *American Antiquity* 64:231–242.

Bigelow, R. S.
1958   Classification and Phylogeny. *Systematic Zoology* 7:49–59.

Binford, L. R.
1962   Archaeology as Anthropology. *American Antiquity* 28:217–225.
1965   Archaeological Systematics and the Study of Culture Process. *American Antiquity* 31:203–210.

Blackmore, S.
1999   *The Meme Machine.* Oxford University Press, Oxford.

Blum, H. F.
1963   On the Origin and Evolution of Human Culture. *American Scientist* 51:32–47.

Boas, F.
1895   The Aims of Anthropology. *Science* 2:241–252.
1904   The History of Anthropology. *Science* 20:513–524.
1911   Review of "Methode der Ethnologie" by F. Graebner. *Science* 34:804–810.
1940   *Race, Language and Culture.* Macmillan, New York.

Bock, W. J.
1973   Philosophical Foundations of Classical Evolutionary Classification. *Systematic Zoology* 22:375–392.

Bonner, J. T.
1980   *The Evolution of Culture in Animals.* Princeton University Press, Princeton, N.J.
1988   *The Evolution of Complexity.* Princeton University Press, Princeton, N.J.

Borgerhoff Mulder, M.
2001   Using Phylogenetically Based Comparative Methods in Anthropology: More Questions Than Answers. *Evolutionary Anthropology* 10:99–111.

Borgerhoff Mulder, M., M. George-Cramer, J. Eshelman, and A. Ortolani
2001   A Study of East African Kinship and Marriage Using Phylogenetically Based Comparative Methods. *American Anthropologist* 103:1059–1082.

Borgmeier, T.
1957   Basic Questions of Systematics. *Systematic Zoology* 6:53–69.

Boyd, R., M. Borgerhoff Mulder, W. H. Durham, and P. J. Richerson
1997   Are Cultural Phylogenies Possible? In *Human by Nature: Between Biology and the Social Sciences,* edited by P. Weingart, S. D. Mitchell, P. J. Richerson, and S. Maasen, pp. 355–386. Erlbaum, Mahwah, N.J.

Boyd, R., and P. J. Richerson
1982   Cultural Transmission and the Evolution of Cooperative Behavior. *Human Ecology* 10:325–351.

1983   The Cultural Transmission of Acquired Variation: Effects on Genetic Fitness. *Journal of Theoretical Biology* 100:567–596.

1985   *Culture and the Evolutionary Process.* University of Chicago Press, Chicago.

1987   The Evolution of Ethnic Markers. *Cultural Anthropology* 2:65–79.

Bradley, B. A.

1997   Sloan Site Biface and Projectile Point Technology. In *Sloan: A Paleoindian Dalton Cemetery in Arkansas,* by D. F. Morse, pp. 53–57. Smithsonian Institution Press, Washington, D.C.

Brady, R. H.

1985   On the Independence of Systematics. *Cladistics* 1:113–126.

Bremer, K.

1990   Combinable Component Consensus. *Cladistics* 6:369–372.

Brew, J. O.

1946   *Archaeology of Alkali Ridge, Southeastern Utah.* Papers 21. Peabody Museum of American Archaeology and Ethnology, Harvard University, Cambridge, Mass.

Brooks, D. R., and D. A. McLennan

1991   *Phylogeny, Ecology, and Behavior: A Research Program in Comparative Biology.* University of Chicago Press, Chicago.

Brower, A. V. Z.

1999   Delimitation of Phylogenetic Species with DNA Sequences: A Critique of Davis and Nixon's Population Aggregation Analysis. *Systematic Biology* 48:199–213.

2000   Evolution Is Not a Necessary Assumption of Cladistics. *Cladistics* 16:143–154.

Brower, A. V. Z., R. DeSalle, and A. Vogler

1996   Gene Trees, Species Trees, and Systematics: A Cladistic Perspective. *Annual Review of Ecology and Systematics* 27:423–450.

Brown, J. H., and M. V. Lomolino

1998   *Biogeography.* 2nd ed. Sinauer, Sunderland, Mass.

Brummitt, R. K.

1996   In Defence of Paraphyletic Taxa. In *The Biodiversity of African Plants,* edited by L. J. G. van der Maesen, X. M. van der Burgt, and J. M. van der Medenbach de Rooy, pp. 371–384. Kluwer, Dordrecht, the Netherlands.

1997   The BioCode Is Unnecessary and Unwanted. *Systematic Botany* 22:182–186.

Bryan, A. L.

1988   The Relationship of the Stemmed Point and Fluted Point Traditions in the Great Basin. In *Early Human Occupation in Far Western North America: The Clovis-Archaic Interface,* edited by J. A. Willig, C. M. Aikens, and J. L. Fagan, pp. 373–387. Anthropological Papers, no. 21. Nevada State Museum, Reno.

1991   The Fluted-Point Tradition in the Americas—One of Several Adaptations to Late Pleistocene American Environments. In *Clovis: Origins and Adaptations,* edited by R. Bonnichsen and K. L. Turnmire, pp. 15–33. Center for the Study of the First Americans, Corvallis, Ore.

Buck, R. C., and D. L. Hull
    1966   The Logical Structure of the Linnaean Hierarchy. *Systematic Zoology* 15:97–111.

Bullen, R. P.
    1968   *A Guide to the Identification of Florida Projectile Points.* Florida State Museum, Gainesville.

Cain, A. J.
    1956   The Genus in Evolutionary Taxonomy. *Systematic Zoology* 5:97–109.
    1959   The Post-Linnaean Development of Taxonomy. *Proceedings of the Linnean Society, London* 170:234–244.

Cain, A. J., and G. A. Harrison
    1958   An Analysis of the Taxonomist's Judgement of Affinity. *Proceedings of the Linnean Society, London* 131:85–98.

Cambron, J. W., and D. C. Hulse
    1964   *Handbook of Alabama Archaeology, Part 1: Point Types.* Archaeological Research Association of Alabama, Moundville.

Cameron, H. D.
    1987   The Upside-Down Cladogram: Problems in Manuscript Affiliation. In *Biological Metaphor and Cladistic Classification,* edited by H. M. Hoenigswald and L. F. Wiener, pp. 227–242. University of Pennsylvania Press, Philadelphia.

Camin, J. H., and R. R. Sokal
    1965   A Method for Deducing Branching Sequences in Phylogeny. *Evolution* 19:311–326.

Cann, R. L., M. Stoneking, and A. C. Wilson
    1987   Mitochondrial DNA and Human Evolution. *Nature* 325:31–35.

Cantino, P. D.
    2000   Phylogenetic Nomenclature: Addressing Some Concerns. *Taxon* 49:85–93.

Cantino, P. D., H. N. Bryant, K. de Queiroz, M. J. Donoghue, T. Eriksson, D. M. Hillis, and M. S. Y. Lee
    1999 Species Names in Phylogenetic Nomenclature. *Systematic Biology* 48:790–807.

Cavalli-Sforza, L. L., and A. W. F. Edwards
    1967   Phylogenetic Analysis: Models and Estimation Procedures. *Evolution* 21:550–570.

Cavalli-Sforza, L. L., and M. Feldman
    1981   *Cultural Transmission and Evolution: A Quantitative Approach.* Princeton University Press, Princeton, N.J.

Cavalli-Sforza, L. L., A. Piazza, and P. Menozzi
    1994   *History and Geography of Genes.* Princeton University Press, Princeton, N.J.

Cavalli-Sforza, L. L., A. Piazza, P. Menozzi, and J. Mountain
    1988   Reconstruction of Human Evolution: Bringing Together Genetic, Archaeological, and Linguistic Data. *National Academy of Sciences, Proceedings* 85:6002–6006.

Chapman, C. H.
    1948   A Preliminary Survey of Missouri Archaeology (Part IV): Ancient Cultures and Sequence. *Missouri Archaeologist* 10:133–164.

1975   *The Archaeology of Missouri, I.* University of Missouri Press, Columbia.

Clarke, D. L.
1978   *Analytical Archaeology.* 2nd ed. Columbia University Press, New York.

Cloak, F. T., Jr.
1973   Elementary Self-Replicating Instructions and Their Works: Toward a Radical Reconstruction of General Anthropology through a General Theory of Natural Selection. Paper presented at the Ninth International Congress of Anthropological and Ethnographical Sciences, Chicago.
1975   Is a Cultural Ethology Possible? *Human Ecology* 3:161–182.

Clyde, W. C., and D. C. Fisher
1997   Comparing the Fit of Stratigraphic and Morphologic Data in Phylogenetic Analysis. *Paleobiology* 23:1–19.

Coe, J. L.
1964   *The Formative Cultures of the Carolina Piedmont.* American Philosophical Society, Transactions 54(5). Philadelphia.

Collard, M., and S. Shennan
2000   Processes of Culture Change in Prehistory: A Case Study from the European Neolithic. In *Archaeogenetics: DNA and the Population Prehistory of Europe,* edited by C. Renfrew and K. Boyle, pp. 89–97. McDonald Institute for Archaeological Research, Cambridge.

Colless, D. H.
1967   An Examination of Certain Concepts in Phenetic Taxonomy. *Systematic Zoology* 16:6–27.
1970   The Phylogram as an Estimate of Phylogeny. *Systematic Zoology* 19:352–362.
1971   "Phenetic," "Phylogenetic," and "Weighting." *Systematic Zoology* 20:73–76.

Colton, H. S., and L. L. Hargrave
1937   *Handbook of Northern Arizona Pottery Wares.* Bulletin 11. Museum of Northern Arizona, Flagstaff.

Conway Morris, S.
1998   *The Crucible of Creation: The Burgess Shale and the Rise of Animals.* Oxford University Press, Oxford.

Cotter, J. L.
1937   The Occurrence of Flints and Extinct Animals in Pluvial Deposits near Clovis, New Mexico. In Report on Excavation at the Gravel Pit, 1936 (Part 4). *Academy of Natural Sciences of Philadelphia, Proceedings* 89:1–16.

Cracraft, J.
1981   The Use of Functional and Adaptive Criteria in Phylogenetic Systematics. *American Zoologist* 21:21–36.
2000   Species Concepts in Theoretical and Applied Biology: A Systematic Debate with Consequences. In *Species Concepts and Phylogenetic Theory: A Debate,* edited by Q. D. Wheeler and R. Meier, pp. 3–14. Columbia University Press, New York.

Crowe, T. M.
1994 Morphometrics, Phylogenetic Models and Cladistics: Means to an End or Much to Do about Nothing? *Cladistics* 10:77–84.

Cullen, B.
1993 The Darwinian Resurgence and the Cultural Virus Critique. *Cambridge Archaeological Journal* 3:179–202.

Darwent, J., and M. J. O'Brien
2003 Using Cladistics to Reconstruct Lineages of Archaic Projectile Points in Northeastern Missouri. Paper presented at the 65th annual meeting of the Society for American Archaeology, Milwaukee, Wis.

Darwent, J., M. J. O'Brien, and R. L. Lyman
2000 Southeastern Fluted-Point Lineages. Paper presented at the 65th annual meeting of the Society for American Archaeology, Philadelphia.

Darwin, C.
1859 *On the Origin of Species by Means of Natural Selection; or the Preservation of Favoured Races in the Struggle for Life.* Murray, London.

Davis, J. I., and K. C. Nixon
1992 Populations, Genetic Variation, and the Delimitation of Phylogenetic Species. *Systematic Biology* 41:421–435.

Dawkins, R.
1976 *The Selfish Gene.* Oxford University Press, New York.
1990 *The Extended Phenotype: The Long Reach of the Gene.* New ed. Oxford University Press, Oxford.

DeJarnette, D. L., E. B. Kurjack, and J. W. Cambron
1962 Stanfield-Worley Bluff Shelter Excavations. *Journal of Alabama Archaeology* 8(1–2).

Dempsey, P., and M. Baumhoff
1963 The Statistical Use of Artifact Distributions to Establish Chronological Sequence. *American Antiquity* 28:496–509.

de Queiroz, K.
1998 The General Lineage Concept of Species, Species Criteria, and the Process of Speciation: A Conceptual Unification and Terminological Recommendations. In *Endless Forms: Species and Speciation,* edited by D. J. Howard and S. H. Berlocher, pp. 57–75. Oxford University Press, New York.

de Queiroz, K., and J. Gauthier
1992 Phylogenetic Taxonomy. *Annual Review of Ecology and Systematics* 23:449–480.
1994 Toward a Phylogenetic System of Biological Nomenclature. *Trends in Ecology and Evolution* 9:27–31.

Dewar, R. E.
1995 Of Nets and Trees: Untangling the Reticulate and Dendritic in Madagascar Prehistory. *World Archaeology* 26:301–318.

Dollo, L.
1893 Les lois de l'évolution. *Société Belge de Géologie, de Paléontologie et d'Hydrologie, Bulletin* 7:164–166.

Dominguez, E., and Q. D. Wheeler
  1997   Taxonomic Stability Is Ignorance. *Cladistics* 13:367–372.
Doolittle, W. F.
  1999   Phylogenetic Classification and the Universal Tree. *Science* 284:2124–2128.
Dunnell, R. C.
  1971   *Systematics in Prehistory.* Free Press, New York.
  1978   Style and Function: A Fundamental Dichotomy. *American Antiquity* 43:192–202.
  1980   Evolutionary Theory and Archaeology. *Advances in Archaeological Method and Theory* 3:35–99.
  1986   Methodological Issues in Americanist Artifact Classification. *Advances in Archaeological Method and Theory* 9:149–207.
  1991   Methodological Impacts of Catastrophic Depopulation on American Archaeology and Ethnology. In *Columbian Consequences,* vol. 3: *The Spanish Borderlands in Pan-American Perspective,* edited by D. H. Thomas, pp. 561–580. Smithsonian Institution Press, Washington, D.C.
DuPraw, E. J.
  1964   Non-Linnaean Taxonomy. *Nature* 202:849–852.
Durham, W. H.
  1976   The Adaptive Significance of Cultural Behavior. *Human Ecology* 4:89–121.
  1978   Toward a Coevolutionary View of Human Biology and Culture. In *The Sociobiology Debate,* edited by A. Caplan, pp. 428–448. Harper and Row, New York.
  1982   Interactions of Genetic and Cultural Evolution: Models and Examples. *Human Ecology* 10:289–323.
  1990   Advances in Evolutionary Culture Theory. *Annual Review of Anthropology* 19:187–210.
  1991   *Coevolution: Genes, Culture, and Human Diversity.* Stanford University Press, Stanford, Calif.
Edwards, A. W. F., and L. L. Cavalli-Sforza
  1964   Reconstruction of Evolutionary Trees. In *Phenetic and Phylogenetic Classification,* edited by V. H. Heywood and J. McNeill, pp. 67–76. Systematics Association, Vol. 6. Systematics Association, London.
Eggan, F.
  1954   Social Anthropology and the Method of Controlled Comparison. *American Anthropologist* 56:743–763.
Eldredge, N.
  1989   Punctuated Equilibria, Rates of Change, and Large-Scale Entities in Evolutionary Systems. *Journal of Biological and Social Structures* 12:173–184.
Eldredge, N., and J. Cracraft
  1980   *Phylogenetic Patterns and the Evolutionary Process.* Columbia University Press, New York.
Eldredge, N., and S. J. Gould
  1972   Punctuated Equilibria: An Alternative to Phyletic Gradualism. In

Models in Paleobiology, edited by T. J. M. Schopf, pp. 82–115. Freeman, Cooper, San Francisco.

1977 Evolutionary Models and Biostratigraphic Strategies. In *Concepts and Methods of Biostratigraphy,* edited by E. G. Kauffman and J. E. Hazel, pp. 25–40. Dowden, Hutchinson and Ross, Stroudsburg, Penn.

1997 On Punctuated Equilibria. *Science* 276:338–339.

Eldredge, N., and M. J. Novacek

1985 Systematics and Paleobiology. *Paleobiology* 11:65–74.

Endler, J. A.

1986 *Natural Selection in the Wild.* Princeton University Press, Princeton, N.J.

1998 The Place of Hybridization in Evolution. *Evolution* 52:640–644.

Engelmann, G. F., and E. O. Wiley

1977 The Place of Ancestor-Descendant Relationships in Phylogenetic Reconstruction. *Systematic Zoology* 26:1–11.

Ereshefsky, M.

1994 Some Problems with the Linnaean Hierarchy. *Philosophy of Science* 61:186–205.

1997 The Evolution of the Linnaean Hierarchy. *Biology and Philosophy* 12:493–519.

2001 *The Poverty of the Linnaean Hierarchy: A Philosophical Study of Biological Taxonomy.* Cambridge University Press, Cambridge.

Evans, J.

1850 On the Date of British Coins. *Numismatic Chronicle and Journal of the Numismatic Society* 12(4):127–137.

Farris, J. S.

1982 Outgroups and Parsimony. *Systematic Zoology* 31:328–334.

1983 The Logical Basis of Phylogenetic Analysis. In *Advances in Cladistics,* edited by N. I. Platnick and V. A. Funk, pp. 1–36. Columbia University Press, New York.

1989a The Retention Index and Homoplasy Excess. *Systematic Zoology* 38:406–407.

1989b The Retention Index and the Rescaled Consistency Index. *Cladistics* 5:417–419.

Faught, M. K., D. G. Anderson, and A. Gisiger

1994 North American Paleoindian Database: An Update. *Current Research in the Pleistocene* 11:32–35.

Felsenstein, J.

2001 The Troubled Growth of Statistical Phylogenetics. *Systematic Biology* 50:465–467.

Fiedel, S. J.

1999 Older Than We Thought: Implications of Corrected Dates for Paleoindians. *American Antiquity* 64:95–115.

Fisher, D. C.

1991 Phylogenetic Analysis and Its Application in Evolutionary Paleobiology. In *Analytical Paleobiology,* edited by N. L. Gilinsky and P. W. Signor, pp. 103–122. Short Courses in Paleobiology, no. 4. Paleontological Society, Washington, D.C.

1992   Stratigraphic Parsimony. In *MacClade: Analysis of Phylogeny and Character Evolution* (version 3), edited by W. P. Maddison and D. R. Maddison, pp. 124–129. Sinauer, Sunderland, Mass.

1994   Stratocladistics: Morphological and Temporal Patterns and Their Relation to Phylogenetic Process. In *Interpreting the Hierarchy of Nature,* edited by L. Grande and O. Rieppel, pp. 133–171. Academic Press, San Diego.

Fisher, D. C., M. Foote, D. L. Fox, and L. R. Leighton

2002   Stratigraphy in Phylogeny Reconstruction—Comment on Smith (2000). *Journal of Paleontology* 76:585–586.

Flannery, K. V., and J. Marcus

1983   *The Cloud People: Divergent Evolution of the Zapotec and Mixtec Civilizations.* Academic Press, New York.

Foley, R.

1987   Hominid Species and Stone-Tool Assemblages: How Are They Related? *Antiquity* 61:380–392.

Foley, R., and M. M. Lahr

1997   Mode 3 Technologies and the Evolution of Modern Humans. *Cambridge Archaeological Journal* 7:3–36.

Ford, J. A.

1962   *A Quantitative Method for Deriving Cultural Chronology.* Technical Bulletin, no. 1, Pan American Union, Washington, D.C.

Fox, D. L., D. C. Fisher, and L. R. Leighton

1999   Reconstructing Phylogeny with and without Temporal Data. *Science* 284:1816–1819.

Freeman, D.

1974   The Evolutionary Theories of Charles Darwin and Herbert Spencer. *Current Anthropology* 15:211–237.

Frison, G.

1991   *Prehistoric Hunters of the High Plains.* 2nd ed. Academic Press, New York.

Frison, G., and B. Bradley

1999   *The Fenn Cache: Clovis Weapons and Tools.* One Horse Land and Cattle Company, Santa Fe, N.M.

Frison, G. C., C. V. Haynes, Jr., and M. L. Larson

1996   Discussion and Conclusions. In *The Mill Iron Site,* edited by G. Frison, pp. 205–216. University of New Mexico Press, Albuquerque.

Frison, G. C., and L. C. Todd

1986   *The Colby Mammoth Site: Taphonomy and Archaeology of a Clovis Kill in Northern Wyoming.* University of New Mexico Press, Albuquerque.

Funk, V. A., and W. L. Wagner

1995   Biogeographic Patterns in the Hawaiian Islands. In *Hawaiian Biogeography: Evolution on a Hot Spot Archipelago,* edited by W. L. Wagner and V. A. Funk, pp. 379–419. Smithsonian Institution Press, Washington, D.C.

Futuyma, D. J.

1986   *Evolutionary Biology.* 2nd ed. Sinauer, Sunderland, Mass.

Gamkrelidze, T. V., and V. V. Ivanov
    1990   The Early History of Indo-European Languages. *Scientific American* 262(3):110–116.
Garbarino, M. S.
    1977   *Sociocultural Theory in Anthropology: A Short History.* Waveland, Prospect Heights, Ill.
Gilmour, J. S. L.
    1937   A Taxonomic Problem. *Nature* 139:1040–1042.
    1940   Taxonomy and Philosophy. In *The New Systematics,* edited by J. S. Huxley, pp. 461–474. Clarendon Press, Oxford, England.
    1951   The Development of Taxonomic Theory since 1851. *Nature* 168:400–402.
Gladwin, H. S.
    1936   Methodology in the Southwest. *American Antiquity* 1:256–259.
Gladwin, W., and H. S. Gladwin
    1934   *A Method for the Designation of Cultures and Their Variations.* Medallion Papers No. 15. Globe, Ariz.
Goldenweiser, A. A.
    1916   Diffusion vs. Independent Invention: A Rejoinder to Professor G. Elliot Smith. *Science* 44:531–533.
Goldman, N.
    1990   Maximum Likelihood Inference of Phylogenetic Trees, with Special Reference to a Poisson Process Model of DNA Substitution and to Parsimony Analysis. *Systematic Zoology* 39:345–361.
Goldstein, P. Z., and R. DeSalle
    2000   Phylogenetic Species, Nested Hierarchies, and Character Fixation. *Cladistics* 16:364–384.
Goloboff, P. A.
    1991   Homoplasy and the Choice among Cladograms. *Cladistics* 7:215–232.
Goodenough, W. H.
    1957   Oceania and the Problem of Controls in the Study of Cultural and Human Evolution. *Journal of the Polynesian Society* 66:146–155.
    1997   Comment on "The Dimensions of Social Life in the Pacific: Human Diversity and the Myth of the Primitive Isolate" by J. E. Terrell, T. L. Hunt, and C. Gosden. *Current Anthropology* 38:177–178.
Goodyear, A. C.
    1982   The Chronological Position of the Dalton Horizon in the Southeastern United States. *American Antiquity* 47:382–395.
Gould, S. J.
    1982   Darwinism and the Expansion of Evolutionary Theory. *Science* 216:380–387.
    1986   Evolution and the Triumph of Homology, or Why History Matters. *American Scientist* 74:60–69.
    1987   *Time's Arrow, Time's Cycle: Myth and Metaphor in the Discovery of Geological Time.* Harvard University Press, Cambridge, Mass.
    1991   The Disparity of the Burgess Shale Arthropod Fauna and the Limits of Cladistic Analysis: Why We Must Strive to Quantify Morphospace. *Paleobiology* 17:411–423.

1996   *Full House: The Spread of Excellence from Plato to Darwin.* Harmony, New York.

1997   A Tale of Two Worksites. *Natural History* 106(9):18–22, 29, 62–68.

2002   *The Structure of Evolutionary Theory.* Belknap, Cambridge, Mass.

Gould, S. J., and N. Eldredge

1977   Punctuated Equilibria: The Tempo and Mode of Evolution Reconsidered. *Paleobiology* 3:115–151.

1986   Punctuated Equilibrium at the Third Stage. *Systematic Zoology* 35:143–148.

1993   Punctuated Equilibrium Comes of Age. *Nature* 366:223–227.

Green, R. L.

1991   Near and Remote Oceania: Disestablishing "Melanesia" in Culture History. In *Man and a Half: Essays in Pacific Anthropology and Ethnobiology in Honour of Ralph Bulmer,* edited by A. Pawley, pp. 491–502. Polynesian Society, Auckland, New Zealand.

Griffiths, G. C. D.

1973   Some Fundamental Problems in Biological Classification. *Systematic Zoology* 22:338–343.

Guglielmino, C. R., C. Viganotti, B. Hewlett, and L. L. Cavalli-Sforza

1995   Cultural Variation in Africa: Role of Mechanisms of Transmission and Adaptation. *National Academy of Sciences, Proceedings* 92:7585–7589.

Hall, B. G.

2001   *Phylogenetic Trees Made Easy: A How-To Manual for Molecular Biologists.* Sinauer, Sunderland, Mass.

Hall, B. K.

1996   *Baupläne,* Phylotypic Stages, and Constraint: Why There Are So Few Types of Animals. *Evolutionary Biology* 29:215–261.

Hallowell, A. I.

1960   The Beginnings of Anthropology in America. In *Selected Papers from the American Anthropologist 1888–1920,* edited by F. de Laguna, pp. 1–90. American Anthropological Association, Washington, D.C.

Harmon, M. J., R. D. Leonard, C. S. VanPool, and T. L. VanPool

2000   Cultural Transmission: Shared Intellectual Traditions in Ceramics of the Prehistoric American Southwest and Northern Mexico. Paper presented at the 65th annual meeting of the Society for American Archaeology, Philadelphia.

Harmon, M. J., T. L. VanPool, R. D. Leonard, C. S. VanPool, and L. Salter

2003   Maximum Parsimony vs. Maximum Likelihood: A Comparison in the Reconstruction of Cultural Phylogenies. Paper presented at the 65th annual meeting of the Society for American Archaeology, Milwaukee, Wis.

Harris, M.

1968   *The Rise of Anthropological Theory.* Crowell, New York.

Harvey, P. H., and M. D. Pagel

1991   *The Comparative Method in Evolutionary Biology.* Oxford University Press, Oxford.

Haynes, C. V.
1991 Geoarchaeological and Paleohydrological Evidence for a Clovis-Age Drought in North America and Its Bearing on Extinction. *Quaternary Research* 35:438–450.

Hedberg, O.
1995 Cladistics in Taxonomic Botany—Master or Servant? *Taxon* 44:3–11.

Hendy, M. D., and D. Penny
1989 A Framework for the Quantitative Study of Evolutionary Trees. *Systematic Zoology* 38:297–309.

Hennig, W.
1950 *Grundzüge einer Theorie der Phylogenetischen Systematik*. Deutscher Zentralverlag, Berlin.
1965 Phylogenetic Systematics. *Annual Review of Entomology* 10:97–116.
1966 *Phylogenetic Systematics*. University of Illinois Press, Urbana.

Hintze, J. L.
1999 *NCSS 2000 Statistical System for Windows*. Number Cruncher Statistical Systems, Kaysville, Utah.

Hoelzer, G. A., and D. J. Melnick
1994 Patterns of Speciation and Limits to Phylogenetic Resolution. *Trends in Ecology and Evolution* 9:104–107.

Holden, C., and R. Mace
1997 Phylogenetic Analysis of the Evolution of Lactose Digestion in Adults. *Human Biology* 69:605–628.
1999 Sexual Dimorphism in Stature and Women's Work: A Phylogenetic Cross-Cultural Analysis. *American Journal of Physical Anthropology* 110:27–45.

Howard, C. D.
1995 Projectile Point and Hafting Design Review. *North American Archaeologist* 16:291–301.

Howard, D. J., and S. H. Berlocher (editors)
1998 *Endless Forms: Species and Speciation*. Oxford University Press, New York.

Huelsenbeck, J. P., and J. Bollback
2001 Application of the Likelihood Function in Phylogenetic Analysis. In *Handbook of Statistical Genetics,* edited by D. J. Balding, M. Bishop, and C. Cannings, pp. 415–439. Wiley, New York.

Hughes, S. S.
1998 Getting to the Point: Evolutionary Change in Prehistoric Weaponry. *Journal of Archaeological Method and Theory* 5:345–408.

Hull, D.
1970 Contemporary Systematic Philosophies. *Annual Review of Ecology and Systematics* 1:19–54.
1979 The Limits of Cladism. *Systematic Zoology* 28:416–440.
1987 Genealogical Actors in Ecological Plays. *Biology and Philosophy* 1:44–60.
1988a Interactors versus Vehicles. In *The Role of Behavior in Evolution,* edited by H. C. Plotkin, pp. 19–50. MIT Press, Cambridge, Mass.

1988b   *Science as a Process: An Evolutionary Account of the Social and Conceptual Development of Science*. University of Chicago Press, Chicago.

Hurt, T. D., and G. F. M. Rakita (editors)

2001   *Style and Function: Conceptual Issues in Evolutionary Archaeology*. Bergin and Garvey, Westport, Conn.

Huxley, J. S.

1942   *Evolution, the Modern Synthesis*. Allen and Unwin, London.

Jardine, N.

1969   A Logical Basis for Biological Classification. *Systematic Zoology* 18:37–52.

Kaufman, T.

1990   Language History in South America. In *Amazonian Linguistics*, edited by D. L. Payne, pp. 13–73. University of Texas Press, Austin.

Kehoe, A. B.

1990   The Monumental Midwestern Taxonomic Method. In *The Woodland Tradition in the Western Great Lakes: Papers Presented to Elden Johnson*, edited by G. E. Gibbon, pp. 31–36. Publications in Anthropology, no. 4. University of Minnesota, Minneapolis.

Kidder, A. V.

1915   Pottery of the Pajarito Plateau and of Some Adjacent Regions in New Mexico. *American Anthropological Association, Memoir* 2:407–462.

1917   A Design-Sequence from New Mexico. *National Academy of Sciences, Proceedings* 3:369–370.

1932   *The Artifacts of Pecos*. Papers of the Southwestern Expedition, Phillips Academy, no. 6. Yale University Press, New Haven, Conn.

Kirch, P. V.

1997   *The Lapita Peoples: Ancestors of the Oceanic World*. Blackwell, Oxford, England.

Kirch, P. V., and R. L. Green

1987   History, Phylogeny, and Evolution in Polynesia. *Current Anthropology* 28:431–456.

2001   *Hawaiki, Ancestral Polynesia: An Essay in Historical Anthropology*. Cambridge University Press, Cambridge.

Kiriakoff, S. G.

1965   Some Remarks on Sokal and Sneath's *Principles of Numerical Taxonomy*. *Systematic Zoology* 14:61–64.

Kitching, I. J., P. L. Forey, C. J. Humphries, and D. M. Williams

1998   *Cladistics: The Theory and Practice of Parsimony Analysis*. Oxford University Press, Oxford.

Kluge, A. G.

2001   Parsimony with and without Scientific Justification. *Cladistics* 17:199–210.

Knox, E. B.

1998   The Use of Hierarchies as Organizational Models in Systematics. *Biological Journal of the Linnean Society* 63:1–49.

Kroeber, A. L.

1916a   Zuñi Culture Sequences. *National Academy of Sciences, Proceedings* 2:42–45.

1916b   Zuñi Potsherds. *American Museum of Natural History, Anthropological Papers* 18(1):1–37.

1940a   Statistical Classification. *American Antiquity* 6:29–44.

1940b   Stimulus Diffusion. *American Anthropologist* 42:1–20.

1942   Tapajó Pottery. *American Antiquity* 7:403–405.

1948   *Anthropology.* Revised ed. Harcourt Brace, New York.

Lathrap, D. W. (editor)

1956   An Archaeological Classification of Culture Contact Situations. In *Seminars in Archaeology: 1955,* pp. 1–30. Memoirs, no. 11. Society for American Archaeology, Menasha, Wis.

Leaf, M. L.

1979   *Man, Mind, and Science: A History of Anthropology.* Columbia University Press, New York.

Lee, A.

1989   Numerical Taxonomy Revisited: John Griffith, Cladistic Analysis and St. Augustine's Quaestiones in Heptateuchum. *Studia Patristica* 20:24–32.

Lee, M. S. Y., and P. Doughty

1997   The Relationship between Evolutionary Theory and Phylogenetic Analysis. *Biological Reviews* 72:471–495.

Leonard, R. D.

2001   Evolutionary Archaeology. In *Archaeological Theory Today,* edited by I. Hodder, pp. 65–97. Polity Press, Cambridge.

Leonard, R. D., and G. T. Jones

1987   Elements of an Inclusive Evolutionary Model for Archaeology. *Journal of Anthropological Archaeology* 6:199–219.

Levin, D. A.

2002   Hybridization and Extinction. *American Scientist* 90:254–261.

Lewis, P. O.

2001   A Likelihood Approach to Estimating Phylogeny from Discrete Morphological Character Data. *Systematic Biology* 50:913–925.

Lewis, T. M. N.

1954   The Cumberland Point. *Oklahoma Anthropological Society, Bulletin* 2:7–8.

Lewis, T. M. N., and M. Kneberg

1958   The Nuckolls Site. *Tennessee Archaeologist* 14(2):60–79.

Lipo, C. P.

2001   *Science, Style and the Study of Community Structure: An Example from the Central Mississippi River Valley.* British Archaeological Reports, International Series, no. 918. Oxford.

Lipo, C. P., and M. E. Madsen

2001   Neutrality, "Style," and Drift: Building Models for Studying Cultural Transmission in the Archaeological Record. In *Style and Function: Conceptual Issues in Evolutionary Archaeology,* edited by T. D. Hurt and G. F. M. Rakita, pp. 91–118. Bergin and Garvey, Westport, Conn.

Lipo, C. P., M. E. Madsen, R. L. Dunnell, and T. Hunt

1997   Population Structure, Cultural Transmission, and Frequency Seriation. *Journal of Anthropological Archaeology* 16:301–334.

Lipscomb, D.
1998   Basics of Cladistic Analysis. Manuscript in possession of the author (available on the Web at http://www.gwu.edu/~clade/faculty/lipscomb/Cladistics.pdf).

Lowie, R. H.
1912   On the Principle of Convergence in Ethnology. *Journal of American Folk-Lore* 25:24–42.
1918   Survivals and the Historical Method. *American Journal of Sociology* 23:529–535.
1937   *A History of Ethnological Theory*. Rinehart, New York.
1956   Reminiscences of Anthropological Currents in America Half a Century Ago. *American Anthropologist* 58:995–1016.

Lumsden, C. J., and E. O. Wilson
1981   *Genes, Mind, and Culture: The Coevolutionary Process*. Harvard University Press, Cambridge, Mass.

Lyman, R. L.
2001   Culture Historical and Biological Approaches to Identifying Homologous Traits. In *Style and Function: Conceptual Issues in Evolutionary Archaeology*, edited by T. D. Hurt and G. F. M. Rakita, pp. 69–89. Bergin and Garvey, Westport, Conn.

Lyman, R. L., and M. J. O'Brien
1997   The Concept of Evolution in Early Twentieth-Century Americanist Archaeology. In *Rediscovering Darwin: Evolutionary Theory in Archeological Explanation*, edited by C. M. Barton and G. A. Clark, pp. 21–48. Archeological Papers, no. 7. American Anthropological Association, Washington, D.C.
1998   The Goals of Evolutionary Archaeology: History and Explanation. *Current Anthropology* 39:615–652.
2000a   Chronometers and Units in Early Archaeology and Paleontology. *American Antiquity* 65:691–707.
2000b   Measuring and Explaining Change in Artifact Variation with Clade-Diversity Diagrams. *Journal of Anthropological Archaeology* 19:39–74.
2001a   The Direct Historical Approach, Analogical Reasoning and Theory in Americanist Archaeology. *Journal of Archaeological Method and Theory* 8:303–342.
2001b   On Misconceptions of Evolutionary Archaeology: Confusing Macroevolution and Microevolution. *Current Anthropology* 42:408–409.
2002   Classification. In *A Handbook of Concepts in Modern Evolutionary Archaeology*, edited by J. P. Hart and J. E. Terrell, pp. 69–88. Greenwood Press, Westport, Conn.
2003   *W. C. McKern and the Midwestern Taxonomic Method*. University of Alabama Press, Tuscaloosa.

Lyman, R. L., M. J. O'Brien, and R. L. Dunnell
1997   *The Rise and Fall of Culture History*. Plenum, New York.

Lyman, R. L., M. J. O'Brien, and V. Hayes
1998   A Mechanical and Functional Study of Bone Rods from the Richey-Roberts Clovis Cache, Washington, U.S.A. *Journal of Archaeological Science* 25:887–906.

Lyman, R. L., S. Wolverton, and M. J. O'Brien
  1998   Seriation, Superposition, and Interdigitation: A History of Americanist Graphic Depictions of Culture Change. *American Antiquity* 63:239–261.
Lyons-Weiler, J., and G. A. Hoelzer
  1997   Escaping from the Felsenstein Zone prior to the Inference of a Phylogenetic Tree. *Molecular Phylogenetics and Evolution* 8: 375–384.
Lyons-Weiler, J., G. A. Hoelzer, and R. J. Tausch
  1996   Relative Apparent Synapomorphy Analysis (RASA) I: The Statistical Measurement of Phylogenetic Signal. *Molecular Biological Evolution* 13:749–757.
Mace, R., and M. Pagel
  1994   The Comparative Method in Anthropology. *Current Anthropology* 35:549–564.
Maddison, D. R., and W. P. Maddison
  2001   *MacClade 4: Analysis of Phylogeny and Character Evolution.* Sinauer, Sunderland, Mass.
Mason, R. J.
  1962   The Paleo-Indian Tradition in Eastern North America. *Current Anthropology* 3:227–278.
Mayden, R. L.
  1997   A Hierarchy of Species Concepts: The Denouement in the Saga of the Species Problem. In *Species: The Units of Biodiversity,* edited by M. F. Claridge, H. A. Dawah, and M. R. Wilson, pp. 381–424. Chapman and Hall, London.
Mayr, E.
  1942   *Systematics and the Origin of Species.* Columbia University Press, New York.
  1965a   Classification and Phylogeny. *American Zoologist* 5:165–174.
  1965b   Numerical Phenetics and Taxonomic Theory. *Systematic Zoology* 14:73–97.
  1969   *Principles of Systematic Zoology.* McGraw-Hill, New York.
  1981   Biological Classification: Toward a Synthesis of Opposing Methodologies. *Science* 214:510–516.
  1982   *The Growth of Biological Thought: Diversity, Evolution, and Inheritance.* Harvard University Press, Cambridge, Mass.
  1995   Systems of Ordering Data. *Biology and Philosophy* 10:419–434.
  1997   *This is Biology: The Science of the Living World.* Harvard University Press, Cambridge, Mass.
Mayr, E., and P. D. Ashlock
  1991   *Principles of Systematic Zoology.* 2nd ed. McGraw-Hill, New York.
McKern, W. C.
  1939   The Midwestern Taxonomic Method as an Aid to Archaeological Culture Study. *American Antiquity* 4:301–313.
Meltzer, D. J.
  1981   A Study of Style and Function in a Class of Tools. *Journal of Field Archaeology* 8:313–326.
  1988   Late Pleistocene Human Adaptations in Eastern North America. *Journal of World Prehistory* 2:1–52.

Michener, C. D., and R. R. Sokal
  1957   A Quantitative Approach to a Problem in Classification. *Evolution* 11:130–162.

Mitra, P.
  1933   *History of American Anthropology.* Calcutta University Press, Calcutta.

Moore, C., and A. K. Romney
  1994   Material Culture, Geographic Propinquity, and Linguistic Affiliation on the North Coast of New Guinea: A Reanalysis of Welsch, Terrell & Nadolski (1992). *American Anthropologist* 96:370–396.

Moore, J. A.
  1993   *Science as a Way of Knowing: The Foundations of Modern Biology.* Harvard University Press, Cambridge, Mass.

Moore, J. H.
  1994a   Ethnogenetic Theories of Human Evolution. *Research and Exploration* 10:10–23.
  1994b   Putting Anthropology Back Together Again: The Ethnogenetic Critique of Cladistic Theory. *American Anthropologist* 96:925–948.
  2001   Ethnogenetic Patterns in Native North America. In *Archaeology, Language, and History: Essays on Culture and Ethnicity,* edited by J. E. Terrell, pp. 31–56. Bergin and Garvey, Westport, Conn.

Morgan, L. H.
  1877   *Ancient Society.* Holt, New York.

Morrow, J. E., and T. A. Morrow
  1999   Geographic Variation in Fluted Projectile Points: A Hemispheric Perspective. *American Antiquity* 64:215–230.

Musil, R. R.
  1988   Functional Efficiency and Technological Change: A Hafting Tradition Model for Prehistoric North America. In *Early Human Occupation in Far Western North America: The Clovis-Archaic Interface,* edited by J. A. Willig, C. M. Aikens, and J. L. Fagan, pp. 373–387. Anthropological Papers, no. 21. Nevada State Museum, Reno.

Naroll, R.
  1970   Galton's Problem. In *A Handbook of Method in Cultural Anthropology,* edited by R. Naroll and R. Cohen, pp. 974–989. Columbia University Press, New York.

Neff, H.
  1992   Ceramics and Evolution. *Archaeological Method and Theory* 4:141–193.

Neiman, F. D.
  1995   Stylistic Variation in Evolutionary Perspective: Inferences from Decorative Diversity and Interassemblage Distance in Illinois Woodland Ceramic Assemblages. *American Antiquity* 60:7–36.

Nelson, G.
  1983   Reticulation in Cladograms. In *Advances in Cladistics,* vol. 2, edited by N. I. Platnick and V. A. Funk, pp. 105–111. Columbia University Press, New York.

Nelson, G., and N. I. Platnick
　1981　*Systematics and Biogeography: Cladistics and Vicariance.* Columbia University Press, New York.

Nichols, J.
　1996　The Comparative Method as Heuristic. In *The Comparative Method Reviewed: Regularity and Irregularity in Language Change,* edited by M. Durie and M. Ross, pp. 39–71. Oxford University Press, New York.

Nixon, K. C., and J. M. Carpenter
　1993　On Outgroups. *Cladistics* 9:413–426.
　1996　On Consensus, Collapsibility and Clade Concordance. *Cladistics* 305–321.

Norell, M. A., and M. J. Novacek
　1992a　Congruence between Superpositional and Phylogenetic Patterns: Comparing Cladistic Patterns with Fossil Records. *Cladistics* 8:319–337.
　1992b　The Fossil Record and Evolution: Comparing Cladistic and Paleontologic Evidence for Vertebrate History. *Science* 255:1690–1693.
　1997　The Ghost Dance: A Cladistic Critique of Stratigraphic Approaches to Paleobiology and Phylogeny. *Journal of Vertebrate Paleontology* 17, Suppl. 3:67A.

O'Brien, M. J.
　2001　Constructing Phylogenetic Hypotheses in Archaeology: The Case for Cladistics. Paper presented at the annual meeting of the Human Behavior and Evolution Society, London.

O'Brien, M. J., J. Darwent, and R. L. Lyman
　2001　Cladistics Is Useful for Reconstructing Archaeological Phylogenies: Paleoindian Points from the Southeastern United States. *Journal of Archaeological Science* 28:1115–1136.

O'Brien, M. J., and T. D. Holland
　1990　Variation, Selection, and the Archaeological Record. *Archaeological Method and Theory* 2:31–79.
　1992　The Role of Adaptation in Archaeological Explanation. *American Antiquity* 57:3–59.
　1995　Behavioral Archaeology and the Extended Phenotype. In *Expanding Archaeology,* edited by J. M. Skibo, W. H. Walker, and A. E. Nielsen, pp. 143–161. University of Utah Press, Salt Lake City.

O'Brien, M. J., T. D. Holland, R. J. Hoard, and G. L. Fox
　1994　Evolutionary Implications of Design and Performance Characteristics of Prehistoric Pottery. *Journal of Archaeological Method and Theory* 1:259–304.

O'Brien, M. J., and R. D. Leonard
　2001　Style and Function: An Introduction. In *Style and Function: Conceptual Issues in Evolutionary Archaeology,* edited by T. D. Hurt and G. F. M. Rakita, pp. 1–23. Bergin and Garvey, Westport, Conn.

O'Brien, M. J., and R. L. Lyman
　1998　*James A. Ford and the Growth of Americanist Archaeology.* University of Missouri Press, Columbia.

1999   *Seriation, Stratigraphy, and Index Fossils: The Backbone of Archaeo-logical Dating.* Kluwer Academic/Plenum, New York.

2000   *Applying Evolutionary Archaeology: A Systematic Approach.* Kluwer Academic/Plenum, New York.

2002a   The Epistemological Nature of Archaeological Units. *Anthropological Theory* 2:37–57.

2002b   Evolutionary Archeology: Current Status and Future Prospects. *Evolutionary Anthropology* 11:26–36.

2003a   Resolving Phylogeny: Evolutionary Archaeology's Fundamental Issue. In *Essential Tensions in Archaeological Method and Theory,* edited by T. L. VanPool and C. S. VanPool, pp. 115–135. University of Utah Press, Salt Lake City.

2003b   Style, Function, Transmission: An Introduction. In *Style, Function, Transmission: Evolutionary Archaeological Perspectives,* edited by M. J. O'Brien and R. L. Lyman, pp. 1–32. University of Utah Press, Salt Lake City.

O'Brien, M. J., R. L. Lyman, and J. Darwent

2000   Cladistics and Archaeological Phylogeny. Paper presented at the 2do Reunión Internacional de Teoría Arqueológica en América del Sur, Olavarría, Argentina.

O'Brien, M. J., R. L. Lyman, and R. D. Leonard

1998   Basic Incompatibilities between Evolutionary and Behavioral Archaeology. *American Antiquity* 63:485–498.

2003   What Is Evolution? A Reply to Bamforth. *American Antiquity* 68:__–__.

O'Brien, M. J., R. L. Lyman, Y. Saab, E. Saab, J. Darwent, and D. S. Glover

2002   Two Issues in Archaeological Phylogenetics: Taxon Construction and Outgroup Selection. *Journal of Theoretical Biology* 215:133–150.

O'Brien, M. J., and W. R. Wood

1998   *The Prehistory of Missouri.* University of Missouri Press, Columbia.

O'Hara, R. J.

1988   Homage to Clio, or, toward an Historical Philosophy for Evolutionary Biology. *Systematic Zoology* 37:142–155.

Padian, K.

1997   The Rehabilitation of Sir Richard Owen. *BioScience* 47:446–453.

1999   Charles Darwin's Views of Classification in Theoretical Perspective. *Systematic Biology* 48:352–364.

Patterson, C.

1988   Homology in Classical and Molecular Biology. *Molecular Biology and Evolution* 5:603–625.

Perino, G.

1971   *Guide to the Identification of Certain American Indian Projectile Points.* Oklahoma Anthropological Society, Special Bulletin 4. Norman.

1985   *Selected Preforms, Points and Knives of the North American Indians.* Vol. 1. Points and Barbs Press, Idabel, Okla.

Petrie, W. M. F.

1899   Sequences in Prehistoric Remains. *Journal of the Royal Anthropological Institute of Great Britain and Ireland* 29:295–301.

1901   *Diospolis Parva, the Cemeteries of Abadiyeh and Hu, 1898–9.* Egypt
         Exploration Fund, Memoir 20. Egypt Exploration Fund, London.

Phillips, P., J. A. Ford, and J. B. Griffin
  1951   *Archaeological Survey in the Lower Mississippi Alluvial Valley,*
         1940–1947. Papers, no. 25. Peabody Museum of Archaeology and
         Ethnology, Harvard University, Cambridge, Mass.

Platnick, N. I.
  1977   The Hypochiloid Spiders: A Cladistic Analysis, with Notes on the
         Atypoidea (Arachnida, Araneae). *American Museum Novitates*
         2627:1–23.
  1979   Philosophy and the Transformation of Cladistics. *Systematic Zoology*
         28:537–546.
  1985   Philosophy and the Transformation of Cladistics Revisited. *Cladistics*
         1:87–94.

Platnick, N. I., and D. Cameron
  1977   Cladistic Methods in Textual, Linguistic, and Phylogenetic Analysis.
         Systematic Zoology 26:380–385.

Pleijel, F., and G. W. Rouse
  2000   Least-Inclusive Taxonomic Unit: A New Taxonomic Concept for Bi-
         ology. *Royal Society of London (Biological Sciences), Proceedings*
         267:627–630.

Poe, S., and J. J. Wiens
  2000   Character Selection and the Methodology of Morphological Phylo-
         genetics. In *Phylogenetic Analysis of Morphological Data,* edited by
         J. J. Wiens, pp. 20–36. Smithsonian Institution Press, Washington,
         D.C.

Pogue, M. G., and M. F. Mickevich
  1990   Character Definitions and Character State Delineation: The Bête Noir
         of Phylogenetic Inference. *Cladistics* 6:319–361.

Politis, G. G.
  1991   Fishtail Projectile Points in the Southern Cone of South America: An
         Overview. In *Clovis: Origins and Adaptations,* edited by R. Bonnich-
         sen and K. L. Turnmire, pp. 287–301. Center for the Study of the First
         Americans, Corvallis, Ore.

Polly, P. D.
  1997   Ancestry and Species Definition in Paleontology: A Stratocladistic
         Analysis of Paleocene-Eocene Viverravidae (Mammalia, Carnivora)
         from Wyoming. *University of Michigan, Museum of Paleontology,*
         Contributions 30:1–53.

Popper, K. R.
  1974   Darwinism as a Metaphysical Research Programme. In *The Philoso-*
         phy of Karl Popper, edited by P. A. Schillp, pp. 133–143. Open Court,
         La Salle, Ill.

Pulliam, H. R., and C. Dunford
  1980   *Programmed to Learn: An Essay on the Evolution of Culture.* Co-
         lumbia University Press, New York.

Radin, P.
  1929   History of Ethnological Theories. *American Anthropologist* 31:9–33.

Reif, W.-E.

1986 Evolutionary Theory in German Paleontology. In *Dimensions of Darwinism*, edited by M. Grene, pp. 173–204. Cambridge University Press, Cambridge.

Renfrew, C.

1987 *Archaeology and Language: The Puzzle of Indo-European Origins*. Cape, London.

1992 Archaeology, Genetics and Linguistic Diversity. *Man* 27:445–478.

1998 Applications of DNA in Archaeology: A Review of the DNA Studies of the Ancient Biomolecules Initiative. *Ancient Biomolecules* 2:107–116.

1999 Time Depth, Convergence Theory and Innovation in Proto-Indo-European: "Old Europe" as a PIE Linguistic Area. *Journal of Indo-European Studies* 27:257–293.

2000a At the Edge of Knowability: Towards a Prehistory of Languages. *Cambridge Archaeological Journal* 10:7–34.

2000b (editor) *America Past, America Present: Genes and Languages in the Americas and Beyond*. McDonald Institute for Archaeological Research, Cambridge.

Renfrew, C., and K. Boyle (editors)

2000 *Archaeogenetics: DNA and the Population Prehistory of Europe*. McDonald Institute for Archaeological Research, Cambridge.

Renfrew, C., A. McMahon, and L. Trask (editors)

2000 *Time Depth in Historical Linguistics*. McDonald Institute for Archaeological Research, Cambridge.

Rhymer, J., and D. Simberloff

1996 Extinction by Hybridization and Introgression. *Annual Review of Ecology and Systematics* 27:83–109.

Richerson, P. J., and R. Boyd

1992 Cultural Inheritance and Evolutionary Ecology. In *Evolutionary Ecology and Human Behavior*, edited by E. A. Smith and B. Winterhalder, pp. 61–92. Aldine, Hawthorne, N.Y.

Ridley, M.

1986 *Evolution and Classification: The Reformation of Cladism*. Longman, London.

1996 *Evolution*. 2nd ed. Blackwell, Cambridge, Mass.

Rieppel, O.

1997 Falsificationist versus Verificationist Approaches to History. *Journal of Vertebrate Paleontology* 17, Suppl. 3:71A.

Ritvo, H.

1997 *The Platypus and the Mermaid and Other Figments of the Classifying Imagination*. Harvard University Press, Cambridge, Mass.

Robinson, P. M. W., and R. J. O'Hara

1996 Cladistic Analysis of an Old Norse Manuscript Tradition. *Research in Humanities Computing* 4:115–137.

Romney, A. K.

1957 The Genetic Model and Uto-Aztecan Time Perspective. *Davidson Journal of Anthropology* 3:35–41.

Rosen, D. E.

1982　Do Current Theories of Evolution Satisfy the Basic Requirements of Explanation? *Systematic Biology* 31:76–85.

Ross, M.

1989　Early Oceanic Linguistic Prehistory. *Journal of Pacific History* 24:135–149.

Rouse, I. B.

1954　Review of "Measurements of Some Prehistoric Design Developments in the Southeastern States" by J. A. Ford. *American Antiquity* 19:296–297.

1955　On the Correlation of Phases of Culture. *American Anthropologist* 57:713–722.

Rowe, J. H.

1959　Archaeological Dating and Cultural Process. *Southwestern Journal of Anthropology* 15:317–324.

Ruhlen, M.

1987　*A Guide to the World's Languages,* vol. 1: *Classification.* Stanford University Press, Stanford, Calif.

Rushforth, S., and J. S. Chisolm

1991　*Cultural Persistence: Continuity in Meaning and Moral Responsibility among Bearlake Athapaskans.* University of Arizona Press, Tucson.

Russell, P.

1992　*Gila Cliff Dwellings National Monument: An Administrative History.* Professional Papers, no. 46. National Park Service, Southwest Cultural Resources Center, Santa Fe, N.M.

Sackett, J. R.

1981　From de Mortillet to Bordes: A Century of French Paleolithic Research. In *Towards a History of Archaeology,* edited by G. Daniel, pp. 85–99. Thames and Hudson, London.

Sahlins, M. D.

1958　*Social Stratification in Polynesia.* University of Washington Press, Seattle.

Sapir, E.

1916　*Time Perspective in Aboriginal American Culture, a Study in Method.* Canada Department of Mines, Geological Survey, Memoir 90. Government Printing Bureau, Ottawa.

Schiffer, M. B., and J. M. Skibo

1987　Theory and Experiment in the Study of Technological Change. *Current Anthropology* 28:595–622.

Schuh, R. T.

2000　*Biological Systematics: Principles and Applications.* Cornell University Press, Ithaca, N.Y.

Sellen, D. W., and R. Mace

1997　Fertility and Mode of Subsistence: A Phylogenetic Analysis. *Current Anthropology* 38:878–889.

Shaw, A. B.

1969　Adam and Eve, Paleontology, and the Non-Objective Arts. *Journal of Paleontology* 43:1085–1098.

Shennan, S.
   2002   *Genes, Memes and Human History: Darwinian Archaeology and Cultural Evolution.* Thames and Hudson, London.
Siddall, M. E.
   1996   Stratigraphic Consistency and the Shape of Things. *Systematic Biology* 45:111–115.
   1997   Stratigraphic Indices in the Balance: A Reply to Hitchin and Benton. *Systematic Biology* 46:569–573.
Simpson, G. G.
   1944   *Tempo and Mode in Evolution.* Columbia University Press, New York.
   1945   *The Principles of Classification and a Classification of Mammals.* American Museum of Natural History, Bulletin 85. New York.
   1951   The Species Concept. *Evolution* 5:285–298.
   1959   Anatomy and Morphology: Classification and Evolution: 1859 and 1959. *American Philosophical Society, Proceedings* 103:286–306.
   1961   *Principles of Animal Taxonomy.* Columbia University Press, New York.
   1963   The Meaning of Taxonomic Statements. In *Classification and Human Evolution,* edited by S. L. Washburn, pp. 1–31. Publications in Anthropology, no. 37. Viking Fund, New York.
Skála, Z., and J. Zrzavý
   1994   Phylogenetic Reticulations and Cladistics: Discussion of Methodological Concepts. *Cladistics* 10:305–313.
Smith, A. B.
   2000   Stratigraphy in Phylogeny Reconstruction. *Journal of Paleontology* 74:763–766.
   2002   Stratigraphy in Phylogeny Reconstruction—Response. *Journal of Paleontology* 76:594–595.
Smith, H. M.
   1967   Biological Similarities and Homologies. *Systematic Zoology* 16:101–102.
Sneath, P. H. A.
   1957   The Application of Computers to Taxonomy. *Journal of General Microbiology* 17:201–226.
Sneath, P. H. A., and R. R. Sokal
   1973   *Numerical Taxonomy.* Freeman, San Francisco.
Sober, E.
   1983   Parsimony Methods in Systematics. In *Advances in Cladistics,* vol. 2, edited by N. I. Platnick and V. A. Funk, pp. 37–47. Columbia University Press, New York.
   1988   *Reconstructing the Past: Parsimony, Evolution, and Inference.* MIT Press, Cambridge, Mass.
Sokal, R. R.
   1966   Numerical Taxonomy. *Scientific American* 215(6):106–116.
   1974   Classification: Purposes, Principles, Progress, Prospects. *Science* 185:1115–1123.

Sokal, R. R., and J. H. Camin
  1965   The Two Taxonomies: Areas of Agreement and of Conflict. *Systematic Zoology* 14:176–195.
Sokal, R. R., J. H. Camin, F. J. Rohlf, and P. H. A. Sneath
  1965   Numerical Taxonomy: Some Points of View. *Systematic Zoology* 14:237–243.
Sokal, R. R., and P. H. A. Sneath
  1963   *Principles of Numerical Taxonomy.* Freeman, San Francisco.
Sosef, M. S. M.
  1997   Hierarchical Models, Reticulate Evolution and the Inevitability of Paraphyletic Supraspecific Taxa. *Taxon* 46:75–85.
Spaulding, A. C.
  1954   Prehistoric Cultural Development in the Eastern United States. In *New Interpretations of Aboriginal American Culture History,* edited by B. J. Meggers and C. Evans, pp. 12–27. Anthropological Society of Washington, Washington, D.C.
Stanford, D.
  1991   Clovis Origins and Adaptations: An Introductory Perspective. In *Clovis: Origins and Adaptations,* edited by R. Bonnichsen and K. L. Turnmire, pp. 1–13. Center for the Study of the First Americans, Corvallis, Ore.
Stearn, W. T.
  1959   The Background of Linnaeus's Contributions to the Nomenclature and Methods of Systematic Biology. *Systematic Zoology* 8:4–22.
Stevens, P. F.
  1991   Character States, Morphological Variation, and Phylogenetic Analysis: A Review. *Systematic Botany* 16:553–583.
Steward, J. H.
  1929   Diffusion and Independent Invention: A Critique of Logic. *American Anthropologist* 31:491–495.
  1941   Review of "Prehistoric Culture Units and Their Relationships in Northern Arizona" by H. S. Colton. *American Antiquity* 6:366–367.
  1944   Re: Archaeological Tools and Jobs. *American Antiquity* 10:99–100.
  1955   *Theory of Culture Change: The Methodology of Multilinear Evolution.* University of Illinois Press, Urbana.
Stocking, G. W., Jr.
  1987   *Victorian Anthropology.* Free Press, New York.
Stoneking, M.
  1993   DNA and Recent Human Evolution. *Evolutionary Anthropology* 2:60–73.
Strait, D., and F. Grine
  1999   Cladistics and Early Hominid Phylogeny. *Science* 285:1210.
Straus, L. G.
  2000   Solutrean Settlement of North America? A Review of Reality. *American Antiquity* 65:219–226.
Strong, W. D.
  1935   An Introduction to Nebraska Archaeology. *Smithsonian Miscellaneous Collections* 93(10):1–323.

1953   Historical Approach in Anthropology. In *Anthropology Today,* edited by A. L. Kroeber, pp. 386–397. University of Chicago Press, Chicago.

Swadesh, M.

1964   Diffusional Cumulation and Archaic Residue as Historical Explanations. In *Language in Culture and Society,* edited by D. Hymes, pp. 624–637. Harper and Row, New York.

Swofford, D. L.

1991   When Are Phylogeny Estimates from Morphological and Molecular Data Incongruent? In *Phylogenetic Analysis of DNA Sequences,* edited by M. M. Miyamoto and J. Cracraft, pp. 295–333. Oxford University Press, New York.

1998   *PAUP*: Phylogenetic Analysis Using Parsimony (*and Other Methods)* (version 4). Sinauer, Sunderland, Mass.

Swofford, D. L., G. J. Olsen, P. J. Waddell, and D. M. Hillis

1996   Phylogenetic Inference. In *Molecular Systematics,* 2nd ed., edited by D. M. Hillis, C. Moritz, and B. K. Mable, pp. 407–514. Sinauer, Sunderland, Mass.

Swofford, D. L., P. J. Waddell, J. P. Huelsenbeck, P. G. Foster, P. O. Lewis, and J. S. Rogers

2001   Bias in Phylogenetic Estimation and Its Relevance to the Choice between Parsimony and Likelihood Methods. *Systematic Biology* 50:525–539.

Szalay, F. S., and W. J. Bock

1991   Evolutionary Theory and Systematics: Relationships between Process and Patterns. *Zeitschrift für Zoologische Systematik und Evolutionsforschung* 29:1–39.

Tattersall, I.

1995   *The Fossil Trail: How We Know What We Think We Know about Human Evolution.* Oxford University Press, New York.

2000   Paleoanthropology: The Last Half-Century. *Evolutionary Anthropology* 9:2–16.

Taylor, R. E., C. V. Haynes, Jr., and M. Stuiver

1996   Clovis and Folsom Age Estimates: Stratigraphic Context and Radiocarbon Calibration. *Antiquity* 70:515–525.

Tehrani, J., and M. Collard

2002   Investigating Cultural Evolution through Biological Phylogenetic Analysis of Turkmen Textiles. *Journal of Anthropological Archaeology* 21:443–63.

Terrell, J. E.

1988   History as a Family Tree, History as an Entangled Bank: Constructing Images and Interpretations of Prehistory in the South Pacific. *Antiquity* 62:642–657.

2001a   Introduction. In *Archaeology, Language, and History: Essays on Culture and Ethnicity,* edited by J. E. Terrell, pp. 1–10. Bergin and Garvey, Westport, Conn.

2001b   (editor) *Archaeology, Language, and History: Essays on Culture and Ethnicity.* Bergin and Garvey, Westport, Conn.

Terrell, J. E., T. L. Hunt, and C. Gosden
  1997   The Dimensions of Social Life in the Pacific: Human Diversity and the Myth of the Primitive Isolate. *Current Anthropology* 38:155–195.
Terrell, J. E., and P. J. Stewart
  1996   The Paradox of Human Population Genetics at the End of the Twentieth Century. *Reviews in Anthropology* 26:13–33.
Thomas, D. H.
  1998   *Archaeology.* 3rd ed. Harcourt Brace, Fort Worth, Texas.
Thompson, R. H.
  1956   An Archaeological Approach to Cultural Stability. In *Seminars in Archaeology: 1955*, pp. 31–57. Memoirs, no. 11. Society for American Archaeology, Menasha, Wis.
  1958   (editor) *Migrations in New World Culture History.* Social Science Bulletin 27. University of Arizona, Tucson.
Tompkins, C. N.
  1993   Classifying Clovis Points: A Study in Metric Variability. M.A. thesis, Department of Anthropology, University of Arizona, Tucson.
Turner, J. S.
  2000   *The Extended Organism: The Physiology of Animal-Built Structures.* Harvard University Press, Cambridge, Mass.
Tylor, E. B.
  1871   *Primitive Culture.* Murray, London.
Valentine, J. W., and C. L. May
  1996   Hierarchies in Biology and Paleobiology. *Paleobiology* 22:23–33.
Van Buren, G. E.
  1974   *Arrowheads and Projectile Points.* Arrowhead, Garden Grove, Calif.
VanPool, C. S., T. L. VanPool, D. A. Phillips Jr., and M. J. Harmon
  2000   The Changing Faces of Horned/Plumed Serpents in the Greater North American Southwest. Paper presented at the 33rd annual Chacmool Conference, Calgary, Canada.
Vansina, J.
  1990   *Paths in the Rainforests: Toward a History of Political Tradition in Equatorial Africa.* University of Wisconsin Press, Madison.
van Welzen, P. C.
  1997   Paraphyletic Groups or What Should a Classification Entail. *Taxon* 46:99–103.
Vogt, E. Z.
  1964   The Genetic Model and Maya Cultural Development. In *Desarrollo cultural de los Mayas*, edited by E. Z. Vogt and A. Ruz, pp. 9–48. Universidad Nacional Autónoma de México, Mexico City.
von Frisch, K., and O. von Frisch
  1974   *Animal Architecture.* Harcourt, Brace, Jovanovich, New York.
Wagner, W. H., Jr.
  1983   Reticulistics: The Recognition of Hybrids and Their Role in Cladistics and Classification. In *Advances in Cladistics*, vol. 2, edited by N. I. Platnick and V. A. Funk, pp. 63–79. Columbia University Press, New York.

Wedel, W. R.
  1938   The Direct-Historical Approach in Pawnee Archaeology. *Smithsonian Miscellaneous Collections* 97(7):1–21.
Wells, R. S.
  1987   The Life and Growth of Language: Metaphors in Biology and Linguistics. In *Biological Metaphor and Cladistic Classification,* edited by H. M. Hoenigswald and L. F. Wiener, pp. 39–80. University of Pennsylvania Press, Philadelphia.
Welsch, R. L., and J. E. Terrell
  1994   Reply to Moore & Romney. *American Anthropologist* 96:392–396.
Welsch, R. L., J. E. Terrell, and J. A. Nadolski
  1992   Language and Culture on the North Coast of New Guinea. *American Anthropologist* 94:568–600.
Wheeler, Q. D., and R. Meier (editors)
  2000   *Species Concepts and Phylogenetic Theory: A Debate.* Columbia University Press, New York.
Wheeler, W. C.
  1990   Nucleic Acid Sequence Phylogeny and Random Outgroups. *Cladistics* 6:269–275.
White, L. A.
  1949   *The Science of Culture: A Study of Man and Civilization.* Grove Press, New York.
  1959a   The Concept of Evolution in Anthropology. In *Evolution and Anthropology: A Centennial Appraisal,* edited by B. J. Meggers, pp. 106–124. Anthropological Society of Washington, Washington, D.C.
  1959b   *The Evolution of Culture: The Development of Civilization to the Fall of Rome.* McGraw-Hill, New York.
Wiener, L. F.
  1987   Of Phonetics and Genetics: A Comparison of Classification in Linguistic and Organic Systems. In *Biological Metaphor and Cladistic Classification,* edited by H. M. Hoenigswald and L. F. Wiener, pp. 217–226. University of Pennsylvania Press, Philadelphia.
Wiley, E. O.
  1981   *Phylogenetics: The Theory and Practice of Phylogenetic Systematics.* Wiley-InterScience, New York.
Wiley, E. O., D. J. Siegel-Causey, D. R. Brooks, and V. A. Funk
  1991   *The Compleat Cladist: A Primer of Phylogenetic Procedures.* University of Kansas, Museum of Natural History, Lawrence.
Wilhelmsen, K.
  2001   Building the Framework for an Evolutionary Explanation of Projectile Point Variation: An Example from the Central Mississippi River Valley. In *Archaeology for the Third Millennium,* edited by T. L. Hunt, C. P. Lipo, and S. L. Sterling, pp. 97–144. Bergin and Garvey, Westport, Conn.
Willey, G. R.
  1945   Horizon Styles and Pottery Traditions in Peruvian Archaeology. *American Antiquity* 10:49–56.
  1953   Archaeological Theories and Interpretation: New World. In *Anthro-*

pology Today, edited by A. L. Kroeber, pp. 361–385. University of Chicago Press, Chicago.

Willey, G. R., and P. Phillips
1958   *Method and Theory in American Archaeology.* University of Chicago Press, Chicago.

Wills, M. A.
1999   Congruence between Phylogeny and Stratigraphy: Randomization Tests and Gap Excess Ratio. *Systematic Biology* 48:559–580.

Winterhalder, B., and E. A. Smith
2000   Analyzing Adaptive Strategies: Human Behavioral Ecology at Twenty-Five. *Evolutionary Anthropology* 9:51–72.

Wissler, C.
1917   *The American Indian.* McMurtie, New York.
1923   *Man and Culture.* Crowell, New York.

Wolverton, S., and R. L. Lyman
2000   Immanence and Configuration in Analogical Reasoning. *North American Archaeologist* 21:233–247.

Wormington, H. M.
1957   *Ancient Man in North America.* 4th ed. Popular Series, no. 4. Denver Museum of Natural History, Denver.

Index

adaptation, 231
affinity, 23, 31, 34, 231
Agate Basin points, 211
Alberta points, 211
allele, 108, 231
Alroy, J., 90
anagenetic evolution/anagenesis, 7, 8, 12, 13, 117, 231
analogous characters/analogues, 29, 231; behavioral, 101; distinguishing from homologous characters/homologues, 40; function and, 153–54
ancestors: how treated by cladists, 82–83; real vs. hypothetical, 56–57, 81–82, 86
Anderson, D. G., 128, 165, 199
apomorphies. *See* homologous characters, derived
archaeology: cladistics in, 225–28; constrained to study macroevolution, 113; evolutionary, 18; examples of cultural phylogeny in, 7–13, 115–21; as historical science, 227; processual, 4; role of evolutionary theory in, xv; similarity in, 14, 15
Archaeopteryx, 82, 83
archetype, 25, 26, 231
Arkabutla points, 193
Arnold, M. L., 105
artifacts: change in, 5–7; cultural transmission of characters of, 16–17; as phenotypic characters, 103; phylogenetic sequences of, 7–13; as subjects of evolutionary study, 98–101
atlatl, 208
autapomorphies, 45, 52, 232
auxiliary principle, 64, 68–69, 232

Baupläne, 51, 213, 215, 232
Beaver Lake points, 129, 130, 192, 193, 212
Bell, G., 227
Bellwood, P., 113
Benton, M. J., 221
Bigelow, R. S., 31, 46
binomial system, 25
Blackwater Draw, New Mexico, 127, 133, 135, 136, 137
Boas, F., 101, 122, 124
Bollback, J., 64
Borgerhoff Mulder, M., 94, 123
Borgmeier, T., 39
borrowing, 110
Boyd, R., 16, 19, 124; on models of cultures, 118, 119–20; on tracing cultural phylogenies, 117
Bradley, B. A., 134, 137, 165
branch-and-bound search, 75, 232
branches, 36, 37, 232
branch swapping, 75, 185, 232
Brew, J. O., 13, 18, 98, 112, 225
Brooks, D. R., 65–66, 67, 166, 199
Brower, A. V. Z., 55, 90, 149
Brown, J. H., 189, 199
Bryan, A. L., 217

Cain, A. J., 46
camel herding, 94–95
Cameron, D., 102, 103, 124
Carpenter, J. M., 90
Casas Grandes tradition, xiv
Cavalli-Sforza, L. L., 16, 64